CAMPING AND RVING WITH DOGS

Jack and Julee Meltzer

DESERT WINDS PRESS, LLC
PMB 5968
428 Childers Street
Pensacola, Florida 32534
www.petsrv.com

Dedicated to Leela for her patience with our nomadic life and her gentleness with animals.

TABLE OF CONTENTS

CHAPTER 1

INTRODUCTION

In the U.S. alone, more than 30 million people each year take their pets with them while camping. Yet, when we first started RVing with our dogs, we were unable to find much written on the subject. Sure, there were the occasional articles in magazines that reminded us to use pet ID tags, bring plenty of water, and take their favorite toy. But in terms of providing genuine support or bottom-line information, there was nothing out there. Since it was something that we felt was badly needed, we decided to write this book.

Over two years later, after thousands of miles, hundreds of campgrounds, and months of research, we were finally able to piece together the first true reference book on the subject of camping and RVing with dogs.

If you look at the table of contents, you'll see that this book is basically organized along the same lines that you might take when preparing for a trip. In addition, it includes the most comprehensive listing of pet-friendly campgrounds in existence.

Loaded with practical advice and invaluable information, this book will give you the heads up on the unwritten rules and established etiquette that exist at every campground. In addition, chapter seven covers the practical challenges associated with camping in unusual and unfamiliar places. Based on extensive research and real life experience, we could've really used this section before hitting the road with our dogs.

With this book, you now have a reliable source of indispensable information that is specifically designed to make traveling and camping with dogs easier, safer, and more enjoyable.

This symbol, appearing throughout the book, is used to highlight important information.

CHAPTER 2

THE 10 COMMANDMENTS

While there are numerous issues to consider while camping with dogs, these are some of the most important.

1. Make Sure that Your Dog Can't Get Lost

It's one thing if your dog gets free in your neighborhood. It's another when you're at a rest stop, nine hundred miles from home. Either train your dog to come when called or make absolutely sure that they're on a leash at all times.

2. Get All of their Vaccinations Up to Date

If your dog gets into an altercation with another animal (or a person), the central issue will become their rabies shots. If you stay at a campground that has a demanding pet policy, you'll need to verify your dog's vaccination records. If you cross into Canada, you'll have to confirm that your dogs have had their shots. You get the idea.

3. Make Your Dogs Easy to Identify

If your dog does get lost (unfortunately, it happens all the time), the ability to easily identify them will become critical. For permanent identification purposes, consider tattoos or microchips. At a minimum, make sure they wear tags that show their name, your current phone number, and the date of their last rabies vaccination.

4. Clean Up After Your Dog

The biggest complaint about dogs has nothing to do with their bark, their bite, or their behavior. If you pick up after your dog, you'll be helping dog owners everywhere.

5. Learn How to Provide First Aid to Your Dog

If a medical crisis occurs while at home, you drive to your local veterinarian. But if you're heading down a dark highway in a strange town, it will seem like a bad dream. Although there are ways to get help while on the road, it always takes more time. In the meantime, your ability to provide competent first aid could save your dog's life.

6. Involve Your Dog in Everything You Do

If you really want your dogs to have a good time, include them in your activities. Take them with you on long walks. Buy a cheap plastic wading pool and let them play in the water. Throw a ball. Cook them up a hamburger. If you do stuff like that, they'll do cartwheels the next time you decide to take them camping.

7. Call the Campgrounds Before You Go

Even if a park claims they're pet-friendly, always call ahead to confirm their policy regarding *your* dogs. We've arrived at parks (with our two German Shepard dogs) after a long day on the road only to discover that "pet-friendly" meant dogs under 20 pounds.

8. Plan Ahead for the Unexpected

Have a plan (for your dogs) in case of a flat tire, a serious accident, or a fire in your RV. Start with a few extra leashes, a pet carrier, and an extra fire extinguisher. Then have a fire drill to identify potential problems.

9. Learn About Your Camping Environment

The U.S. is a huge country with a vast assortment of dangerous wildlife, treacherous plants, unpredictable weather conditions, and demanding environmental challenges. If you don't know what you're doing, you might inadvertently be putting yourself and your dog in danger.

10. Recognize and Respect the Views of Others

While some of us can't imaging traveling *without* dogs, others can't imaging traveling *with* them. If you keep your dog under control and clean up after them, you won't give others much to grumble about.

CHAPTER 3

GETTING READY FOR YOUR TRIP

This chapter deals with the issue of getting things ready for the road. The principal reason for writing this book was to provide pet owners with the guidance and information they need to keep their dogs happy, healthy, and safe. To that end, this chapter is one of the most important.

Getting Your Dogs Ready

If your dogs aren't used to traveling, there are a few tricks you can try. First, get them accustomed to the vehicle you're taking by sitting with them in the driveway. After that, take them for a few short trips in order to become familiar with actually riding in your vehicle. In most cases, this should be enough to prepare them for the real thing.

In the meantime, you should also make arrangements to take your dogs to a veterinarian for a thorough check up. Bring all their vaccinations up to date and make sure that your dogs are tested for heartworm disease. Purchase any medications that they'll need and get an extra copy of their health and vaccination records to take with you.

If you have the time, give your dog a bath before you leave since it may be a while before you have another opportunity. If your dog suffers from motion sickness, don't feed them or give them large quantities of water before you leave. You might also try limiting their view of the outside world by keeping them in a crate or strategically covering some of the windows in your vehicle.

Pet Identification Requirements

Although there are a number of risks associated with traveling with dogs, the most serious threat (and the most common) is the possibility of your dog getting lost. While no one ever expects to lose their dog, here are some measures that you can take (before you leave) to improve your odds of finding a lost dog:

Photograph Your Dog   Before leaving, take a digital snapshot of your dog and put a copy of it on a 3.5" diskette. If you lose your dog, you'll be able to use the photo to generate lost pet flyers that can be posted in public places.

Get a Pet ID Tag   Most pet stores have vending machines that can produce an engraved ID tag in a matter of minutes. Make sure that the engraved information is correct and current.

Get a Secure Collar   Make sure that your dog has a secure collar that can't inadvertently come off. The collar should have an engraved ID tag that shows the dog's name and your current telephone number.

Register with a Travel Club   Consider registering your dog with the Good Sam Club's pet finder program. They'll send you an engraved tag that has an 800 number to call if someone finds your dog.

Utilize Microchips or Tattoos   Get your dog tattooed or have a microchip surgically imbedded under their skin to facilitate the process of identifying your dog. Many veterinarians now offer this service.

RV Layout Issues

While it's crucial to get your dog prepared for the trip, it's just as important to get your camper or RV ready for your dog. For starters, the floor plan of your RV should be capable of meeting your dog's specific requirements. For example, if your dog is older and has problems climbing stairs, you might have to use a ramp or a step stool. If you plan on crating your dog, make sure that the crate can fit through the door of your RV. If not, you'll have to consider using a crate that can be disassembled (a major hassle). You'll also need to provide your dog with a place to sleep inside the vehicle. Some people put a blanket or a mat under a table or their dinette.

This Winnebago is home to the authors along with their two dogs and three cats.

In terms of where to keep bulky items like portable pens, consider installing a roof mounted storage box or a hitch–mounted rack. For other miscellaneous pet–related items, devote one compartment outside and one cabinet inside.

 To eliminate the possibility of getting locked outside your RV, hide an extra key in a location where it can be easily accessed from the outside. One option is to use a plastic cable tie to secure the key to a stationary object. If you lock yourself out, simply cut the tie to release the spare key.

Food and Water

There are two decisions regarding your dog's food and water supply. The first is where to put their bowls and the second is where to store the extra food.

As a start, place your dog's food and water bowls in a convenient location that is relatively out of the way. Then, expect to move them several times until they're where they should be. We call it "evolutionary engineering".

 If you have large dogs, consider using a bowl stand to raise the bowls off the ground. Available at most pet stores, these devices make it easier for large breeds to access their food. In addition, if you secure the stand to a wall (or the floor), it will keep the bowls from sliding around while you're on the road.

This stand makes it easier for our dogs to access their food. It also keeps the bowls in place during travel. The plastic mat under the water bowl serves to contain spilled water and the box to the left holds all their toys.

Be sure to keep your dog's water bowl on a plastic pet food placemat. These inexpensive mats have a small lip for containing spilled liquids. Use non–slip drawer liners to prevent the bowls (and the mat) from sliding around.

In terms of food storage, we keep a week's supply of dry food in a covered container that sits next to the dog's food bowl. We refill the container from a larger supply that we keep in our RV's cargo bin. Wherever you store their food, make sure that it's kept in a sealed container to keep out insects, rodents, and moisture.

 Always bring an extra quantity of your dog's regular food. If you switch brands while on the road, your dog may experience digestive problems.

Water can be another challenging issue since a 40 pound dog requires more than a gallon of fresh water each day. If you have a good supply of clean water, be sure to fill your water tank before you head out. Once you're on the road, always use a good water filter when filling your tank. Plus, be sure to disinfect your RV's water tank periodically.

When we're traveling, we rely on a "no–spill" pet bowl that keeps the water in, no matter how rough the ride. They're available at most pet stores. When we set up camp, we switch to a larger stainless steel bowl that holds more water and is easier to clean. Be sure to clean and refill your dog's water bowl often, especially if you're staying in an area that's hot and dry.

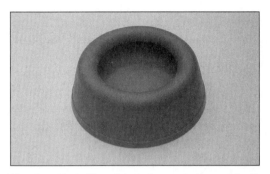

This spill-proof bowl will keep the water in, no matter how rough the ride.

If you're traveling a lot (especially outside the U.S.), you may have some difficulty in finding a reliable source of drinking water. Commercial water filters *can* improve the taste and odor of a water supply, but they're not typically designed to eliminate dangerous pathogens or reduce harmful contaminants. As a result, never fill your tank with water of questionable quality, regardless of the filter.

Because we often stay at locations with poor water quality, we have a water cooler in our RV that dispenses hot or cold water from refillable 5 gallon plastic jugs. We get the jugs filled at water supply stores or from water dispensing vending machines. When we do find a campground with good drinking water, we use a high quality filter and a special (EPA approved) hose to fill the jugs for future use.

Sleeping Accommodations

It doesn't take a government study to realize that dogs, like people, want to be comfortable when they sleep. Fortunately, dog beds are inexpensive and readily available. Alternatively, you can fashion your own dog bed from a piece of foam and a some fabric. Some folks (who will remain nameless) even let their dogs sleep on the couch at night. Whatever you come up with, make sure it's comfortable and has a removable cover that can be washed.

Dog Toys

When we originally got our first German Shepard Dogs years ago, we bought each one of them a toy from the pet shop. To our surprise, they proceeded to play with these toys for hours at a time. We now realize that dogs value their toys just as kids cherish theirs. In addition, toys help to keep dogs busy, active, and amused. Plus, some chew toys can even help to keep your dog's teeth clean. So before you hit the road, purchase some toys, find a box, and put all of your dog's toys in it. They'll derive endless enjoyment rummaging through the box looking for a favorite chew toy or a ball they forgot they had.

Dog Safety Issues

Due to stringent product liability laws, most RVs are inherently safe in terms of obvious hazards. However, it always pays to take a close look around to eliminate any hidden risks that might exist. For instance, look for heavy objects that can pose a hazard if they fall (while you're traveling). Identify and eliminate any possible pathways to the outside including heating and cooling ducts and windows without screens. We once had a kitten that escaped through an open window. Although we searched for days, we never saw her again.

Similarly, look for things that could potentially snag your dog's collar. Each year, a significant number of dogs are accidentally strangled in this manner.

If you have a puppy (or a very immature dog), you'll need to "puppy-proof" your RV. Our full-grown German Shepard male literally devoured one of our seatbelts, buckle and all. Always keep household chemical and cleaning agents out of reach and avoid using extension cords. If your RV has a screen door, consider installing a grill to prevent your dog from accidentally breaking through. Try to use your imagination without becoming outright paranoid.

Preparing for Problems on the Road

At some point in your travels, you will most likely have a problem while on the road. It could be a tire blowout, a dead battery, or something that requires your RV to be towed to the nearest repair shop. When a problem does occur, having a dog with you can complicate matters, particularly if you're not prepared. For the most part, there are three potential scenarios that you should be prepared for: Unexpected breakdowns; lengthy repairs; and fires.

Unexpected Breakdowns

Almost everyone experiences problems on the road at one time or another. Our first major incident occurred in the parking lot of a Wal-Mart in Pecos, Texas. The two slide-outs in our RV became stuck while extended. As a result, we were trapped in the parking lot for three days. The folks at the Wal-Mart were great but it took a cell phone and a resourceful technician from a local RV repair shop to get us going again.

In short, minor roadside problems can quickly escalate if you're not adequately prepared. In our case, it was a cell phone that provided us with a crucial link to the outside world.

There are a few books as well as online forums that cover the issue of what to take with you while on the road. At a minimum, you should have a serviceable spare tire, a cell phone, a container for carrying fuel, and a good roadside assistance plan. You might also want to consider bringing a laptop computer that has wireless internet access. Many RVers now consider laptops to be indispensable for keeping in touch with friends and family, locating businesses, monitoring the weather, and getting directions. In addition, you should consider purchasing an external cell phone antenna for those times when you're out of range. Most truckers depend on them.

In terms of dealing with your dogs during a breakdown, develop a plan *before* you need one. The primary goal is to keep your dogs safe and out of the way until you're back on the road. At times, we've had to put our dogs in the tow vehicle. If you don't have a separate vehicle, use crates or leashes to keep your dogs out of the way until the repairs have been made. If repairs have to be performed *inside* your RV, consider locking your dogs in a bathroom or put them in a crate or pet carrier to ensure they don't get free.

Lengthy Repairs

If and when your RV does require lengthy repairs, you'll need to work out a plan for dealing with your dog. We have some friends with dogs that had to endure several weeks of on–going repairs. Throughout the entire episode, they stayed in their RV *inside* the repair shop each night while their dogs remained in their car in the parking lot (the repair shop had a policy restricting pets). Some companies, including Camping World, allow you to dry camp in their parking lot while your RV is being serviced. At any rate, consider what you might do if *you* had to deal with a similar situation.

Fires in RVs

Whether you have dogs or not, you should take the time to devise a feasible strategy for dealing with a fire. First, make sure that you have enough fire extinguishers to handle most situations. We keep one in the living area and another in the bedroom. Some folks keep one outside their RV to deal with external fires (i.e. engine fires).

Second, figure out how your safety exits actually work. If your emergency escape window is seven feet off the ground, find a way to get out without breaking your neck *before* you actually have a fire. Third, know precisely what to do with your dogs if a fire does break out. In our case, we keep several leashes throughout the RV. If a fire does occur (and we have enough time), we plan to tie the dogs to the nearest tree or sign post away from harm. Letting your dogs out should only be considered as a last resort since most pets tend to run away (out of fear).

The Canine Camper™ is perfect for holding small dogs. It also serves as a makeshift shelter in the event of a fire or other emergency (courtesy Midwest Homes for Pets).

Perform a fire drill to see if your emergency plan will actually work. For example, if your extra leashes are in a locked storage bin, it's unlikely that you'll have enough time to get the key.

What to Bring for Your Dogs

Checklists are the most effective way to ensure that you bring the things you need. You can make a copy of this checklist, improve on it, and use it whenever you're preparing for a trip.

- ❑ Clothing (for dogs)
- ❑ Collars
- ❑ Containers for Food
- ❑ Description of Dog's Tattoo
- ❑ Digital Photograph of Your Dogs
- ❑ Dog Bed
- ❑ Dog Blanket
- ❑ Dog Booties
- ❑ Dog Leads
- ❑ Dog Treats
- ❑ Extra Food
- ❑ Flashlight (for walks at night)
- ❑ Flea and Tick Medication
- ❑ Flea Comb
- ❑ Food and Water Bowls
- ❑ Food Mat
- ❑ Heartworm Medication
- ❑ ID Tags
- ❑ Insect Repellant
- ❑ Leashes
- ❑ Medical and Vaccination Records (from vet)
- ❑ Nail Clippers
- ❑ Orange Scarf (for hunting season)
- ❑ Dog Bed
- ❑ Dog Brush
- ❑ Pet Crate
- ❑ Dog Shampoo
- ❑ Dog Toys (and toy box)
- ❑ Pet Waste Bags
- ❑ Proof of Rabies Vaccination
- ❑ Special Medications
- ❑ Vet's Telephone Number

CHAPTER 4

TRAVELING WITH YOUR DOGS

This chapter deals with life on the road with a dog. If you've addressed some of the important issues described in the previous chapter, you'll find that traveling with dogs can be safe, fun, and rewarding.

Where to Keep Your Dog While Traveling

The top priority when traveling with dogs is to ensure that they're kept safe and comfortable at all times. That being said, you have two basic choices in terms of *where* to keep your dog while traveling. The ideal option is to have your dog travel in the same vehicle that you're driving. For example, many campers routinely keep their dog in the back seat of their truck cab or in their motorhome. With this approach, you can keep an eye on them while they benefit from the company and comfort that you enjoy.

Muffin, owned by John and Phyllis Sadler, knows exactly where she'll be riding when they hit the road.

 For an added measure of safety, consider using a pet harness that secures your dog to a vehicle's seatbelt. In addition to protecting your dog during a collision, these harnesses provide another crucial benefit after an accident. When medics arrive at the scene, they typically open the door of the vehicle to assess the condition of the occupants. When this happens, most dogs jump out of the vehicle and run off, only to become lost or get hit by a car.

The second option, when traveling with dogs, is to have them stay in a towed vehicle such as a travel trailer, fifth wheel, or towed car. People with small vehicles, large dogs, or multiple pets often use this strategy with considerable success. However, this approach has one major drawback. It can be difficult to adequately control and monitor your dog's comfort, health, and safety when they're in a separate vehicle. Unless you have some way to effectively cool or heat the towed vehicle, this approach should be avoided in extreme weather.

This van, used by dog show participants, is outfitted with secured cages and various pet supplies.

 When keeping dogs in a separate vehicle, some dog show professionals use baby monitors or web cameras to keep an eye on their pets. Some of these devices even have speakers enabling you to communicate with your pets as well.

Some campers rely on cages or crates to keep their dogs from getting hurt (or getting into trouble). If you do decide to use this strategy, make sure there's plenty of fresh air, clean water, and a comfortable place for your dog to sleep while in the crate. You'll also need to find a way to secure the crate while you're traveling.

Whichever strategy you use, make sure that it can be sustained under most reasonable circumstances. Remember, if your RV breaks down and must go in for lengthy repairs, you'll need to find a temporary place for your dogs.

If you keep your dog in a crate, you'll have to secure it
during travel (courtesy Midwest Homes for Pets).

Similarly, if the weather becomes unseasonably hot and your air
conditioner breaks down, you're going to have to find some way
to keep your dogs comfortable. Traveling with dogs, in our
opinion, is the only way to go. But as you can see, it does require a
considerable amount of forethought, planning, and effort.

Stopping to Give Your Dogs a Break

Regardless of where you keep your dog, you'll still need to take
them out for a walk every few hours to relieve themselves (and
stretch their legs). This will give you a break as well. Although
taking your dog for a walk is generally straightforward, there are
a few things to keep in mind when you're on the road:

**Take Them Out
When You Have
the Chance**

Traveling, like everything else, is subject to
unexpected change. Rest stops are occasionally
closed for repairs and major highways are
sometimes diverted towards unknown roads
and unfamiliar towns. So if you see a good place
to walk your dog, pull over. It might be a while
before you have another opportunity.

**Use Common
Sense**

There's a true story about a couple that created a
three hour backup on the New Jersey Turnpike
as a result of taking their dog for a walk on the
interstate's center strip. You get the point.

**Hang On to
Your Dog**

You need to make sure that your dog never gets
loose while you're on the road. One trick is to
put their leash on *before* you open the door. If

you do get separated from your dog, please refer to the section in Chapter 6 that describes various ways to find lost dogs.

Pick Up After Your Dog

If you're stopping at a public rest stop, pick up after your dog. If you don't, you're effectively leaving it for others to clean up (or step in).

This retractable leash has been fitted with a small saddlebag that can hold pet waste bags (shown) and other useful items.

Watch Out for Vehicles

Watch out for cars and trucks. A friend of ours lost his English Sheepdog while walking near a road. The dog was on a leash when a passing car came too close and killed the dog.

Give them Plenty of Air

Be sure to lock your vehicle's doors and crack the windows whenever you go to the restroom or grab something to eat.

Park in the Shade

At a rest stop, try to park in the shade. If there aren't any shade trees, park next to a building, tractor trailer, or dumpster.

Give Them Lots of Fresh Water

Give your dogs an opportunity to drink water whenever possible. Keep a spare bowl and a container of water in the vehicle. For some reason, traveling seem to make dogs thirsty.

Prepare for Rain

In rainy weather, keep a towel nearby to dry off your dog. Also, place an umbrella near the door for walks in the rain.

Crossing the U.S. Border With Your Dogs

Even if you don't have any plans to travel into Canada or Mexico, it always pays to be prepared. We've met travelers who have decided, on a whim, to join an RV caravan that was going down to Mexico. Fortunately, with a little planning, it's easy to prepare for a border crossing with dogs. The regulations described in this section are subject to change. As a result, we would suggest that you confirm these requirements prior to leaving.

The Canadian Border

Dogs can enter Canada if accompanied by a valid rabies vaccination certificate issued by a licensed veterinarian. The certificate must identify the dog in terms of its breed, color, sex, and weight. It must also indicate the name of the licensed rabies vaccine used (trade name), serial number, and duration of validity (up to three years). If a validity date doesn't appear on the certificate, it will be considered a one–year vaccine. If you don't have a rabies certificate, an inspector will order you to have your dog vaccinated for rabies and to provide the vaccination certificate at the border.

Special Purpose Dogs

Assistance dogs that are certified as a guide, hearing, seizure, or other service dog, are not subject to any restrictions for importation if the person importing the dog is the user of the dog and accompanies the dog into Canada.

The Mexican Border

Both Mexico and the U.S. enforce rather stringent regulations about pets. That being said, many people routinely bring their dogs across the Mexican border without any problems. For dogs taken into Mexico and returned to the U.S., owners must present a rabies vaccination certificate dated not less than one month nor longer than twelve months (from the current date) along with an International Health Certificate (form 77–043) signed by a veterinarian. The certificate will be stamped at the border or at the Mexican consulate where tourist cards are obtained.

CHAPTER 5

FINDING PLACES TO STAY WITH YOUR DOGS

This chapter deals with the issue of finding suitable places to stay when camping and RVing with dogs. For a comprehensive listing of pet-friendly campgrounds and parks throughout the United States, please refer to Appendix A.

Pet–Related Policies and Restrictions

It should be easy to figure out which campgrounds accept dogs and which don't. However, as a practical matter, the task can be surprisingly complicated. The reason for this has to do with the way that campgrounds depict their actual policy towards pets. Since few campgrounds want to turn away potential customers, they rarely state outright that they don't accept pets. Instead, they effectively restrict pets on the basis of their number, weight, and breed.

To make matters worse, many published campground directories fail to address the issue adequately or they simply indicate that a particular campground has "pet restrictions". As a result, most dog owners are unable to determine a campground's policy towards pets unless they call and ask. On that note, here are some things to keep in mind:

Keep High Standards	Places that are genuinely pet–friendly are a pleasure to stay at. They appreciate what it's like to travel and camp with animals and best of all, they sincerely enjoy dogs. When you find places like this, spread the word.
Ask Other Dog Owners	Talk to other campers with dogs. They can be a great source of valuable information regarding pet–friendly (or unfriendly) places.

**Call Before
You Go**

Even if a campground states that it's pet friendly, give them a call before you go. This way, you'll be able to make sure that *your* dogs are actually accepted.

**Look for Simple
Pet Policies**

Places that are genuinely pet–friendly typically have uncomplicated policies. One common example reads: *All dogs must be on a leash and owners are required to pick up after their dogs.*

**Be Careful of
One–sided Pet
Restrictions**

In our opinion, parks and campgrounds that have size restrictions (i.e. nothing over 25 pounds) or limit the number of pets you can have, are not *entirely* pet friendly. Dogs come in all sizes and quantities. If you want to stay at a campground that genuinely welcomes you and your dogs, avoid places with overly ambitious pet policies.

Believe it or not, some campgrounds won't allow Poquita to spend the night (courtesy of Wilmer and Judy Pittman).

**Avoid Unrealistic
Pet Rules**

Some places state that you cannot leave your dog unattended. This policy may be pet–friendly but it's not particularly *people*–friendly. There are times when you must leave your dog alone. Besides, the vast majority of campers are able to leave their dogs alone in their RV without incident.

Scrutinize Breed Restrictions
There are very few breeds of dogs that could be considered fundamentally dangerous. While we understand the thinking behind banning certain breeds, it makes us wonder how the vast majority of pet–friendly campgrounds somehow get by without these same restrictions.

Campground Layouts and Amenities

Even if a campground *does* demonstrate a positive attitude regarding dogs, there are other critical factors that can make or break a campground's actual suitability for campers with pets. Here are a few suggestions regarding this issue:

Avoid Crowded Sites
Many campgrounds, regrettably, have sites that are small, jam–packed, and short on privacy. Places like these can be stressful for dogs and their owners. Before making a reservation, talk with the hosts to get a sense of the campground's layout and amenities.

Check Out the Reviews
There is a web site that posts reviews and comments about specific campgrounds (www.rvparkreviews.com). While some reviews may lack fairness, they can be very illuminating.

Don't Judge a Campground by its Site Plan
You can't always judge a park on the basis of its published site plan because the individual sites might be very suitable. For instance, there's a campground in Lexington, KY that shows a site plan on their web site (www.kyhorsepark.com) that gives the impression that the park is severely congested. In reality, the sites are spacious and attractive with manicured lawns and beautiful shade trees. They're also genuinely pet–friendly.

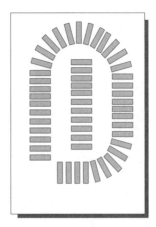

On paper, this park looks crowded. In reality, it might be spacious, depending on the map's scale, the level of site privacy, and the actual size of each site.

Seek Out Publicly Owned Parks

Parks and campgrounds that are owned and operated by federal, state, or local authorities tend to be less crowded and more spacious than privately owned places. Thus, many veteran campers and RVers with dogs look for publicly owned facilities. One drawback is that many of these parks lack the full hookups that are often available at privately owned campgrounds.

Look for Isolated Sites

When you arrive at a campground, ask if there are sites that offer more privacy than others. It's always easier with dogs when you have a little breathing room.

Assess Their Pet Provisions

The best pet–friendly campgrounds have special provisions for dogs such as walking trails, planned activities, pet supplies, dedicated play areas, boarding facilities, and dog–sitting services. One highly regarded example is Four Paws Kingdom in Rutherfordton, NC.

Dog show participants often travel from show to show in recreational vehicles. They depend on campgrounds that are extremely tolerant of pets. These beautiful Salukis belong to Rachel and John Cohee, Sharon Gause, Suzie Henson, Destany Navarro, Aimee Reed, Tajia Taylor, Mara Utterback, and Andrew Wood.

Look at the Big Picture

Sometimes, unsuitable campgrounds can be tolerated in the short run if there are mitigating factors. For example, we once stayed at a campground in Las Vegas that was exceptionally crowded. However, it was convenient to the strip, had full hookups, and was adjacent to a large public park that was perfect for walking the dogs.

CHAPTER 6

STAYING AT CAMPGROUNDS WITH YOUR DOGS

The purpose of this chapter is to help you make the most out of the parks and campgrounds that you stay at. It will give you some idea of what to expect when you arrive, what to watch out for, what to do with your dogs, and how to deal with other campers (and *their* dogs).

Checking In at the Campground

Whether staying at a campground for a single night or spending an entire season, there are a few things to take care of before you check in.

If you have a dog that barks, enjoys frightening people, or bounces off the wall when they get to a new place, find some way to calm them down *before* registering. For example, in our case, when we first pull up to a campground, one of us begins to threaten the dogs within an inch of their life if they make a sound, while the other handles the registration process. The idea isn't to sneak your dogs in. It's simply about making life easier for everyone.

 You should keep a copy of your dog's medical records in a convenient location because some campgrounds require proof of vaccination when checking in.

There's also something you should do *before* you start setting up camp. Right after you turn off the engine, take your dog for a quick walk. They're apt to be apprehensive about their new surroundings and will undoubtedly need to relieve themselves. A quick walk will alleviate both concerns. Also, give your dogs some water. Besides quenching their thirst, this simple gesture will let them know that this place is going to be their home for a little while.

These two Weimaraners, owned by Jeni Roosen, are enjoying their afternoon nap (inside an enclosure). Notice that the furniture includes a dog bed and a fold–out cot.

Lining Up Emergency Medical Care

If you plan on staying in an area for a while, it's imperative that you find the location of the nearest emergency care facility, especially if you're in a region that has poisonous snakes. Each year, more than 15,000 dogs are bitten by snakes (80% are rattlesnakes). If your dog is bitten, you normally have less than half an hour to obtain medical care. Assuming that you'll have to first get your dog into a vehicle and then drive somewhere, it doesn't give you much time to figure out *where* to go.

 When you first arrive, obtain the yellow pages from the campground to secure the address and phone number of the nearest emergency pet care facility. Then tape this information (along with driving directions) onto your refrigerator.

Caring for Your Dogs When You Can't

If your dogs are at a campground, there could be a serious problem if you get hurt when you're away from the park. Fortunately, there's a simple way to address this scenario. Simply fill out two cards like the one shown on the following page. Place one copy in your wallet (or purse) and place another in your vehicle, where someone can easily find it. These instructions will enable someone to make arrangements for your pet's care, should you need it.

My name is Bob Smith. I'm currently staying in an RV (Winnebago Brave) at the Big Valley Campground in Springdale, Virginia (302–524–9016). Currently, there is one dog (Max) and one cat (Pudge) in the motorhome. If you find this note, please call the campground to make sure that someone can take care of my pets. My cell phone number is 417–869–7233. If you can't get through, please call my brother Ray at 417–862–0488 (raysmith@hotmail.com). Thank you !

A well–placed note like this one can eliminate the possibility of your dogs being inadvertently abandoned if something happens to you. Place one copy in your vehicle and keep another on your person.

Securing Your Dogs

Virtually all parks and campgrounds have rules that require dogs to be on a leash at all times. While this requirement may seem overly restrictive at times, it does make sense for one important reason. Your dog won't get lost if it's always on a leash. The fact is, every year, a significant number of people lose their dogs while camping. The circumstances vary but one fact is always the same. The lost dog was not on a leash.

 Before you devise a way to secure your dog while at the campground, make sure that they can't get loose when you open the door of your vehicle. The easiest way is to put on your dog's leash before opening the door. Also, to keep people from inadvertently letting your dog out, place a sign on the door of your RV that lets visitors know that you have a dog inside.

There are numerous methods for containing your dogs at a campground. We've seen everything from ropes tied to picnic tables to elaborate kennels consisting of multiple sections of portable pet fencing. One particularly elegant solution entailed the use of a portable deck that came with its own aluminum railing (www.wingdeck.com).

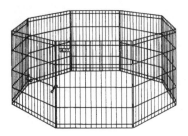

This ExPen™ is portable, easy to set up, and very secure
(courtesy of Midwest Homes for Pets).

The following table summarizes the most commonly used approaches for securing dogs:

Table 1 – Options for Securing Dogs at a Campsite

Method	Benefits	Drawbacks
Chain, cable, or rope	Can be secured to any stationary object.	Tend to get tangled.
Dog runs	Provides good mobility and minimizes tangling.	Many parks ban the securing of leads to trees.
Portable pet fencing	Expandable, easy to set up, and secure for most dogs.	Requires dedicated storage space.
Pet cages and crates	Easy to set up. Very secure.	Offers little mobility. Needs dedicated storage space.
Chain-link fencing based enclosures	Extremely secure and expandable.	Heavy, bulky, and needs dedicated storage space.
Screen rooms (free standing or fixed to RV)	Roomy, bug–free, rain proof, holds multiple dogs.	Needs dedicated storage. Must be set up and stored.
Portable decking (www.wingdeck.com)	Expandable, secure, and can serve as a porch.	Needs dedicated storage. Must be set up and stored.

 Never leave a dog tied to a rope or chain outside when you're not around since the risk of strangulation is greater than you think. Furthermore, in some areas of the country, coyotes and mountain lions will take advantage of a tied–up dog, even in broad daylight. If it's warm, make sure that your dog has access to some shade and plenty of water.

This portable kennel, used by show dog professionals, consists of chain link fencing and a removable roof.

What to Do if Your Dog Gets Lost

Losing a dog in a campground is unfortunately a common occurrence. Here are some of the things that can help to find a lost dog:

Get Help from the Locals   In many cases, the best approach for finding your dog is to seek the advice of people that are familiar with the area. This might include animal control authorities; local police; animal shelters; emergency pet care clinics; campground hosts; and area vets.

Look Around and Shout   Some people automatically dash off in their car to look for their dog when they might be better off focusing their search on the immediate area. If your voice doesn't carry, create a makeshift megaphone out of cardboard. If it's dark, bring a strong flashlight.

Leave Something Behind   If you have to leave the area without finding your dog, leave a piece of clothing with your scent on it (i.e. nail it to a tree). If your dog comes back, they'll often stay by the object assuming that you'll be back to retrieve it. We've seen this approach used very successfully.

Post Flyers
If you have a photo of your dog, take it to a Kinkos or an office supply store. They'll help you to create a missing pet poster. Be sure to offer a reward because they tend to improve the odds of finding a lost dog. Don't forget to take the posters down when they're no longer needed.

Talk to Other Campers
Walk around and talk to other campers. If you can, give them a picture of your dog and be sure to leave your cell phone number.

Use the Press
Place a "Lost Pet" ad in the local papers. Also, be sure to check the "Found" section in the newspaper each day.

Don't Get Swindled
There are con artists that will rip–off people with lost dogs. As a result, never meet someone alone, never give out your address, and don't give anybody the reward money until you actually have your dog back.

Leaving Your Dogs Alone at the Campground

Despite rules about leaving dogs unattended, there are often times when you'll need to leave your dogs alone. In this case, make sure that your dog won't be a nuisance while your away. These are some of the methods used by others to deal with this situation:

Never Let Them Roam
Never let your dogs wander freely around a campground. It's not only the best way to lose your dog, it will also inevitably result in complaints.

Keep Them Inside

When leaving your dogs alone, always keep them inside your camper or RV. Never, ever leave them outside tied up.

Have a Backup Plan

In hot weather, many campers leave their dogs in a camper or RV with the air conditioner running. While this is a good way to keep your dog cool, you should have a contingency plan for dealing with power outages or equipment failures. Try to park in a shady spot and always leave a few windows open. Leave them plenty of water and consider installing a thermostatically controlled (12 volt) ventilation fan that automatically turns on when the temperature gets too high. If at all possible, leave a key with an obliging neighbor. If there's a problem, they can call you, open more windows, and generally look after your dogs until you return.

Block Their View

To minimize barking, restrict your dog's view of the outside world by closing the shades in your RV.

Karen Martin's Great Dane "Glory" keeps a watchful eye on the outside world through the opening in her RV's screen door.

Play Some Tunes

Some dogs that are afraid to be alone suffer from separation anxiety. Try leaving the radio or TV on. It may help to calm them down.

Consider a Crate	Some people leave their dog in its crate. Be sure to provide plenty of water. Refer to the previous comment regarding a backup plan.
Try Using Medications	To minimize anxiety, some dog owners have had success with amitriptyline, dog appeasing pheromones, St. John's Wort, or homeopathic pet medicines.
Consider Getting an 2nd Dog	If drugs, distractions, and window blocking techniques don't seem to work, consider getting a second dog. After all, everything is easier when you're not alone.
Take Them With You	If you have a dog that barks constantly when you're away, don't leave them alone. It's hard on the dog and even harder on other campers.

Dealing with Other Campers and Dogs

Once you get settled into a campground, you'll soon be mingling with other campers (and their dogs). While few campgrounds actually distribute detailed pet regulations, here are a few "unwritten" rules that you should try to comply with:

Control Your Dogs	One of the most common complaints involves dogs that run freely within a campground. If you can't see your dogs, you can't control them.
Respect the Views of Others	Bear in mind, many campers and RVers don't travel with dogs. In fact, some see dogs as a nuisance. That's one reason why it's important to be a responsible and thoughtful dog owner.
Be Careful of Other Dogs	Some dogs find other dogs to be a threat, especially when they're on a leash. As a result, try not to approach other campers with dogs when you're out walking your dog.
Get Out and	If you're out walking *without* your dog, it's

Socialize

perfectly acceptable to mingle with other dog owners. People love to talk about their dogs and will be interested in hearing all about yours.

Limit Your Dog's View

If your dog always barks at people and dogs, configure your RV or camper in such a way as to reduce their view of the road. You can also close the blinds when your dog is inside.

Clean Up After Your Dogs

Always pick up after your dog. This helps to keep the area clean, making it more enjoyable for others. It also ensures that dogs will always be welcome in the years to come.

Respect Other People's Apprehension about Dogs

If you have a breed that may be perceived as aggressive (like our German Shepard Dogs), give people an opportunity to steer clear of your dogs. For example, when we're taking them for a walk, we usually cross the road when we pass other people.

These three dogs are camping friends. The two dogs are on the left (Fearless and Lilac) belong to the authors. The dog on the right, Bingo, is owned by Lyle and Helen Kingsbury. Helen (shown above) is giving the group a little advice.

Reduce Persistent Barking	People want to relax when they're camping. If your dog barks a lot, find a way to calm them down, especially at night. It's not reasonable to expect others to put up with nonstop barking.
Handle Complaints Sensibly	If someone does complain about your dog, keep cool and focus on the complaint, not the person complaining. If you become defensive or combative, you'll give the campground one more reason to restrict pets.

Activities for Your Dogs

Playing with your dog is not just fun and games. It can also provide exercise, enforce training goals, reduce stress, and lower the incidence of problematic behaviors (such as barking). Plus, camping trips are ideal times to have fun with your dog because there's normally lots of space and plenty of time. While the number of potential pet–related activities is virtually unlimited, the following list should be enough to get you started:

Walks, Jogging, and Hiking	Dogs are always a great excuse to go on a hike. Bring plenty of water, take some treats, keep them on their leash, and stay on the trails.
Picnics	Our dog's favorite pastime is begging. What better activity for the begging dog than a picnic. Be sure to bring some food (and a few toys) for them. That way, you'll be able to eat as well.
Ball or Frisbee Toss	Even if your dog isn't a champion athlete, they'll still enjoy chasing after a Frisbee or a tennis ball. It's great exercise and maybe you can even teach them to give it back once in a while.
Agility Training	We've seen people set up chairs, hoops, and other camping gear to create a makeshift obstacle course for their dogs. It's a blast to watch the dogs soar over chairs, hammocks, and coolers (or not).

Swimming   If your dog enjoys the water, let them go in for a dip. Better yet, if you're on a lake with a dock, show them how to dive into the water. Bring plenty of towels and watch out for fishing lines, power boats, and broken glass (along the shore).

Boating   If your dog likes the water, they'll really enjoy boating. If you plan on fishing though, be careful when you haul in your catch because some dogs like to help.

Most dogs love everything to do with the water including fishing, swimming, and boating.

Campfires   There's something timeless about sitting around a campfire at night with your dog. You can then celebrate the occasion by cooking up a few hotdogs. Needless to say, this treasured moment will also require some beer.

Screen Rooms   Dogs love watching the world go by in bug–free, weather–proof comfort. There are stand–alone models that function like a tent and others that work in conjunction with an RV's awning.

Playing with Other Dogs   If you're really fortunate, you'll meet some folks with well–adjusted dogs that will play with your dog. There's nothing like watching a group of dogs having the time of their life playing with their own kind.

CHAPTER 7

COPING WITH DIVERSE ENVIRONMENTS

Campers and RVers are inherently some of the most mobile people in the world. In fact, many full–time RVers spend their entire life traveling from place to place. While mobility is clearly one of the things that makes RVing so attractive, it also means that you and your dogs will inevitably end up staying in places that are very different from what you're used to.

Although this desert campground is beautiful, it does have its share of treacherous plant life, dangerous predators, and challenging conditions. If you plan on camping in the desert, be sure to read the next section.

Accordingly, this chapter includes information and insight that can help you cope with some of the nation's more challenging environments. It's possible that this chapter may inadvertently serve to depict the U.S. as an exceptionally dangerous place for dogs. As a practical matter, it's no more dangerous than other comparable places in the world. In any case, when it comes to dealing with unfamiliar places, a little knowledge can go a long way. That's precisely what this chapter is about.

The Desert

Deserts represent one of the most challenging environments in the world due to an extreme lack of water, intense heat, treacherous plant life, and deadly predators. Here are some things that you should consider when camping in the desert with dogs:

Bring Lots of Water   When going for a walk with your dog, bring plenty of water and a container for drinking. If your dog starts panting and seems out of breath, find some shade, give them some water, and then head back. Some camping stores sell specialized backpacks that are designed to hold and dispense water. Plus, most pet stores sell collapsible bowls that can be kept in a daypack.

This specialized backpack from CamelBak™ holds more than a gallon of water. The tube (shown on the right) can be used for sipping or dispensing. There's also room in the backpack for other items such as a folding bowl.

Clean Up After Your Dog   If you're on an established path or in a campground, pick up and properly dispose of your dog's waste.

Be Aware of Valley Fever   If you're staying in the southwestern United States, you should be aware of a debilitating infectious disease known as Valley Fever. Since the disease is caused by a fungus in the soil, dogs tend to become infected as a result of digging and playing in dry, dusty areas. Contact a local vet to see if the area has a high occurrence of this disease. If it does, keep a tight rein on your dog's activities.

Watch Out for Hot Surfaces	When walking your dog on a paved surface, make sure that it's not too hot for their paws. In the warmer months, the sun can quickly turn an asphalt road into a sizzling hot plate. If there's some question, use the palm of your hand to assess the pavement's temperature.
Use Current ID Tags	Make sure that your dog's collar has an ID tag with their name and your current telephone number.

Dealing with Dangerous Desert Plants

Since water is such a precious commodity in the desert, most of the plants that grow there are specifically designed to keep living things away. Hence, desert plants can be a real challenge to campers with dogs. Here are some of the tricks used by experienced desert campers:

Get an Illustrated Field Guide	If you plan on staying in the desert for a while, you'll need the ability to properly identify the plants and animals that live there.
Bring a Plastic Comb and a Pair of Pliers	When taking your dog for a walk in the desert, bring a comb and a small pair of needle–nose pliers. The comb is highly effective at flicking away the fragments of cholla cactus (called "joints") that will inevitably latch onto your dog. The pliers are used for pulling out individual thorns. Never remove any joints or thorns with your fingers or you'll find yourself in the same prickly predicament as your dog.
Test the Ground for Thorns	Before taking your dog down a path, gently press the palm of your hand on the ground in a few different locations. If small thorns, needles, or prickly seeds stick to your hand, don't proceed. If you do, your dog's paws will quickly become imbedded with these same thorns and needles.

Remove Stray Cholla Joints

Once you get settled in, conduct a visual survey of the immediate area to identify and remove any stray pieces of cactus that are on the ground. Use barbeque tongs, a rake, sticks, or pliers to move them out of the way. Don't use your foot to move them because they'll simply stick to your shoe.

Watch Out for Wind and Rain

After a windy or rainy night, avoid walking anywhere near cholla bushes. The wind and rain will knock off dozens of prickly cholla joints that will then lay in waiting like Velcro™ land mines.

Consider Using Booties

If you're going to be walking in the desert with your dog, consider getting them some booties. Many pet stores sell leather or vinyl versions that are highly effective at protecting your dog's paws. However, be prepared to remove thorns that stick to the booties.

Train Your Dog to Avoid Cactus

Begin to teach your dog to stay away from dangerous plants. Whenever they approach the plant, quickly pull on their leash while using a consistent and recognizable command.

Observe Your Dog's Behavior

Watch your dog's behavior closely when walking in the desert. If they begin to limp, favor one leg, or start lifting a paw, stop immediately and examine their paws for thorns. Be sure to run your fingers between their toes. When you get back, use a flashlight to check for burrs, barbs, and thorns that you might have missed.

Watch for Swelling

Some cactus thorns are capable of producing severe physical reactions. If you see any swelling or inflammation in your dog's paws, take them to a vet immediately. Antibiotics and anti-inflammatory drugs will usually clear things up in a couple of days. For minor irritations, apply a small amount of hydrocortisone ointment.

Fearless, the author's male German Shepard dog, learned about cactus the hard way. His rear paw grew to twice its normal size when a hardly visible thorn imbedded itself between his toes.

Avoiding Predators

The creatures that live in the desert represent some of the toughest survivors on the planet. In comparison, family dogs are like pampered rich kids from the suburbs. Therefore, pay close attention to the following advice:

Keep an Eye on the Brush   Don't walk your dog through shrubs, thick brush, or tall grass between March and October when the weather is warm. These locations will often harbor poisonous snakes.

Prepare for Snake Bites   If your dog does get bitten by a snake, keep them calm and take them to a local vet or emergency care facility immediately. For further details, please refer to Chapter 8.

Don't Tie Them Out Alone   Never leave your dog tied outside when you're not around. There are predators that will take advantage of a dog that is unable to escape or defend itself effectively.

Be Careful of the Dark   Most desert predators are partially nocturnal. In fact, snakes, scorpions, coyotes, and tarantulas do most of their hunting on warm summer nights. We tend to walk our dogs on the road at night.

Make a Little Noise   When you're walking in the desert, talk to your dog, whistle, or sing. This will give the snakes and coyotes time to either hide or move on.

Watch Out for Coyotes   Coyotes tend to be very timid in small groups but can be very formidable when in a pack. Therefore, never let a pack of coyotes encircle you or your dog. If you do encounter a pack of coyotes, take a firm hold of your dog's leash and leave the area. Never, ever let your dog off its leash in this scenario.

Use a Flashlight   When walking your dog at night, always use a flashlight in order to see where you're going. The flashlight will also enable moving vehicles, other campers, and wildlife to see you coming.

Forest Lands

The woods are a magical place for dogs because there's an infinite variety of exciting smells and a strong abundance of fascinating wildlife. However, like all natural environments, forests have their own unique set of challenges and natural laws.

Use Pet IDs   Be sure that your dog has a current ID tag. If they get lost in the woods, the tag will become a crucial source of hope and optimism.

Be Careful About Letting Your Dog Off Its Leash   The decision to let your dog off its leash should be made sensibly. For instance, if there are deer in the area, you should always keep your dog on a leash. Dogs frequently get lost when they chase deer too far into the woods.

**Stay Off
Posted Land**
If the area you're hiking in is posted with "No Trespassing" signs, take another route. In some areas of the country, there are people that will shoot dogs that trespass on their property.

**Avoid Hunting
Season**
Never go into the woods during hunting season. If you're camping during hunting season, put a brightly colored orange handkerchief around your dog's neck.

**Be Aware of
Unsafe Terrain**
Ask around or use a topographic map to determine if there are any dangerous cliffs or steep terrain in the area.

**Be Careful
of the Plants**
Don't let your dog eat mushrooms or other strange looking plants. They may be toxic. Likewise, keep an eye open for bushes with thorns, burdock, patches of thistle, poison ivy, poison sumac, or poison oak. There are illustrated guide books that can help you to identify dangerous plants. If your dog does become exposed to poison ivy, bathe the dog immediately using a gentle shampoo and warm water. Be sure to wear rubber gloves and keep the soap and water away from your dog's eyes (to reduce the possibility of spreading the plant's caustic oils).

**Watch Out for
the Water**
Many natural water bodies contain microorganisms that can make you and your dog deathly ill. As a result, don't swallow untreated water from shallow wells, lakes, rivers, springs, ponds, or streams.

**Watch Out
for Bees**
Bee keeping is a popular activity in many rural areas. If you encounter a collection of stacked boxes or stacked crates (called supers) sitting in a sunny location, stay clear. They're probably somebody's bee collection.

Exciting smells and wild animals make the woods a magical place for dogs.
However, become familiar with the area before you let your dog off its leash.

Dealing with Insects

Most wooded environments have an abundant supply of stinging and biting insects. That's why it's important to be prepared.

Use Heartworm Medication

Heartworm is a deadly disease in dogs that is transmitted by mosquitoes. Consequently, if you're in an area with an active mosquito population, make sure that your dog has been tested for and subsequently medicated to prevent heartworm disease.

Use Bug Repellant

If you're in an area with biting insects, rub bug repellant on your dog. Their ears, eyes, mouth, and stomach are the most vulnerable. Follow the instructions on the repellant.

Use Flea and Tick Medication

If you're staying in a wooded area during the summer months, make sure that your dog is being treated with a topical flea and tick medication such as Frontline™. Avoid camping in areas that are notoriously infested with deer ticks (i.e. Cape Cod, Massachusetts). Deer ticks are the primary carriers of Lyme disease, a serious illness that can affect both dogs and people. If you are in such an area, examine your dog for ticks at least once a day.

Remove Ticks
Immediately

For Lyme disease to spread to a dog, ticks must be attached for two days. Therefore, if you find a tick on your dog (or on you), remove it right away. First try using an alcohol soaked swab which may cause the tick to lose its grip. If this doesn't work, use tweezers to take hold of the tick where its mouth is attached to your dog's skin. Try not to squeeze the tick since it could release more bacteria into your dog. If the tick's head stays under the dog's skin, leave it, since it will eventually fall out on its own.

Use Bug
Repellant

If you're in an area with biting insects, rub bug repellant on your dog. Their ears, eyes, mouth, and stomach are the most vulnerable. Follow the instructions on the repellant.

Bring
Hydrocortisone

When your dog is bit or stung, they often make matters worse by licking at the affected area. Hydrocortisone, available at pharmacies, is highly effective at reducing the itching and burning that occurs. Keep a tube handy.

Watch Out for
Insect Nests

Keep an eye out for bee hives, wasps, and hornet nests. They're often attached to tree limbs but sometimes fall to the ground. Yellow jackets, on the other hand, often reside in ground nests that can't be seen until you're on top of them.

Dealing with Animals in Wooded Areas

The vast majority of animals that pose a threat to your dogs are nocturnal. Thus, if you keep your dog out of the woods from dusk to dawn, you'll be in good shape. Here are a few other ways to keep your dog out of trouble:

Make Sure
Your Dog Has
its Shots

Since many wild animals are rabid, make sure that your dog has been vaccinated for rabies.

Stay Clear of Skunks

If your dog gets sprayed by a skunk, bathe them in soda, fruit juice, diluted vinegar, or tomato juice (always avoiding the eyes). You can also use special pet products that are theoretically effective at reducing skunk odors. At any rate, expect to live with the smell for several weeks.

If you keep your dog on a leash and stay out of the woods between dusk and dawn, you'll reduce the likelihood of encountering one of these little guys. If your dog does get sprayed by a skunk, expect to live with the smell for a while.

Be Careful of Porcupines

If your dog gets skewered by a porcupine, get them to a vet as quickly as possible. If this isn't an option, use wire cutters or a similar device to trim off all but an inch of each quill. Then, while someone holds your dog, use pliers to quickly yank out each quill, one at a time. Examine the *inside* of your dog's mouth to make sure that you haven't missed any. Quills that inadvertently break off will eventually soften, dissolve, or fall out.

Watch Out for Bears

Bears are formidable animals. If there are bears in the area, educate yourself about them. Use extreme caution when taking walks and make some noise when moving through thick brush. Consider purchasing a pepper spray device that is designed specifically for bears. Do not let your dog off its leash if you encounter a bear.

Freshwater and Marine Environments

Most dogs love water. Whether it's the ocean, a lake, or even a puddle, dogs like to splash around and get wet. If you're staying at a park or a campground near a body of water, there are some things that you should keep in mind:

Comply With Local Ordinances	Most beach environments are highly regulated. As a result, make sure that you're complying with local ordinances relating to dogs.
Clean Up After Your Dog	While on the beach, clean up after your dog. Don't simply bury it in the sand.

Water–Related Hazards

The following comments and suggestions are intended to increase your awareness of the unique risks associated with freshwater and marine environments:

Avoid Fishing Areas	Watch out for fisherman. Sometimes it's hard to see a line in the water. In marine environments, make sure that your dog doesn't get tangled in buoy lines, fish nets, and other subsurface utility lines.
Be Careful of Power Boats	If your dog likes to swim, make sure they're protected from power boats and jet skis.
Learn What's In the Water	Keep your dog out of any pond or lake that supports snapping turtles or water moccasins (a poisonous freshwater snake). These creatures can easily injure or kill a dog. Similarly, some coastal beaches in warm climates have problems with stinging jellyfish. Check with the locals before you go in.
Don't Let Dogs Chase Wildlife	Don't allow your dog to chase ducks and geese in the water. They might encounter a beaver that has the skills to drown a dog.

Don't Assume the Water's Safe

If you're staying near a lake or pond that's located within a populated area, the water will probably be polluted. If your dog does go in, give them a bath and clean their ears with a pet product that is designed for this purpose.

Avoid Certain Beaches

There are beaches with barnacle–covered rocks and razor-sharp shells that can damage your dog's paws. Before your dog hits the beach, check it out.

Watch Out for Broken Glass

Lakes and ponds in populated areas often have broken glass along the shoreline. If your dog is wading in the water, examine their paws for cuts when they come out.

Be Aware of Leeches

Warm, shallow, grassy bottom lakes are often teeming with leaches and other bloodsuckers. Ask around. If they are present, think twice about letting your dog go in for a swim. If they do, be sure to examine and wash them thoroughly when they come out.

Watch Out for Hidden Currents

Calm looking ocean beaches can often conceal dangerous currents and rip tides. If a beach is deserted or there are warning signs about dangerous tides, stay out of the water. If you do get carried out by rip tides, don't try to swim back to shore. Instead, swim to your left or right (parallel to the shore) until you feel yourself being carried back towards the shore. The idea is to first get out of the rip tide's region of influence before attempting to swim back.

Gentle waves and deserted beaches can mask dangerous rip tides that can carry you and your dog far out into the ocean in a matter of seconds.

Bathe Your Dog When it Comes Out

If your dog has been playing in the ocean, wash them thoroughly when they get out. Salt water will leave your dog's coat feeling greasy and can often take days to dry completely. In the meantime, your dog will smell like an old plate of fried clams.

Cities

Cities are considered, by some, to be one of the more challenging environments for people with dogs. However, take a close look at any major urban area and you'll observe an endless variety of well adjusted "city" dogs.

Even though some dog owners find cities challenging, they can actually be a lot of fun. Most metropolitan centers have large public parks and some cities even promote formal activities for pets.

In the late 1990's, we lived in Boston with our female German Shepard dog and have fond memories of taking her to the Boston Common for long walks. There were several informal "dog groups" that gave us a chance to socialize a little while she frolicked with the other dogs.

With respect to camping, most dog owners stay in campgrounds *outside* the metropolitan area and simply take their dog with them when they go into the city. The following suggestions are based on extensive experience with dogs in the city:

Keep a Tight Rein on Your Dog	Never let your dog off its leash unless you're in a designated dog area. If your dog gets lost in the city, you're in for a long, stressful ordeal.
Have a Current Pet ID Tag	Make sure that your dog has an ID tag that's up to date. Our dogs have two. One from the Good Sam Club and another engraved pet tag that includes their name and our cell phone number.
Make Sure Your Dog is Vaccinated	Rabies are a big deal to animal control authorities. Consequently, make sure that your dog has a tag indicating the date of its last rabies vaccination.
Rely on the Experts if Your Dog Gets Loose	If you do lose your dog, you'll need to notify the local animal control authorities. They should be able to tell you the best way to proceed.
Locate Grassy Parks	If your dog isn't accustomed to the city, it can often be difficult to get them to do their business on paved surfaces. Every few hours, we take our dogs to the small parks that exist in most cities. There, they can enjoy the benefits of real grass.
Comply With Dog Curbing Laws	Because cities are crowded, it's imperative that you always pick up after your dog. Plus, most cities have strict ordinances that include stiff fines for dog owners that don't curb their dog.

$200 Fine

For Failure to
Curb Your Dog

Signs like these, common in most cities, provide a
compelling incentive for picking up after your dog.

Watch Where You Walk and Always Use a Leash	Most cities impose very strict leash laws. Pay close attention to street signs in the area. If you don't, you might get a nice fat ticket from the local animal control police.

Urban Hazards and Environmental Risks

The following recommendations are intended to increase your awareness of the various risks that dogs in the city often face:

Avoid Empty City Lots	Abandoned city lots often contain hazardous chemicals, toxic substances, and a wide array of physical hazards. Consequently, keep your dogs away from them.
Stay Away From Puddles	Never let your dog drink from a puddle in the city. It could contain antifreeze, transmission fluid, motor oil, or other dangerous substances.
Teach Your Dog to Drop Things	Cities tend to have a lot of debris, trash, and garbage. As a result, train your dog to drop things that they pick up. Otherwise, they could become sick or choke on something.
Watch Out for Hot Asphalt	If you're walking your dog in the summer, watch out for hot asphalt. Some paved surfaces get so hot, they'll blister your dog's paws in a matter of seconds.

Protect Your Dog from Theft If you must leave your dog in a parked vehicle, lock the car and leave the windows open just a little (assuming it's not too warm). If your dog is aggressive, make sure that a child can't slip their hands through the open window. If your dog is a sought–after breed (but relatively defenseless), avoid parking in public areas. Instead, stay in a parking garage or a private parking lot.

Learn to Cross Streets Like a Local When crossing busy city streets, keep your dog's leash short and hold them close to your side. Always obey traffic signals and wait until there's a crowd before you cross (there's safety in numbers). Never *run* across the street.

Dealing with People

One of the most challenging aspects of taking a dog into the city is the endless stream of people that will inevitably approach your dog. As a result, consider the following advice:

Consider Using a Muzzle If your dog has aggressive tendencies, put a muzzle on them while in the city. It might look a little intimidating but it beats the alternative.

Respect Your Dog's Limits Some dogs shouldn't be taken into an urban environment. This includes dogs that are exceptionally protective, overly aggressive, or frightened of people.

Don't Let People Feed Your Dog Your dog should never take food from strangers. If people offer, politely tell them that you're trying to train your dog to refuse food in order to avoid the possibility of malicious poisoning.

Don't Be Afraid to Warn People Away If your dog is wary of strangers, it's ok to tell people that your dog isn't friendly. Most people will understand and appreciate the heads up.

CHAPTER 8

MEDICAL PROBLEMS

While this chapter is not a substitute for formal medical training or veterinarian care, it is designed to help you deal with the most common pet–related medical emergencies. It includes practical advice and simple instructions for handling problems such as choking, bleeding, broken bones, dehydration, snake bites, poisons, and car accidents. This chapter also contains a list of medical supplies that should be included in a first aid kit for dogs.

Handling Emergencies

There are some medical conditions that you can sometimes treat yourself. On the other hand, there are situations that *always* require a veterinarian, including the following:

Seizures	Abrupt Viciousness or Lethargy
Abnormal Lumps	Excessive Water Consumption
Abnormal Posture	Unable to Put Weight on a Limb
Breathing Problems	Discharges from Nose or Eyes
Serious Burns	Persistent Constipation
Car Accidents	Ingesting Poisons
Excessive Diarrhea	Jaundice
Excessive Drooling	Excessive Bleeding
Excessive Vomiting	Loss of Hair or Open Sores
High Fever (>104°F)	Choking
Inability to Urinate	Marked Weight Loss
Loss of Appetite	Excessive Urination
Serious Blow or Fall	Unable to Stand or Get Up
Snake Bites	Excessive Head Shaking

When a medical emergency does occur, it's essential that you remain calm. In these situations, your dog is totally dependent on you. If you become frantic, you may be unable to perform the emergency procedures that they so desperately require. In any serious emergency, there are always certain routines that you must follow:

Make Sure Your Dog is Safe and Secure

Be sure that you're in a safe place. If you're close to traffic, move. You can't do much if you get hit by a car! Whatever you do, don't let go of your dog, even if it struggles or tries to bite you.

Consider a Muzzle

Assess your dog's injuries and make a quick decision regarding whether to use a muzzle. If your dog is in pain or frightened, they may try to bite anyone that gets near. If in doubt, use a muzzle. The following page has instructions for creating an improvised muzzle.

Get Ready to Go

Quickly evaluate your dog's injuries and prepare to transport them to a veterinarian. If you suspect internal injuries or broken bones, secure them (with anything) to a flat surface such as a board or a table. If you don't have a hard surface, use a blanket or a coat.

Get Help Any Way You Can

When you're on the road, try calling the local police, stop at a store, or find some yellow pages. When you do locate a vet, be sure to call first. This will enable them to give you any required instructions and prepare for your arrival. Be sure to get detailed driving instructions. These two organizations can also be extremely helpful in an emergency:

The American Animal Hospital Association
1–800–252–2242

The American Veterinary Medical Association
1–847–925–8070

Use Your Computer

If you have a computer with wireless internet access, you should be able to locate area vets. Start a search by using the three keywords: *Vets, City, State* (i.e. Vets, Richmond, Virginia). In addition, the following web sites maintain that they can help you find a veterinarian:

- www.vetquest.com
- www.vetlocator.petplace.com
- www.healthypet.com

How to Create a Makeshift Muzzle

1. Use a strip of long cloth or a piece of sheeting.

2. Make a noose by tying a knot in the middle of the strip of material, leaving a large loop.

3. Approach the dog from behind and slip the noose over the snout, about halfway up the nose. Then pull it tight.

4. Pull the ends back behind the neck and tie them behind the ears.

5. If you don't have any cloth, use first aid tape to secure your dog's muzzle. Be sure to leave enough space for them to breathe.

Treating an Unconscious Dog

Before you begin CPR procedures on your dog, you must make sure that there isn't an obstruction in their airway. If there is, you must take measures to remove it *before* performing CPR, even if your dog isn't breathing. For details, refer to the subsequent section that deals with choking dogs.

 Never practice CPR on a real dog. While it's okay to use your dog to practice where to place your hands or check a pulse, never perform artificial respiration and cardiac message on a healthy dog. If you do, you could cause serious harm.

How to Perform CPR on Dogs

Make Sure Their Airway is Clear   Open your dog's mouth and confirm that their airway is clear. If not, remove any visible obstruction or perform the procedure for choking dogs that is described further on.

Get Them Breathing   Assuming their airway is clear, tilt your dog's head back and proceed as follows:

- For big dogs, firmly close their jaw and steadily exhale into their nose. Your dog's chest should expand.

- For smaller dogs, cover their nose *and* mouth with your mouth as you exhale. Your dog's chest should expand. For small dogs, be careful not to exhale forcefully as you might injure them.

- Use the following guide to set the number of breaths per minute:

  Dogs over 60 lbs: 1 breath every 6 seconds

  Dogs 10 to 60 lbs: 1 breath every 4 seconds

  Dogs under 10 lbs: 1 breath every 3 seconds

Begin Chest Compressions

- For medium dogs, lay them on their back and compress their chest (as you would for a person).

- For small dogs and large dogs with deep chests, lay your dog on its side and gently compress the side of its rib cage. Alternatively, you can lay your dog on its back and press on both sides of its rib cage.

- The rate of chest compressions is based on the dog's size:

  Dogs over 60 lbs: 60 compressions per minute (one compression every second)

  Dogs 10 to 60 lbs: 80 to 100 compressions per minute (three compressions every two seconds)

  Dogs under 10 lbs: 120 compressions per minute (two compressions every second)

Alternate Breaths with Compressions

The ratio of compressions to breaths varies with the size (and age) of the dog. For puppies, use one breath per two compressions. For medium dogs, use one breath per three compressions. Large dogs (over 120 lbs.) require one breath per five compressions. Continue until your dog begins to breathe on their own.

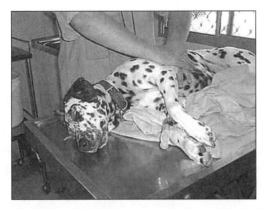

This Dalmatian is receiving chest compressions. Be sure to use the ratio of breaths to chest compressions that is appropriate for your dog's size and age. Also, never practice CPR on a healthy dog (courtesy www.petalert.com).

Dealing with Choking Dogs

If your dog is choking, you don't have a lot of time. Reach into your dog's mouth and remove any foreign objects. If necessary, pull their tongue out and sweep your fingers around. If you feel something, try to hook it with your fingers and pull it out. If you can't, perform the Heimlich Maneuver as described below:

Performing the Heimlich Maneuver on Dogs

- If your dog is choking and you can't manually remove the obstruction, place your dog with his back against your chest or lay them on their side. Then lie down behind them and put both arms just below their rib cage.

- Hug the dog with one fist in the other hand and give five sharp thrusts (bear hugs) to their abdomen.

- Check to see if there's something in the dog's airway.

- If the object is still not dislodged, try using the heel of your hand to give them a sharp thump on the back (between their shoulder blades).

- If you find something, remove it. If your dog isn't breathing, proceed with CPR as described previously.

Checking Your Dog's Vitals

Checking Their Pulse

The easiest place to locate a pulse is along the femoral artery in your dog's groin area. Place your fingers on the inside of their hind leg and slide your hand upward until the back of your fingers touch their abdomen. Gently move your fingers back and forth on the inside of the hind leg until you feel a pulse. Count the number of pulses in fifteen seconds and multiply that number by four. This will give you the number of beats per minute (bpm). These are the normal resting heart rates for dogs:

- Small dogs: 90 to 160 bpm
- Medium dogs: 70 to 110 bpm
- Large dogs: 60 to 90 bpm

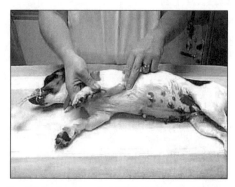

You can also check your dog's heart rate by gently placing your fingers in the location shown above (courtesy www.petalert.com).

Checking a Dog's Temperature

To measure your dog's temperature, use a rectal thermometer. First shake the thermometer with a quick flick of your wrist until it reads less than 94°F. Then apply a small amount of petroleum jelly. Lift your dog's tail and slowly insert the thermometer approximately one inch into their rectum for two minutes. The normal temperature range for dogs is between 100°F and 102.5°F.

Handling Specific Medical Emergencies

This section describes the proper procedures for handling the most common medical emergencies.

Bleeding

Bleeding can result from an accident, a fight with another animal, or from contact with a sharp object. These are general directions:

Apply Direct Pressure to the Wound	Gently press a clean compress or cloth over the bleeding area, allowing it to clot. Do not break up the clot. Instead, keep adding more material or gauze as needed. If a section of bone is exposed or protruding from a wound, cover it with a bandage and apply gentle pressure.
Don't Clean the Wound	Cleaning a wound should only be done by a vet at a hospital. If *you* attempt to clean a wound, it could increase the likelihood of an infection.
Elevate the Point of Bleeding	In conjunction with applying direct pressure, elevate the area that's bleeding. This is very important for larger dogs.
Apply Pressure to the Artery Supplying the Blood	Apply pressure to the femoral artery (groin area) for bleeding in the rear leg; the brachial artery (on the inside of the front leg) for front leg bleeding; and the caudal artery (at the inside base of the tail) for tail bleeding.
Only Apply a Tourniquet as a last Resort	Only use a tourniquet as a last resort because it often results in severe tissue damage or loss of a limb. Tighten the tourniquet around the affected limb and loosen for fifteen to twenty seconds approximately every ten minutes.

Broken Bones

Broken bones can be challenging because dogs usually make matters worse by moving. As a result, take the following steps:

Muzzle Your Dog	A dog with broken bones is usually in severe pain. Therefore, use a muzzle to prevent the possibility of someone getting bitten while attempting to help.

Secure Them to a Board

Gently lay your dog on a padded plank, wooden door, or table top. Carefully secure your dog using sheets, belts, or pieces of clothing.

This unconscious German Shepard dog has been secured to a pet stretcher. If the dog were conscious, there would be more strapping to keep them from moving (courtesy www.petalert.com).

Immobilize the Broken Limb

Never attempt to set a fracture. If a limb is broken, immobilize it (keep it still) by wrapping it in gauze, clothing, or cotton padding. Then create a splint using a magazine, rolled newspaper, towels, or two sticks. The splint should extend one joint above the fracture and one joint below. Secure the area with tape. Make sure that the wrapped splint doesn't constrict blood flow.

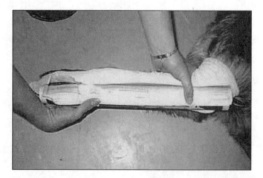

This dog's leg has been immobilized by a makeshift splint. Their leg was first wrapped in a towel. A rolled up tube of newspaper was then strapped to the dog's leg. Never try to actually set a broken limb (courtesy www.petalert.com).

The purpose of a splint it to immobilize the dog's broken bone, not set it. Never try to straighten a broken limb. This must always be performed by a vet in a hospital.

Immobilize Your Pet and Get Them to a Vet
If your pet's spine, ribs, or hips appear injured or broken, gently place them on a stretcher and immobilize them any way you can. Remember, never try to straighten a broken limb. Get them to a vet as quickly as possible.

Burns

Severe burns should always be handled at a hospital. However, for minor burns, do the following:

Apply Cool Water
Run cool water over the affected area. If you're dealing with a chemical burn, rinse the affected area with water for at least 15 to 20 minutes. If necessary, use a mild soap and repeat until the chemical is thoroughly rinsed off.

Don't Apply Lotions
Lotions can often spread burns. As a result, avoid the use of burn ointments or oily lotions.

Cover the Burned Area and Get Them to a Vet
Cover the burned area with a non-stick dressing to keep it clean. The dressing will also serve to prevent your dog from licking the burned area. Then, take your dog to a vet immediately.

Car Accidents

If your dog has been hit by a car or involved in an accident, get them to an emergency care facility or a vet as quickly as possible. In the meantime, follow the procedures described below:

Get Your Dog to a Safe Place
The first priority is to make sure that you and your dog are safe. If you're close to a road, move your dog off to the side.

Keep Them Secure
If possible, place your dog in a carrier or a box and keep them quiet until you get to a vet.

Check for Signs of Shock   Your dog may be in shock. Signs of shock include weakness; collapse, unconsciousness; pale lips, mouth, and eyelids; coolness of skin and legs; rapid but weak pulse; rapid respiration; staring eyes; and dilated pupils. If any of these symptoms occur after an accident, get your dog to a vet immediately.

Elevate Your Dog   Elevate your dog's chest and hindquarters above their head by placing folded towels or a pillow under their chest and body. This will help to increase blood flow to their brain while preventing fluids from filling their chest area.

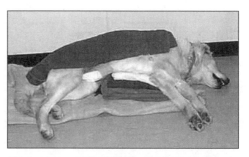

This unconscious dog has folded towels under its rib cage and a piece of clothing over its torso to help keep him warm (courtesy www.petalert.com).

Stop Any Bleeding   Examine your dog and treat any visible signs of bleeding (see the previous section on bleeding).

Perform CPR if Required   If your dog is unconscious, place them on their side with the head extended. Follow the steps for CPR described previously in this chapter.

Keep Them Warm   Try to warm your dog. You can use hot water bottles wrapped in towels, blankets, or clothing. Do not give them any food or water.

Get Them to a Vet   Regardless of your dog's apparent condition, take them to a vet without delay.

Exposure and Hypothermia

Exposure is generally a result of a dog being out in the open for an extended period of time. Consequently, if you're looking for a lost dog, be sure to bring some water, a blanket, and a first aid kit. When you do find them, perform the following procedures:

Confirm Their Condition	Exposure and hypothermia are characterized by violent shaking and shivering followed by lethargy, listlessness, and exhaustion.
Warm Them Up	Warm your dog with blankets, your body, clothing, plastic bottles filled with warm water, a heating pad, a hot water bottle, or a hair dryer.
Monitor Your Dog's Temperature	Monitor your dog's (rectal) temperature every ten to fifteen minutes. When their temperature is back to normal (between 100°F and 102.5°F), stop warming them.
Get Them to a Vet	Even if your dog seems fine, follow up with a visit to the vet immediately.

Dehydration and Heatstroke

Dehydration is normally caused by a dog being exposed to severe conditions for an extended period of time. If you're looking for a lost dog in a hot, dry area, bring plenty of water. When you locate them, take the following steps:

Test for Dehydration	To test for dehydration, lift the skin along your dog's back. It should quickly spring back into place when you let go. If the skin stays up at all, your dog is probably dehydrated.
Pour Lukewarm Water Over Them	If your dog appears heat stressed (excessive panting, staggering, or shaking), take them to a shady place and gently pour water over their head and body. Symptoms of dehydration include dry mouth; sunken eyes; loss of elasticity in the skin; and extreme exhaustion.

Slowly Give Them Water	Provide your dog with water, but don't allow them to guzzle it down because it can result in severe vomiting and increased dehydration. Remove the bowl after a few sips and wait a couple of minutes before letting them take another drink.
Get Them to a Vet	Immediately seek veterinary care. Dehydration is a serious condition and must be treated immediately.

Drowning

The key to treating a drowning dog is to learn how to administer pet CPR. However, you must first clear their airway and empty their lungs as described here:

Open Their Airway	Once your dog is on dry land, clear out their mouth, pull their tongue forward, and extend their neck back to open their airway.
Hold Them Upside Down	If your dog is small, suspend them by their hind legs and gently swing them to drain their lungs. For larger dogs, place them head down on a sloped surface.
Perform CPR	Check for breathing. If necessary, perform rescue breathing and CPR as described previously in this chapter.

Electric Shock

Electrical shocks usually happen quickly and unexpectedly. The faster you can administer CPR, the better. In the meantime, here's what to do first:

Get Them to Safety	Make sure that your dog isn't still in contact with the power source. If they are, don't touch them. Move them with a wooden pole, throw the circuit switch, or do whatever you can to kill the power.

Perform CPR if Required	Follow the steps for CPR described previously in this chapter.
Get Them to a Vet	Quickly seek veterinary care. Shocks can be serious and must be treated immediately.

Snake Bites

The key with snake bites is to keep your dog calm and get them to a hospital immediately. If you already know where the nearest emergency care facility is, you're in good shape. If you don't, find out where the nearest emergency care facility is right now! Here's what to do if your dog gets bitten by a snake:

Make Sure They've Been Bitten	If your dog has been bitten by a snake, they will typically be trembling; drooling; vomiting; have dilated pupils; or collapse. They may also have swelling or bruising at the site of the bite. Never attempt to capture or kill the snake since this frequently results in more bites.
Keep Your Dog Calm	If your dog has been bitten, it's crucial that you keep them calm. Don't let them walk or run and do everything you can to keep them immobile.
Don't Treat Them Yourself	Avoid medications of any type, especially pain medications, cortisone, tranquilizers, or DMSO. Similarly, don't use ice, tourniquets, alcohol, cut and suck techniques, or electrical shock devices.
Get Help Fast	Get your dog to an emergency clinic or hospital as quickly as possible. Call ahead to enable the clinician to prepare the antivenin and make other necessary arrangements.

Poisons

As with snake bites, it helps if you already know where the nearest emergency care facility is. You should also have the poison control hotline telephone number handy where you can find it (1–888–426–4435). Then, follow these directions:

Confirm Their Condition

You should suspect poisoning if your dog has trouble breathing; is having seizures; has severe diarrhea; exhibits a slow or fast heartbeat; has burns around his mouth and lips; or is bleeding from the anus, mouth, or nose.

Call the National Animal Poison Control Center 1–888–426–4435

The National Animal Poison Control Center has one of the largest databases in the U.S.. As a result, they can provide you with crucial information and professional support over the phone. Call them now and follow their advice.

Be Careful About Inducing Vomiting

Never induce vomiting if the ingested substance is either *unknown* or *caustic* (since it could make matters worse). Likewise, never induce vomiting if your dog is having trouble breathing; is having seizures; is unconscious; has a bloated abdomen; or the product label (of the swallowed substance) says *not* to induce vomiting.

Always Induce Vomiting For These Substances

Always induce vomiting for these substances:

- Antifreeze
- Arsenic
- Aspirin
- Insecticides/Pesticides
- Kitchen Matches
- Medications
- Shampoo
- Shoe Polish
- Strychnine (rodent poison)
- Warfarin, but only if *just* consumed.

How to Induce Vomiting (in order of desirability)

Hydrogen Peroxide: Give one teaspoon for every ten pounds of body weight. Wait fifteen minutes. If it doesn't work, repeat the dose.

Dry Mustard: Mix one teaspoon of dry mustard into one cup of lukewarm water. Slowly administer to your dog.

Ipecac: This works, but sometimes the dog will start vomiting and not be able to stop (making it the least desirable option).

Get Them to a
Vet Quickly
Regardless of their outward appearance, get your dog to a vet immediately.

A First Aid Kit for Dogs

This is one possible first-aid kit for dogs. Some people add items and others maintain less. The point is to have one handy and to keep it well stocked.

Tools	Medications
Scissors	Benadryl
Needle Nose Pliers	Glucose Paste or Corn Syrup
Toenail Clippers	Enteric–Coated Aspirin
Latex Gloves	Anti–Diarrhea Medicine
Rectal Thermometer	Pepto–Bismol
Splint Materials	Eye and Ear Drops
Penlight	Oral Antibiotics
Flea Comb	Emetics (to induce vomiting)
Tweezers	Pain Medications (aspirin)
Cleansers & Disinfectants	Anti–inflammatory
3% Hydrogen Peroxide	Hair Ball Ointment
Betadine	Miscellaneous Medications
Sterile Eyewash	**Topical Ointments**
Dressings & Bandages	Hydrogen Peroxide
Non–stick Pads	Rubbing Alcohol
Adhesive Tape	Epsom Salts
Towels	Calamine Lotion
Gauze Pads (4 in.2)	Antibiotic Ointment
Suturing Materials	Baking Soda (for stings)
Cloth Strips	KY Jelly
Cotton Swabs	Stop Bleeding Powder
Gauze Roll	Hydrocortisone Ointment

the use of such information. Readers are encouraged to confirm the information contained herein with other reliable sources and to direct any questions concerning emergency pet care to licensed veterinarians or other appropriate pet health care professionals.

While the authors and Desert Winds Press, LLC have endeavored to make sure the information contained in this site is accurate, we cannot guarantee the accuracy of such information and it is provided without warranty or guarantee of any kind.

This book is not intended as a substitute for medical advice from a licensed veterinarian. The diagnosis and treatment of pet medical and emergency conditions depends upon a comprehensive history, physical examination, and a careful assessment of alternative treatment modalities, including the benefits, risks and limitations of each. Desert Winds Press, LLC and the authors disclaim liability and are not legally responsible if the information provided is incomplete, inaccurate or inapplicable to a reader's specific circumstances.

CHAPTER 9

ADDITIONAL RESOURCES

Useful Telephone Numbers

American Animal Hospital Associations
800–883–6301

American Humane Association
800–227–4645

A.S.P.C.A.
212–876–7700

Emergency Animal Rescue Service
800–440–Ears

Humane Society of the U.S.
202–452–1100

National Animal Poison Control Center
888–426–4435

AKC Companion Animal Recovery
800–252–7894

Awolpet.com
888–743–6465

Pets 911
888–Pets–911

800–Help–4–Pets

800–Help–For–Pets (A tag–based, 24–hour recovery services system)

310–652–9837

AKC–CAR
24–hour recovery services for micro–chipped and tattooed pets

1–800–Tattoos
5580 Centerview Drive, Suite 250
Raleigh, North Carolina 27606–3389

Useful Web Sites

www.healthypet.com

www.campingpet.com

www.travelinpets.com

www.activek9.com

www.petsonthego.com

www.vetquest.com

www.vetlocator.petplace.com

www.petfinder.com

APPENDIX A

DIRECTORY OF PET–FRIENDLY CAMPGROUNDS

While the following directory of pet–friendly parks and campgrounds is substantial, it is not all–inclusive. If you would like to add a pet-friendly campground to this directory or amend any information already included, please contact us at www.petsrv.com. We will include the changes in the next edition.

In addition, this directory may include details that are incomplete, incorrect, or out of date. As a result, you should always call first to confirm their location and their actual policy towards *your* pets.

Alabama

Alexander City, AL
Wind Creek State Park
4325 AL Hwy 128
Alexander City, AL 35010
256-329-0845

Atmore, AL
Claude D. Kelley State Park
580 H. Kyle
Atmore, AL 36502
334-862-2511

Auburn, AL
Chewacla State Park
124 Shell Toomer Parkway
Auburn, AL 36830
334-887-5621

Camden, AL
Roland Cooper State Park
285 Deer Run Drive
Camden, AL 36726
334-682-4050

Childersburg, AL
DeSoto Caverns Park Campground
5181 DeSoto Caverns Parkway
Childersburg, AL 36044
Voice: (256) 378-7252 / (800) 933-2283
Fax: (256) 378-3678
desoto@mindspring.com

Coker, AL
Lake Lurleen State Park
13226 Lake Lurleen
Coker, AL 35452
205-339-1558

Crane Hill, AL
Big Bridge Campground
21899 County Road 222
Crane Hill, AL 35053
256-287-0440

Creola, AL
KOA
2350 Dead Lake Road
Creola, AL 36525
334-675-0320

Decatur, AL
Point Mallard Park

1800 Point Mallard Dr. SE
Decatur, AL 35601
Voice: (256) 351-7772
Fax: (256) 341-4906

Delta, AL
Cheaha State Park
Route 1, Box 77-H
Delta, AL 36258
256-488-5115

Fort Payne, AL
DeSoto State Park
3883 CR 89
Fort Payne, AL 35967
256-845-5075

Gallion, AL
Chickasaw State Park
26955 US Highway 43
Gallion, AL 36742
334-295-8230

Greenville, AL
Sherling Lake
PO Box 158
Greenville, AL 36037
800-810-5253

Grove Oak, AL
Bucks Pocket State Park
393 County Rd 174
Grove Oak 35975
256-659-2000

Gulf Shores, AL
Gulf State Park
20115 State Highway 135
Gulf Shores, AL 36542
334-948-6353

Guntersville, AL
Lake Guntersville State Park
7966 Alabama Hwy 227
Guntersville, AL 35976
256-571-5444

Hope Hull, AL
KOA
250 Fisher Road
Hope Hull, AL 36043
334-288-0728

Huntsville, AL
Monte Sano State Park
5105 Nolen Avenue

Huntsville, AL 35801
256-534-6589

Jasper, AL

Clear Creek Recreation Area
8079 Fall City Road
Jasper, AL 35501
205-384-4792

Jemison, AL

Peach Queen Campground
12986 CR 42
Jemison, AL 35085
Voice: (205) 688-2573
peachqueencamp@mindspring.com

Langston, AL

Mountain Lakes Resort
1345 Murphy Hill Road
Langston, AL 35755
800-330-3550

McCalla, AL

KOA
22191 Hwy 216
McCalla, AL 35111
205-477-2778

Mobile, AL

Chiackasabogue Park and Campground
760 Aldock Road
Mobile, AL 36613
251-574-2267

Shady Acres Campground
2510 Old Military Road
Mobile, AL 36605
Voice: (251) 478-0013
Fax: (251) 478-0013
dogriver13@aol.com

Ozark, AL

Ozark Travel Park
2414 North US 231
Ozark, AL 36360
Toll Free: (800)359-3218
Phone: (334)774-3219
Fax: (334)774-3219
rv@charter.net

Pelham, AL

Birmingham South Campground
222 Hwy. 33
Pelham, AL 35124
Voice: (205) 664-8832 / (800) 772-8832
Fax: (205) 620-1103
bscampground@aol.com

KOA
222 Hwy 33
Pelham, AL 35124
205-664-8832

Oak Mountain State Park
PO Box 278
Pelham, AL 35124
205-620-2527

Pickensville, AL

Pickensville Recreation
61 Camping Road
Pickensville, AL 35447
205-373-6328

Robertsdale, AL

Styx River Resort
25301 Water World Road
Robertsdale, AL 36567
800-330-3550

Rogersville, AL

Joe Wheeler State Park
201 Mc Lean Drive
Rogerville, AL 35652
256-247-1184

Selma, AL

Paul M. Grist State Park
1546 Grist Road
Selma, AL 36701
334-872-5846

Spanish Fort, AL

Meaher State Park
5200 Battleship Parkway East
Spanish Fort, AL 36577
251-626-0798

Warrior, AL

Rickwood Caverns State Park
370 Rickwood Park Road
Warrior, AL 35180
205-647-9692

Woodville, AL

Parnell Creek Campground
10527 Hwy 72 E.
Woodville, AL 35776
256-508-7308

Alaska

Anchorage, AK

Alaska Recreational Management
800 East Diamond Blvd
Anchorage, AK 99515
907-522-8368

Anchorage RV Park
7300 Oilwell Road
Anchorage, AK 99504
907-338-7275

Centennial Park Campground
Glenn Highway
Anchorage, AK 99519
Voice: (907) 343-6986
bishop,t.I.@muni.org

Golden Nugget Camper Park
4100 DeBarr Road
Anchorage, AK 99506
Voice: (907) 333-2012 / (800) 449-2012
Fax: (907) 333-1016
gnugget@alaska.net

The Original Chicken Gold Campground
PO Box 71
Anchorage, AK 99732
907-235-6396

Williwaw Campground
800 East Diamond Blvd.
Anchorage, AK 99515
907-522-8368

Coffman Cove, AK

Oceanview RV Park & Campground
PO Box 18035
Coffman Cove, AK 99918
907-329-2015

Cooper Landing, AK

Kenai Princess RV Park
907-595-1425

Denali National Park, AK

Denali Grizzly Bear Cabins & Campground
Mile 240 Parks Hwy.
Denali National Park, AK 99755
907 683-2696 (SUM) / (866) 583-2696
Fax: (907) 683-2697
info@denaligrizzlybear.com

Denali Rainbow Village & RV Park
Mile 238.6 Parks Hwy.
Denali National Park, AK 99755
Voice: (907) 683-7777
Fax: (907) 683-7275
stayatdenalirainbowrvpark@gci.net
Denali Riverside RV Park
Milepost 240, Parks Hwy
Denali National Park, AK 99755
888-778-7700

Denali RV Park & Motel
Box 155V
Denali National Park, AK 99755
800-478-1501

Fairbanks, AK

Chena Marina RV Park
1145 Shypoke Drive
Fairbanks, Alaska 99709
Voice ~ 907-479-GOLD (4653)
Fax ~ 907-479-0575 (summer only)
chenarv@mosquitonet.com

River's Edge RV Park
4140 Boat St.
Fairbanks, AK 99709
Voice: (907) 474-0286
Fax: (907) 474-3695

Haines, AK

Haines Hitch-Up RV Park
851 Main St.
Haines, AK 99827
Voice: (907) 766-2882
Fax: (907) 766-2515
HitchupRV@aol.com

Healy, AK

McKinley RV & Campground
PO Box 340
Healy, AK 99743
907-683-2379

Homer, AK

The Driftwood Inn RV Park
135 W. Bunnell Ave.
Homer, AK 99603
800-478-8019

Kenai, AK

Riverquest Campground & RV Resort
45933 Porter Road
Kenai, AK 99611
907-283-4991

North Pole, AK

Santaland RV Park
125 St Nicholas Dr.
North Pole, AK 99705
Voice: (907) 488-9123 / (888) 488-9123
Fax: (907) 488-7947
info@santalandrv.com

Palmer, AK

Mountain View RV Park
Mile 1, Smith Road
Palmer, AK 99645
Voice: (907) 745-5747 / (800) 264-4582
Fax: (907) 745-1700
starr1@mtaonline.net

Seward, AK

Bear Creek RV Park
33508 Lincoln St.
Seward, AK 99664
Voice: (907) 224-5725 / (877) 924-5725
Fax: (907) 224-2283
bearcreekrvpk@gci.net

Skagway, AK

Back Track Camper Park
PO Box 375
Skagway, AK 99840
888-778-7700

Soldotna, AK

Centennial Park Municipal Campground
349 Centennial Park
Soldotna, AK 99669
907-262-5299

Diamond M Ranch RV Park, Cabins, B & B
Mile 16.5 Kalifornsky Beach Road
Soldotna, AK 99669
Voice: (907) 283-9424
martin@diamondranch.com

Tok, AK

TOK RV Village
PO Box 739
Tok, AK 99780
907-883-5877

Valdez, AK

Eagle's Rest RV Park
630 E Pioneer Dr.
Valdez, AK 99686
Voice: (907) 835-2373 / (800) 553-7275
Fax: (907) 835-5267
rvpark@alaska.net

Wasilla, AK

Iceworm RV Park & Country Store
Mile 50.2 Parks Hwy.
Wasilla, AK 99687
Voice: (907) 892-8200
Fax: (907) 892-8200
iceworm@icewormrvp.com

Arizona

Apache Junction, AZ

Golden Sun RV Resort
999 W Broadway Ave.
Apache Junction, AZ 85220
Voice - (408) 983-3760
Toll Free - (888) 593-9632
Fax - (480) 983-1721
goldensunrvinfo@mhchomes.com
http://www.mhcrv.com

La Hacienda RV Resort
1797 W 28th Ave.
Apache Junction, AZ 85220
Voice - (480) 982-2808
Fax - (480) 982-2808
info@lahaciendarv.com

Lost Dutchman State Park
6109 N. Apache Trail
Apache Junction, AZ 85219
480-982-4485

Superstition Lookout RV Resort
1371 E 4th Ave.
Apache Junction, AZ 85219
Voice - (480) 982-2008

Superstition Sunrise Luxury RV Resort
702 S Meridian
Apache Junction, AZ 85220
Voice - (480) 986-4524
Toll Free - (800) 624-7027
Fax - (480) 986-4681
supersun01@aol.com
http://www.azrvresort.com

Ash Fork, AZ

KOA
PO Box 357
Ash Fork, AZ 86320
520-637-2521

Benson, AZ

Cochise Terrace RV Resort
1030 South Barrel Cactus Ridge
Benson, AZ 85602
520-586-0600

Kartchner Caverns State Park
HWY 90
Benson, AZ 85602
520-542-4174

KOA
Box 1060
Benson, AZ 85602
520-586-3977

Black Canyon City, AZ

KOA
Box 569
Black Canyon City, AZ 85324
602-374-5318

Casa Grande, AZ

Campground Buena Tierra
1995 S Cox Road
Casa Grande, AZ 85222
Voice - (520) 836-3500
Toll Free - (888) 520-8360
Fax - (520) 836-9723
www.campgroundbuenatierra@yahoo.com

Casita Verde RV Park
2200 N Trekell Road
Casa Grande, AZ 85222
Voice - (520) 836-9031
casitaverde@cgmailbox.com

Fiesta Grande RV Resort
1511 E Florence Blvd.
Casa Grande, AZ 85222
Voice - (520) 836-7222
Fax - (520) 426-7584
fstacwbk@casagrande.com

Foothills West RV Resort
19501 W Hopi Dr.
Casa Grande, AZ 85222
Voice - (520) 836-2531
Fax - (520) 836-0471
foothillswestrv@netbeam.net
http://www.rvinthesun.com

Las Colinas RV Park
7136 S Sunland Gin Road
Casa Grande, AZ 85222
Voice - (520) 836-5050
Fax - (520) 421-9046
grannypat12@juno.com

Sundance 1 RV Resort
1920 N Thornton Road
Casa Grande, AZ 85222
Voice - (520) 426-9662
Fax - (520) 876-2800
sundnce@c2i2.com
http://www.sundance1rv.com

Val Vista Winter Village
16680 W Val Vista Road
Casa Grande, AZ 85222
Voice - (520) 836-7800
Toll Free - (877) 836-7801
Fax - (520) 836-2638
vvwv@cybertrails.com

Ehrenberg, AZ
KOA
Ehrenberg-Parker Hwy
Ehrenberg, AZ 85334
520-923-7863

Flagstaff, AZ
KOA
5803 N. Hwy 89
Flagstaff, AZ 86004
520-526-9926

Florence, AZ
Desert Gardens RV Park
9668 N Hwy 79 at Milepost 128.5 (PO Box 1186)
Florence, AZ 85232
Voice - (520) 868-3800
Toll Free - (888) 868-4888
Fax - (520) 868-3872
desertgardens@cgmailbox.com

Gila Bend, AZ
Painted Rock Petroglyph Site and Campground
2015 West Deer Valley Road
Gila Bend, AZ 85027
602-580-5500

Goodyear, AZ
Destiny Phoenix RV Resort
416 N Citrus Road
Goodyear, AZ 85338
Voice - (623) 853-0537
Toll Free - (888) 667-2454
Fax - (623) 853-0645
destinyphx@earthlink.net

Holbrook, AZ
Cholla Lake County Park
Navajo County Parks and Recreation
Holbrook, AZ 86025
928-288-3717

KOA
102 Hermosa Drive
Holbrook, AZ 86025
520-524-6689

Jacob Lake, AZ

Jacob Lake Inn
US 89A and AZ 67
Jacob Lake, AZ 86022
928-643-7298

Kaibab Camper Village
PO Box 3331
Jacob Lake, AZ 86003
800-525-0924

Kingman, AZ
KOA
3820 N. Roosevelt
Kingman, AZ 86401
520-757-4397

Lake Havasu City, AZ
Lake Havasu State Park
699 London Bridge Road
Lake Havasu City, AZ 86403
928-855-2784

Marble Canyon, AZ
Lees Ferry Campground
US 89
Marble Canyon, AZ
928-355-2234

Mesa, AZ
Good Life RV Resort
3403 E Main St.
Mesa, AZ 85213
Voice - (480) 832-4990
Toll Free - (800) 999-4990
Fax - (480) 832-4992
info@goodliferv.com
http://www.goodliferv.com

Mesa Spirit RV Resort
3020 E Main St.
Mesa, AZ 85213
Voice - (480) 832-1770
Toll Free - (877) 924-6709
Fax - (480) 924-0530
trailervillage@azrvpark.com
http://www.azrvpark.com

Monte Vista Village Resort
8865 E Baseline Road
Mesa, AZ 85208
Voice - (480) 833-2223
Toll Free - (800) 435-7128
Fax - (480) 380-3145

Silveridge RV Resort
8265 E Southern Ave.
Mesa, AZ 85208

Voice - (480) 373-7000
Toll Free - (800) 354-0054
Fax - (480) 373-7847
gcainfo@silveridge.com
http://www.silveridge.com

Usery Mountain Recreation Area
3939 N. Usury Pass Road
Mesa, AZ 85207
480-984-0032

Valle Del Oro RV Resort
1452 S Ellsworth Road
Mesa, AZ 85005
Voice - (480) 984-1146
Toll Free - (800) 626-6686
Fax - (480) 984-0473
vdo@azrvresorts.com

Venture Out at Mesa
5001 E Main St.
Mesa, AZ 85205
Voice - (480) 832-0200
Fax - (480) 832-2360
ventureoutgm@qwest.net
http://www.ventureoutrvresort.com\

Viewpoint RV and Golf Resort
8700 E University Dr.
Mesa, AZ 85204
Voice - (480) 373-8700
Toll Free - (800) 822-4404
Fax - (480) 986-8700
viewPoint@mhchomes.com
http://www.viewpointrv.com

Phoenix, AZ

Desert Sands RV Park
22036 N 27th Ave.
Phoenix, AZ 85027
Voice - (623) 869-8186
Fax - (623) 434-9035

Desert Shadows RV Resort
19203 N 29th Ave.
Phoenix, AZ 85027
Voice - (623) 869-8178
Toll Free - (800) 595-7290
Fax - (623) 869-8179
info@arizonarvresorts.com
http://www.arizonarvresorts.com/ds_index.htm

Desert's Edge RV Village
22623 N Black Canyon Hwy.
Phoenix, AZ 85027
Voice - (623) 587-0940

Toll Free - (888) 633-7677
Fax - (623) 587-0029
desertsedge@desertsedgerv.com
http://www.desertsedgerv.com

Picacho, AZ

KOA
PO Box 368
Picacho, AZ 85241
520-466-7401

Page, AZ

Wahweap Campground
PO Box 1597
Page, AZ 86040
800-528-6154

Patagonia, AZ

Patagonia Lake State Park
400 Patagonia Lake RD
Patagonia, AZ 85624
520-287-6965

Peoria, AZ

Lake Pleasant Regional Park
41835 North Castle Hot Springs Road
Peoria, AZ 85382
928-501-1710

Queen Valley, AZ

Encore RV Resort - Queen Valley
50 W Oro Viejo Dr.
Queen Valley, AZ 85219
Voice - (520) 463-2300
Toll Free - (877) 337-2757
Fax - (520) 463-2331
nhcqv@msn.com

Roosevelt, AZ

Cholla Recreation Site
Tonto Basin Ranger District, HC02, Box 4800
Roosevelt, AZ 85545
928-467-3200

Seligman, AZ

KOA
801 East Hwy 66, Box 156
Seligman, AZ 86337
520-422-3358

Surprise, AZ

Sunflower RV Resort
16501 N El Mirage Road
Surprise, AZ 85371
Voice - (623) 583-0100
Toll Free - (800) 627-8637

Fax - (623) 583-2007
res@sunflowerrvresort.com

Tombstone, AZ

Tombstone Hill RV & Campground
PO Box 99
Tombstone, AZ 85638
520-457-3829

Tucson, AZ

Beaudry RV Resort
5151 S Country Club Road
Tucson, AZ 85706
Voice - (520) 239-1300
Toll Free - (877) 694-9176
Fax - (520) 239-1699
info@beaudryrvresort.com

Catalina State Park
Oracle Road
Tucson, AZ 85740
520-628-5798

Crazy Horse RV Park
6660 S Craycroft Road
Tucson, AZ 85706
Voice - (520) 574-0157
Toll Free - (800) 279-6279
Fax - (520) 574-0157
czyhorse@mindspring.com

Far Horizons Tucson Village
555 Pantano Road
Tucson, AZ 85710
Voice - (520) 296-1234
Fax - (520) 733-9003
vacation@tucsonvillage.com
http://www.tucsonvillage.com

Gilbert Ray Campground
1204 W. Silverlake Road
Tucson, AZ 85713
520-740-5830

Mission View RV Resort
31 Los Reales Road
Tucson, AZ 85706
Voice - (520) 741-1945
Toll Free - (800) 444-8439
Fax - (520) 294-2653
missnview2@aol.com

Prince of Tucson RV Park
3501 N Freeway Road
Tucson, AZ 85705
Voice - (520) 887-3501
Toll Free - (800) 955-3501

Fax - (520) 887-3505
princeoftucson@worldnet.att.net

Rincon Country East RV Resort
8989 E Escalante
Tucson, AZ 85730
Voice - (520) 886-8431
Fax - (520) 294-0303
east@rinconcountry.com
http://www.rinconcountry.com/east

Rincon Country West RV Resort
4555 S Mission Road
Tucson, AZ 85746
Voice - (520) 294-5608
Toll Free - (800) 782-7275
Fax - (520) 294-0303
west@rinconcountry.com
http://www.rinconcountry.com/west/

Voyager RV Resort
8701 S Kolb Road
Tucson, AZ 85706
Voice - (520) 574-5000
Toll Free - (800) 424-9191
Fax - (520) 574-5390
info@voyagerrv.com
http://www.voyagerrv.com

Williams, AZ

KOA
5333 Hwy 64
Williams, AZ 86046
520-635-2307

KOA
1000 Circle Pines Road
Williams, AZ 86046
520-635-2626

Yuma, AZ

Blue Sky RV Park
10247 S Frontage Road
Yuma, AZ 85365
Voice - (928) 342-1444
Toll Free - (877) 367-5220
manager@blueskyyuma.com

Bonita Mesa RV Resort
9400 N Frontage Road
Yuma, AZ 85365
Voice - (928) 342-2999
Fax - (928) 342-4614
bonitamesa@aol.com
http://www.bonitamesa.com

Cactus Gardens RV Park

10657 South Ave., #9B
Yuma, AZ 85365
Voice - (928) 342-9188
Fax - (928) 342-9542
cactusgardensrv@aol.com

Caravan Oasis RV Park
10500 N Frontage Road
Yuma, AZ 85365
Voice - (520) 342-1480
Fax - (520) 342-0755
info@caravanoasisresort.com
http://www.caravanoasisresort.com

Desert Paradise RV Resort
10537 South Ave., #9E
Yuma, AZ 85365
Voice - (520) 342-9313
Fax - (520) 342-0584
dprvresort@aol.com

Las Quintas Oasis RV Park
10442 N Frontage Road
Yuma, AZ 85365
Voice - (520) 305-9005
Fax - (520) 342-1480
info@caravanoasisresort.com
http://www.caravanoasisresort.com

Shangri-La RV Resort
10498 N Frontage Road
Yuma, AZ 85365
Voice - (928) 342-9123
Toll Free - (877) 742-6474
Fax - (928) 342-3513
info@shangrilarv.com
http://www.shangrilarv.com

Arkansas

Alma, AR
KOA
3539 N. Highway 71
Alma, AR 72921
501-632-2704

Arkadelphia, AR
KOA
221 Frost Road
Arkadelphia, AR 71923
870-246-4922

Ashdown, AR
Millwood State Park
1564 Highway 32 East
Ashdown, AR 71822
870-898-2800

Bismark, AR
DeGray Lake Resort
Route 3, Box 490
Bismark, AR 71929
501-865-2801

Bluff City, AR
White Oak Lake
Route 2, Box 28
Bluff City, AR 71722
870-685-2748

Bull Shoals, AR
Bull Shoals State Park
PO Box 205
Bull Shoals, AR 72619
870-431-5521

Clinton, AR
Whispering Pines Rv Park
8575 HWY 65 North
Clinton, AR 72031
888-745-4291

Dardanelle, AR
Mount Nebo State Park
Route 3, Box 374
Dardanelle, AR 72834
501-229-3655

Eldorado, AR
Moro Bay State Park
6071 Hwy 15 South
El Dorado, AR 71651

870-463-8555

Eureka Springs, AR
KOA
15020 Hwy 187 South
Eureka Springs, AR 72632
501-253-8036

Wanderlust RV Park
468 Passion Play Road
Eureka Springs, AR 72632
Voice: (479) 253-7385 / (800) 253-7385
wndrlust@ipa.net
Outside Link: www.eureka-net.com/wanderlust

Greenbrier, AR
Woolly Hollow State Park
82 Woolly Hollow Road
Greenbrier, AR 72058
501-679-2098

Hardy, AR
Hardy Camper Park
South Springs Street
Hardy AR 72542
870-856-2356

Harrisburg, AR
Lake Poinsett State Park
5752 State Park Lane
Harrisburg, AR 72432
870-578-2064

Hazen, AR
T Ricks RV Park
3001 Hwy 11
Hazen, AR 72064
Voice: (870) 255-4914 / (501) 268-1335
Fax: (870) 255-4915

Heth, AR
Lake KOA
P.O. Box 151
Heth, AR 72346
800-562-2140

Horseshoe Bend, AR
Boxhound Resort RV Park
1313 Tri-Lake Drive
Horseshoe Bend, AR 72512
501-670-4496

Hot Springs, AR
KOA
838 McClendon Road
Hot Springs, AR 71901

501-624-5912

Huntsville, AR

Withrow Springs State Park
Route 3, Box 29
Huntsville, AR 72740
501-559-2593

Jacksonport, AR

Jacksonport State Park
PO Box 8
Jacksonport, AR 72075
870-523-2143

Jersey, AR

Moro Bay State Park
6071 Highway 15 South
Jersey, AR 71651
870-463-8555

Jonesboro, AR

Craigshead Forest Park
PO Box 1845
Jonesboro, AR 72403
870-933-4604

Lake Village, AR

Lake Chicot State Park
2542 Highway 257
Lake Village, AR 71653
870-265-5480

Pecan Grove RV Park
3768 Hwy 82 and 65 South
Lake Village, AR 71653
870-265-3005

Lowell, AR

Best Holiday Trav-L-Park
7037 I-55 #1
Lowell, AR 72364
501-739-4801

Marion, AR

Green Country RV Park
110 W Pleasant Grove Road
Lowell, AR 72745
Voice: (479) 659-8850 / (888) 980-8850
Fax: (479) 659-8850
cindyhill@greencountry-rvpark.com Marion, AR

McNeil, AR

Logoly State Park
PO Box 245
McNeil, AR 71752
870-695-3561

Morrilton, AR

KOA
30 Kamper Lane
Morrilton, AR 72110
501-354-8262

Petit Jean State Park
1285 Petit Jean Mountain Road
Morrilton, AR 72110
501-727-5441

Mountain Home, AR

Promise Land Resort & RV Park
323 CR 107
Mountain Home, AR 72653
870-431-5576

Mountain Pine, AR

Lake Ouachita State Park
5451 Mountain Pine Road
Mountain Pine, AR 71956
501-767-9366

Mountainburg, AR

Lake Fort Smith State Park
PO Box 4
Mountainburg, AR 72946
501-369-2469

Murfreesboro, AR

Crater of Diamonds State Park
Route 1
Murfreesboro, AR 71958
870-285-3113

KOA
7820 Crystal Hill Road
Murfreesboro, AR 72118
501-758-4598

Pea Ridge, AR

Battlefield Inn, Motel & RV Park
14753 Highway 62 East
Pea Ridge, AR 72751
501-451-1188

Pocahontas, AR

Old Davidsonville State Park
7953 Highway 166 South
Pocahontas, AR 72455
870-892-4708

Powhatan, AR

Lake Charles State Park
3705 Highway 25
Powhatan, AR 72458

870-878-6595

Rogers, AR

KOA
PO Box 456
Rogers, AR 72757
501-451-8566

Russellville, AR

Lake Dardanelle State Park
2428 Marina Road
Russellville, AR 72801
479-967-5516

Siloam Springs, AR

Wilderness Hills RV Park and Campground
13776 Taylor Orchard Road
Siloam Springs AR 72734
479-524-4955

Star City, AR

Cane Creek State Park
PO Box 96
Star City, 71667
870-628-4714

Texarcana, AR

KOA
8225 Camper Lane
Texarcana, AR 71858
870-772-0751

West Fork, AR

Devil's Den State Park
11333 West Arkansas Highway 74
West Fork, AR 72774
479-761-3325

West Memphis, AR

America's Best Campground
7037 i-55
West Memphis, AR 72364
888-857-4890

Tom Sawyer's RV Park
1287 S 8th St. (Mail Only: PO Box 1055, West
Memphis, AR 72303)
West Memphis, AR 72301
Voice: (870) 735-9770
Fax: (870) 735-6038 Wynne, AR

Village Creek State Park
201 CR 754
West Memphis, AR 72396
870-238-9406

California

Anaheim, CA

Anaheim Resort RV Park
200 W. Midway Drive
Anaheim, CA 92805
Phone: (714)774-3860
Fax: (714)774-5970
RVDR@aol.com

Canyon RV Park
24001 Santa Ana Canyon Road
Anaheim, CA 92808
Phone: (714) 637-0210
Fax: (714) 637-9317
camping@canyonrvpark.com

Angels Camp, CA

Angels Camp RV and Camping Resort
PO Box 847
3069 Hwy 49
Angels Camp, CA 95222
Toll Free: (888)398-0404
Phone: (209) 736-0404
Fax: (209)736-2849
angelscamprv@goldrush.com

Atascadero, CA

Atascadero All Nite RV Park
5000 Marchant Ave.
Atascadero, CA 93422
Phone: (805) 461-0543

Auburn, CA

KOA
3550 KOA Way
Atascadero, CA 95602
530-885-0990

Azusa, CA

Camp Williams
24210 East Fork Road
Azusa, CA 91702
Phone: (626) 910-1126
info@campwilliams.com

Bakersfield, CA

A Country RV Park
622 S. Fairfax Road
Bakersfield, CA 93307
Phone: (661)363-6412
acntryrv@aol.com

Bakersfield Palms RV Resort

250 Fairfax Road
Bakersfield, CA 93307
Toll Free: (888)725-6778
Phone: (661) 366-6700
Fax: (661)366-6704
bakersfield@palmsrv.com

Big River RV Park
1 Marina Street
Big River, CA 92242
Phone: (760) 665-9359
administration@bigriverrvpark.com

Southland RV Park & Mini Storage
9901 Southland Court
Bakersfield, CA 93307
Toll Free: (877)834-4868
Phone: Park: (661) 834-1134
Fax: (661) 834-9198
Foxsouthland@aol.com

Banning, CA

Pine Ranch RV Park
1455 S. San Gorgonio
Banning, CA 92220
Phone: (909) 849-7513
reservations@reynoldsresorts.com

Bethel Island, CA

Sugar Barge RV Park And Marina
1440 Sugar Barge Road
Bethel Island, CA 94511
Toll Free: (800)799-4100
Phone: (925)684-9075
rv@sugarbarge.com

Big Bar, CA

Del Loma RV Park & Campground
Route 1, Box 54
Big Bar, CA 96010
Toll Free: (800)839-0194
Phone: (530)623-2834
delloma@snowcrest.net

Bodega Bay, CA

Porto Bodega
1500 Bay Flat Road
Bodega Bay, CA 94923
Phone: (707)875-2354
Fax: (707) 875-2589

Boulevard, CA

Outdoor World RV Park
37133 Hwy 94
Boulevard, CA 91905
Phone: (888)703-0009

info@outdoorworldrvpark.com

Browns Valley, CA

Sycamore Ranch RV Park & Campground
5390 St Hwy 20
Browns Valley, CA 95918
Toll Free: (800)834-1190
Phone: (530) 741-1190
sycamoreranch@inreach.com

Buellton, CA

Flying Flags RV Resort & Campground
180 Ave. of the Flags
Buellton, CA 93427
Phone: (805)688-3716
Fax: (805)688-9245
info@flyingflags.com

Camptonville, CA

Willow Creek RV CG & Llama Camp
17548 Hwy 49
Camptonville, CA 95922
Phone: (530) 288-0646
Fax: (530)288-3595
info@neonllama.com

Carmel, CA

Saddle Mountain RV Park & Campground
27625 Schulte Road
Carmel, CA 93923
Phone: (831)624-1617

Clearlake, CA

Funtime RV Park & Watersports
6035 Old Hwy 53
Clearlake, CA 95422
Phone: (707) 994-6267
Fax: (707)994-6248
jhansen950@zero.net

Cloverdale, CA

KOA
PO Box 600
Cloverdale, CA 95425
707-894-3337

Coloma, CA

Coloma Resort
PO Box 516
6921 Mt Murphy Road
Coloma, CA 95613
Toll Free: (800)238-2298
Phone: (530) 621-2267
info@colomaresort.com

Columbia, CA

Marble Quarry RV Park

11551 Yankee Hill Road
Columbia, CA 95310
Toll Free: (866)677-8464
Phone: (209) 532-9539
Fax: (209) 532-8631
info@marblequarry.com

49er RV Ranch
23223 Italian Bar Road
PO Box 569
Columbia, CA 95310
Phone: (209)532-4978
Fax: (209)532-4978
stay@49rv.com

Crescent City, CA

KOA
4241 Hwy 101 N.
Crescent City, CA 95531
707-464-5744

El Centro, CA

Sunbeam Lake RV Resort
1716 West Sunbeam Lake Drive
El Centro, CA 92243
Phone: (760) 352-7154
sunbeamlakerv@sbcglobal.net

Escondido, CA

Champagne Lakes RV Resort
8310 Nelson Way
Escondido, CA 92026
Phone: (760) 749-7572

Eureka, CA

KOA
4050 N. Hwy 101
Eureka, CA 95503
707-725-3359

Felton, CA

Cotillion Gardens RV Park
300 Old Big Trees Road
Felton, CA 95018
Phone: (831) 335-7669

Fortuna, CA

KOA
2189 Riverwalk Drive
Fortuna, CA 95540
707-725-3359

Grand Terrace, CA

Terrace Village RV Park
21900 Barton Road
Grand Terrace, CA 92313
Toll Free: (800)427-2441

Phone: (909) 783-4580
Fax: (909) 783-3417
info@terracevillagervpark.com

Groveland, CA

Yosemite Pines RV Resort
20450 Old Hwy 120
Groveland, CA 95321
Toll Free: (877)962-7690
Phone: (209)962-7690
Fax: (209)962-4378
yosemite@yosemitepinesrv.com

Guerneville, CA

Fife's Guest Ranch
16467 Highway 116
Guerneville, CA 95446
707-869-0656Hat Creek, CA

Hat Creek, CA

Rancheria RV Park
15665 Black Angus Lane
Hat Creek, CA 96040
Phone: (530)335-7418
ranchrv@c-zone.net

Huntington Beach, CA

Huntington By The Sea RV Park
21871 Newland St
Huntington Beach, CA 92646
Toll Free: (800)439-3486
Phone: (714)536-8316
hbtsea@hotmail.com

Isleton, CA

Ko-Ket Resort
14174 Isleton Road
Isleton, CA 95641
Phone: (916) 776-1488

Jamestown, CA

Lake Tulloch RV Campground & Marina
14448 Tulloch Road
95327
800-894-2267

Julian, CA

Pinezanita Trailer Ranch
P.O. Box 2380
4446 Highway 79
Julian, CA 92036-2380
Phone: (760)765-0429
questions@pinezanita.com

Kernville, CA

Riverview Trailer Park

PO Box 458
24 Sirretta Street
Kernville, CA 93238
Phone: (760)376-2345
Fax: (760) 376-2715

Klamath, CA

Kamp Klamath
1661 West Klamath Beach Road
PO Box 99
Klamath, CA 95548
Toll Free: (866)552-6284
Phone: (707)482-0227
Fax: (707)482-0147
kampklamath@msn.com

Lakehead, CA

Lakeshore Villa RV Park
20672 Lakeshore Drive
Lakehead, CA 96051
Phone: (530)238-8688

Shasta Lake RV Resort And Campground
PO Box 450
20433 Lakeshore Drive
Lakehead, CA 96051
Phone: 800-374-2782
shastarv@aol.com

Lakeport, CA

Northport Trailer Resort
5020 Lakeshore Blvd
Lakeport, CA 95453
Phone: (707) 263-6311
Fax: (707) 262-1644

Lewiston, CA

Lakeview Terrace Resort
HC01 Box 250C
Lewiston, CA 96052
Phone: (530)778-3803
lvtr@snowcrest.net

Old Lewiston Bridge RV Resort
PO Box 148
Rush Creek Road at Turnpike Coridore Road
Lewiston, CA 96052
Toll Free: (800)922-1924
Phone: (530) 778-3894
Fax: (530)778-3894
olb@snowcrest.net

Lodi, CA

KOA
2851 East 8 Mile Road
Lodi, CA 95420

800-562-1229

Lone Pine, CA

Boulder Creek RV Resort
2550 S. Hwy 395
P.O. Box 870
Lone Pine, CA 93545
Toll Free: (800)648-8965
Phone: (760) 876-4243
Fax: (760)876-5253
hwy395bc@qnet.com

Loomis, CA

KOA
3945 Taylor Road
Loomis, CA 95650
916-652-6737

Lost Hills, CA

KOA
PO Box 276
Lost Hills, CA 93249
805-797-2719

Manchester, CA

KOA
Box 266
Manchester, CA 95459
707-882-2375

Marina, CA

Marina Dunes RV Park
3330 Dunes Drive
Marina, CA 93933
Phone: (831) 384-6914
Fax: (831) 384-0285
info@marinadunesrv.com

McArthur, CA

Lassen Pines RV Resort
548-335 Old Hwy 407
McArthur, CA 96056
Phone: (530) 336-5657
Fax: (530) 336-5652
lassenpines@shasta.com

Midpines, CA

KOA
Box 545, Hwy 140
Midpines, CA 05345
209-966-2201

Morgan Hill, CA

Oak Dell Park
12790 Watsonville Road
Morgan Hill, CA 95037
Phone: (408) 779-7779

kim@oakdellpark.com

Uvas Pines RV Park
13210 Uvas Road
Morgan Hill, CA 95037
Phone: (408) 779-3417
Fax: (408) 778-7281
uvaspinesrvpark@hotmail.com

Moss Landing, CA

Moss Landing RV Park
7905 Sandholdt Road
Moss Landing, CA 95039
Phone: (877)735-7275

Mt. Shasta City, CA

KOA
900 N. Mt. Shasta Blvd.
Mt. Shasta City, CA 96067
800-562-3617

Napa, CA

Spanish Flat Resort
4290 Knoxville Road
Napa, CA 94558
Phone: (707) 966-7700
Fax: (707) 966-7704
sfr@interx.net
Needles, CA

KOA
5400 National Old Trails Hwy
Napa, CA 92363
760-326-4207

Newport Beach, CA

Newport Dunes Waterfront Resort
1131 Back Bay Drive
Newport Beach, CA 92660
Phone: (949) 729-3863
Fax: (949) 729-1133
info@newportdunes.com

Niland, CA

Bashford's Hot Mineral Spa
10590 Hot Mineral Spa Road
Niland, CA 92257
Phone: (760) 354-1315 Ph/fax
bashfordspa@yahoo.com

Fountain Of Youth Spa
10249 Coachella Canal Road
Niland, CA 92257
Phone: 760-354-1340

Oceano, CA

Sand And Surf RV Park

1001 Pacific Blvd, Hwy 1
Oceano, CA 93445
Toll Free: (800)330-2504
Phone: (805)489-2384
info@SANDandSURF.com

Olema, CA

Olema Ranch
10155 Hwy 1
Olema, CA 94950
Toll Free: (800)655-2267
Phone: (415) 663-8001
Fax: (415) 663-8832
camping@nbn.com

Palomar Mountain, CA

Oak Knoll Campground
31718 South Grade Road
PO Box 192
Palomar Mountain, CA 92060
Phone: (760) 742-3437
okcamp@aol.com

Patterson, CA

Kit Fox RV Park
14750 Rogers Road
Patterson, CA 95363
Phone: (209) 892-2638
reservations@kitfoxrv.com

Petaluma, CA

KOA
20 Rainsville Road
Petaluma, CA 94952
800-992-CAMP

Pomona, CA

Fairplex KOA
2200 North White Avenue
Pomona, CA 91768
Toll Free: (888)562-4230
Phone: (909) 593-8915
Fax: (909)593-2685
koa@fairplex.com

Portola, CA

Sierra Springs Trailer Resort
PO Box 595
70099 Hwy 70
Portola, CA 96122
Phone: (530) 836-2747
Fax: (530) 836-2559
sstr@psln.com

Quincy, CA

Pioneer RV Park
1326 Pioneer Road
Quincy, CA 95971
Toll Free: (888)216-3266
Phone: (530)283-0769
Fax: (530)283-3978
pioneerrv@jps.net

Redding, CA

Redding RV Park
11075 Campers Court
Redding, CA 11075
Phone: (530)241-0707
reddingrvpark@aol.com

Redway, CA

Dean Creek Resort
4112 Redwood Drive
PO Box 157
Redway, CA 95560
Toll Free: (877)923-2555
Phone: (707)923-2555
Fax: (707)923-2547
deancrk@humboldt.net

Rio Vista, CA

Rio Viento RV Park
4460 W. Sherman Island Road
Rio Vista, CA 94571
Phone: (925)382-4193
info@rioviento.com

Sacramento, CA

Stillman Adult RV Park
3880 Stillman Park Cir
Sacramento, CA 95824
Phone: (916) 392-2820
San Bernardino, CA

KOA
1707 Cable Canyon Road
Sacramento, CA 92407
909-887-4098

San Juan Bautista, CA

KOA
900 Anzar Road
San Juan Bautista, CA 95045
408-623-4263

Santa Cruz, CA

Santa Cruz KOA
1186 San Andreas Road
Santa Cruz, CA 95076
831-722-2377

Santa Fe Springs, CA

El Monte RV Park
12818 Firestone Blvd.
Santa Fe Springs, CA 90670
562-404-9300

Santa Margarita, CA

KOA
4765 Santa Margarita Lake Road
Santa Margarita, CA 93453
805-438-5618

Saratoga, CA

Saratoga Springs
22801 Big Basin Way (Hwy 9)
Saratoga, CA 95070
Phone: (408) 867-9999
camping@saratoga-springs.com

Scotts Valley, CA

Santa Cruz Ranch RV Park
917 Disc Drive
Scotts Valley, CA 95066
Toll Free: (800)546-1288
Phone: (831)438-1288
Fax: (831) 438-2877
info@santacruzranchrv.com

Shafter, CA

KOA
5101 E. Lerdo Hwy
Shafter, CA 93263
661-399-3107

Shingle Springs, CA

KOA
4655 Rock Barn Road
Shingle Springs, CA 95682
530-676-2267

Soda Springs, CA

Cisco Grove Campground & RV Park
48415 Hampshire Rock Road
PO Box 890
Soda Springs, CA 95728
Phone: (530) 426-1600
Fax: (530)426-1609
info@ciscogrove.com

South Lake Tahoe, CA

KOA
Box 11552
South Lake Tahoe, CA 96155
530-577-3693

Tahoe Valley Campground

PO Box 9026
1175 Melba Drive
South Lake Tahoe, CA 96158
Phone: (530) 541-2222
Tahoevalley@megapathdsl.net

Susanville, CA

Mariner's Resort
509-725 Stone Road
Susanville, CA 96130-9657
Phone: 800-700-5253
mariners@psln.com

Mountain View RV Park
3075 Johnstonville Road
Susanville, CA 96130
Phone: (530)251-4757
Fax: (530) 251-0796

Temecula, CA

Indian Oaks Trailer Ranch
PO Box 922
38120 E. Benton Road
Temecula, CA 92593
Phone: (951)302-5399
indianoaks@aol.com

Truckee, CA

Coachland RV Park
10100 Pioneer Trail
Truckee, CA 96161
Phone: (530) 587-3071

Twain Harte, CA

Sugar Pine RV
23699 Hwy 108
Twain Harte, CA 95383
Phone: (209) 586-4631
Fax: (209)586-7783
eaglesnesting@mlode.com

Vacaville, CA

Vineyard RV Park
4985 Midway Road
Vacaville, CA 95688
Toll Free: (866)447-8797
Phone: (707)693-8797
reservations@vineyardrvpark.com

Vallejo, CA

Tradewinds RV Park
239 Lincoln Road West
Vallejo, CA 94590
Phone: (707) 643-4000
tradewinds@sbcglobal.net

Valley Center, CA

Woods Valley Kampground
15236 Woods Valley Road
Valley Center, CA 92082
Phone: (760)749-2905
Victorville, CA

KOA
16530 Stoddard Wells Road
Valley Center, CA 92392
760-245-6867

Visalia, CA
KOA
7480 Ave. 308
Visalia, CA 94391
800-562-0540

Weldon, CA
KOA
15627 Highway 178
Weldon, CA 93283
760-378-2001

Westport, CA
Westport Beach RV & Camping
37700 N Highway 1
Westport, CA 95488
Phone: (707) 964-2964
Fax: (707)964-8185
camping@westportbeachrv.com

West Sacramento, CA
KOA
3951 Lake Road
95691
800-KOA-2747

Capitol West RV & Mobile Park
715 Glide Avenue
West Sacramento, CA 95691
Phone: (916) 371-6671
elkerner@attbi.com

Whitewater, CA
Whitewater Trout Farm
9160 Whitewater Canyon Road
Whitewater, CA 92282
Phone: (760)325-5570

Williams, CA
Almond Grove MH Park
880 12th Street
Williams, CA 95987
Phone: (530) 473-5620 ph/fax

Willits, CA

KOA
Box 946
Willits, CA 95490
800-KOA-8542

Windsor, CA
Windsorland RV Park
9290 Old Redwood Hwy
Windsor, CA 95492
Toll Free: (800)864-3407
Phone: (707) 838-4882
wlandprk@msn.com

Yermo, CA
KOA
Box 967, 35250 Outer Hwy 15
Yermo, CA 92398
760-254-2311

Colorado

Alamosa, CO

KOA
6900 Juniper Lane
Alamosa, CO 81101
800-562-9157

Aurora, CO

Cherry Creek State Park
4201 S. Parker Road
Aurora, CO 80014
303-699-3860

Buena Vista, CO

Arrowhead Point Camping Resort
33975 US Hwy. 24 N
Buena Vista, CO 81211
Voice: (719) 395-2323 / (800) 888-7320
Fax: (719) 395-4069
reservations@arrowheadpointresort.com

KOA
27700 CR 303
Buena Vista, CO 81211
800-562-2672

Canon City, CO

Buffalo Bill's Royal Gorge Campground
30 County Road 3A
Canon City, CO 81212
Voice: (719) 269-3211 / (800) 787-0880
Fax: (719) 269-3211
buffalo@ris.net
Outside Link: www.camproyalgorge.com

KOA
PO Box 528
Canon City, CO 81215
719-275-6116

Castle Rock, CO

KOA
6527 S I-25
Castle Rock, CO 80104
303-681-2568

Clark, CO

Pearl Lake State Park
PO Box 750
Clark, CO 80428
970-879-3922

Steamboat Lake State Park

PO Box 750
Clark, CO 80428
970-879-3922

Clifton, CO

Colorado River State Park-Island Acres
PO Box 700
Clifton, CO 81520
970-434-3388

KOA
3238 E I-70 Business
Clifton, CO 81520
970-434-6644

Colorado Springs, CO

Garden of the Gods Campground
3704 W Colorado Ave.
Colorado Springs, CO 80904
Voice: (719) 475-9450 / (800) 248-9451
Fax: (719) 633-9643
camp@coloradocampground.com

Golden Eagle Ranch RV Park & Campground
710 Rock Creek Canyon Road
Colorado Springs, CO 80926
Voice: (719) 576-0450 / (800) 666-3841
Fax: (719) 576-3644
maymuseum2001@yahoo.com
Outside Link: www.maymuseum-camp-rvpark.com

Goldfield RV Campground
411 S 26th St
Colorado Springs, CO 80904
Toll Free: (888)471-0495
Phone: (719)471-0495
info@goldfieldrvcampground.com

Mountaindale Campground and Cabins
2000 Barrett Road
Colorado Springs, CO 80926
Voice: (719) 576-0619
Fax: (719) 302-0103
mountaindalecamp@msn.com

Cortez, CO

KOA
27432 E. Hwy 160
Cortez, CO 81321
970-565-9301

Cotopaxi, CO

KOA
21435 US Hwy 50
Cotopaxi, CO 81223

719-275-9308

Craig, CO

KOA
2800 E. US 40
Craig, CO 81625
970-824-5105

Cripple Creek, CO

Cripple Creek Hospitality House & RV Park
600 No. B St.
Cripple Creek, CO 80813
Voice: (719) 689-2513 / (800) 500-2513
Fax: (719) 689-2513
auagsmith@ccvnet.net

KOA
PO Box 699
Cripple Creek, CO 80813
719-689-3376

Delta, CO

KOA
1675 Hwy 92
Delta, CO 81416
970-874-3918

The Flying A RV Park & Motel
676 Hwy 50
Delta, CO 81416
970-874-9659

Divide, CO

Mueller State Park
PO Box 49
Divide, CO 80814
719-687-2366

Durango, CO

Lightner Creek Campground and Cabins
1567 CR 207
Durango, CO 81301
Voice: (970) 247-5406
Fax: (970) 385-5260
camplightner1@mindspring.com

United Campground
1322 Animas View Dr.
Durango, CO 81301
Voice: (970) 247-3853
Fax: (970) 385-7636
Outside Link: www.unitedcampground.com

Estes Park, CO

Elk Meadow Lodge & RV Resort
1665 Colorado Hwy. 66
Estes Park, CO 80517

Voice: (970) 586-5342 / (800) 582-5342
Fax: (970) 586-5013
info@elkmeadowrv.com

Manor RV Park & Motel
815 E Riverside Dr.
Estes Park, CO 80517
Voice: (970) 586-3251 / (800) 344-3256
Fax: (970) 586-9674
elake2@mindspring.com

Mary's Lake Campground
2120 Mary Lake Road
Estes Park, CO 80517
Voice: (970) 586-4411 / (800) 445-6279
Fax: (970) 586-4493
maryslake@aol.com

Spruce Lake RV Park
1050 Marys Lake Road
Estes Park, CO 80517
Voice: (970) 586-2889 / (800) 583-1050
Fax: (970) 586-5100
info@sprucelakerv.com

Yogi Bears Jellystone Park of Estes
5495 US Hwy 36
Estes Park, CO 80517
Toll Free: (800)722-2928
Phone: (970)586-4230
info@jellystoneofestes.com
Falcon, CO

Falcon Meadow RV Campground
11150 Hwy. 24
Falcon, CO 80831
Voice: (719) 495-2694
Fax: (719) 495-7168
falconmeadowcg@aol.com
Fort Collins, CO

Heron Lake RV Park
1910 N Taft Hill Road
Fort Collins, CO 80524
Voice: (970) 484-9880 / (877) 254-4063
Fax: (970) 493-8900
info@heronlakerv.com

Golden, CO

Golden Gate Canyon State Park
3873 Hwy 46
Golden, CO 80403
303-582-3707

KOA
661 Highway 46
Golden, CO 80403

303-582-9979

Grand Lake, CO

Elk Creek Campground, LLC
143 CR 48
Grand Lake, CO 80447
Voice: (970) 527-8502 / (800) 355-2733
Fax: (970) 627-5456
elkcreekcamp@yahoo.com

Winding River Resort Village
1447 CR 491
Grand Lake, CO 80447
Voice: (970) 627-3215 / (800) 282-5121
Fax: (970) 627-5003
trailboss@rkymtnhi.com

Gunnison, CO

KOA
105 Country Road 50
Grand Lake, CO 81230
970-641-1358

La Junta, CO

KOA
26680 Hwy 50
La Junta, CO 81050
719-384-9580

LaPorte, CO

KOA
Box 600, 6670 N. Hwy 287
LaPorte, CO 80535
970-493-9758

Lake George, CO

Eleven Mile State Park
4229 County Road 92
Lake George, CO 80827
719-748-3401

Leadville, CO

Sugar Loafin Campground
2665 County Road 4
Leadville, CO 80461
Phone: (719)486-1031
sugarloafin@leadville.com

Littleton, CO

Chatfield State Park
11500 N. Roxborough Park Road
Littleton, CO 80125
303-791-7275

Loma, CO

Highline State Park

1800 11.8 Road
Loma, CO 81524
970-858-7208

Longmont, CO

Barbour Ponds State Park
4995 Weld County Road 24
Longmont, CO 80501
303-678-9402

Loveland, CO

Boyd Lake State Park
3720 N. County Road 11-C
Loveland, CO 80538
970-669-1739

Mancos, CO

Mesa Verde RV Resort
35303 US Hwy. 160
Mancos, CO 81328
Voice: (970) 533-7421 / (800) 776-7421
mesaverdervresort@starband.net

Mesa Verde Nat'l Park, CO

Morefield Campground
Mile Marker 4
81330
800-449-2288

Montrose, CO

KOA
200 N. Cedar
Montrose, CO 81401
970-249-9177

Mosca, CO

San Luis State Park
PO Box 175
Mosca, CO 81146
719-378-2020

Nathrop, CO

Chalk Creek Campground and RV Park
POB 39
11430 CR 197
Nathrop, CO 81236
Toll Free: (800)643-9727
Phone: (719)395-8301
Fax: (719)395-8337
chalkcreek@realwest.com

Oak Creek, CO

Stagecoach State Park
PO Box 98
Oak Creek, CO 80467
970-736-2436

Orchard, CO

Jackson Lake State Park
26363 County Road 3
Orchard, CO 80649
970-645-2551

Ouray, CO

KOA
PO Box J
Ouray, CO 81427
970-325-4736

Pagosa Springs, CO

Cool Pines RV Park
1501 W Hwy. 160, #3
Pagosa Springs, CO 81147
Voice: (970) 264-9130 / (877) 250-4811
coolpinesrv@frontier.net

Pagosa Riverside Campground
2270 E Hwy. 160
Pagosa Springs, CO 81147
Voice: (970) 264-5874 / (888) 785-3234
Fax: (970) 264-5874
prc-jones@juno.com

Pueblo, CO

Pueblo KOA
4131 I-25 N
Pueblo, CO 81008
Voice: (719) 542-2273 / (800) 562-7453
Fax: (719) 744-0058
pueblokoa@juno.com

Pueblo State Park
640 Pueblo Reservoir Road
Pueblo, CO 81005
719-561-9320

Ridgway, CO

Ridgway State Park
28555 Hwy 550
Ridgway, CO 81432
970-626-5822

Rifle, CO

Rifle Falls State Park
0050 Road 219
Rifle, CO 81650
970-625-1607

Sylvan State Park
0050 Road 219
Rifle, CO 81650
970-625-1607

Salida, CO

Arkansas Headwaters State Park
PO Box 126
Salida, CO 81201
719-539-7289

Steamboat Springs, CO

KOA
3603 Lincoln Ave.
Steamboat Springs, CO 80487
970-879-0273

Sterling, CO

North Sterling State Park
24005 County Road 330
Sterling, CO 80751
970-522-3657

Strasburg, CO

KOA
Box 597
Strasburg, CO 80136
303-622-9274

Trinidad, CO

Trinidad State Park
32610 Hwy 12
Trinidad, CO 81082
719-846-6951

Walden, CO

KOA
53337 Hwy 14
Walden, CO 80480
970-723-4310

State Forest State Park
2746 Jackson County Road 14
Walden, CO 80480
970-723-8366

Walsenburg, CO

Lathrop State Park
70 County Road 502
Walsenburg, CO 81089
719-738-2376

Wellington, CO

KOA
Box 130
Wellington, CO 80549
970-568-7486

100

Connecticut

Ashford, CT

Brialee RV & Tent Park
174 Laurel Lane, Box 125
Ashford, CT 06278
800-303-CAMP

Baltic, CT

Salt Rock Campground
120 Scotland Road
Baltic, CT 06330
860-822-8728

Bozrah, CT

Acorn Acres
135 Lake Road
Bozrah, CT 06334
860-859-1020

Chaplin, CT

Nickerson Park
Rt. 198
Chaplin, CT 06235
860-455-0007

Clinton, CT

River Road Campground
13 River Road
Clinton, CT 06413
860-669-2238

Riverdale Farm Campsite
111 River Road
Clinton, CT 06413
860-669-5388

East Canaan, CT

Lone Oak Campground
360 Norfolk Road
East Canaan, CT 06024
860-824-7051

East Haddam, CT

Wolf's Den Campground
256 Town St.
East Haddam, CT 06423
860-873-9681

East Hampton, CT

Markham Meadows
7 Markham Road
East Hampton, CT 06424
860-267-8012

Nelson's Family Campground
71 Mott Hill Road
East Hampton, CT 06424
860-267-5300

East Killingly, CT

Hide-Away-Cove Family Campground
1060 North Road
East Killingly, CT 06243
860-774-1128

Stateline Campresort
Route 101
East Killingly, CT 06243
860-774-3016

East Lyme, CT

Aces High RV Park
301 Chesterfield Road
East Lyme, CT 06333
860-739-8858

Eastford, CT

Charlie Brown Campground
100 Chaplin Road
Eastford, CT 06242
877-974-0142

Peppertree Camping
Rt. 198
Eastford, CT 06242
860-974-1439

Goshen, CT

Mohawk Campground
Route 4
Goshen, CT 06756
860-491-2231

Valley in the Pines
Lucas Road
Goshen, CT 06756
860-491-2032

Higganum, CT

Little City Campground
741 Little City Road
Higganum, CT 06441
860-345-4886

Jewett City, CT

Campers World
Edmond Road
Jewett City, CT 06351
860-376-2340

Lebanon, CT

Lake Williams Campground
1742 Exeter Road
Lebanon, CT 06249
860-642-7761

Water's Edge Family Campground
271 Leonard Bridge Road
Lebanon, CT 06249
860-642-7470

Lisbon, CT

Deer Haven Campground
15 Kenyon Road
Lisbon, CT 06351
860-376-1081

Ross Hill park
170 Ross Hill Road
Lisbon, CT 06351
860-376-9606

Litchfield, CT

Hemlock Hill Camp Resorts
Hemlock Hill Road
Litchfield, CT 06759
860-567-2267

Looking Glass Hill Campground
Route 202
Litchfield, CT 06759
860-567-2050

White Memorial Family Campground
Bantam Lake
Litchfield, CT 06759
860-567-0089

Niantic, CT

Camp Niantic-By-The-Atlantic
271 W. Main St.
Niantic, CT 06357
860-739-9308

North Grosvenordale, CT

West Thompson Lake Campground
Reardon Road
North Grosvenordale, CT 06255
860-923-2982

North Stonington, CT

Highland Orchards Resort Park
118 Pendleton Hill Road
North Stonington, CT 06359
860-599-5101

M.H.G. RV Park
Route 184
North Stonington, CT 06359
860-535-0501

Oakdale, CT

Pequot ledge Campground & Cabins
157 Doyle Road
Oakdale, CT 06370
860-859-0682

Old Mystic, CT

Seaport Campground
Route 184
Old Mystic, CT 06372
860-536-4044

Oneco, CT

River Bend Campground
41 Pond St.
Oneco, CT 06373
860-564-3440

Preston, CT

Hidden Acres Family Campground
47 River Road
Preston, CT 06365
860-887-9633

Strawberry Park Resort Campground
Pierce Road
Preston, CT 06365
860-886-1944

Salem, CT

Salem Farms Campground
39 Alexander Road
Salem, CT 06420
860-859-2320

Witch Meadow Lake Campground
139 Witch Meadow Road
Salem, CT 06420
860-859-1542

Scotland, CT

Highland Campground
42 Toleration Road, Box 305
Scotland, CT 06264
860-423-5684

Stafford Springs, CT

Mineral Springs Campground
135 Leonard Road
Stafford Springs, CT 06076
860-684-2993

Roaring Brook Campground
8 South Road
Stafford Springs, CT 06076
860-684-7086

Sterling, CT

Sterling Park Campground
177 Gibson Hill Road
Sterling, CT 06377
860-564-8777

Thomaston, CT

Branch Brook Campground
435 Watertown Road
Thomaston, CT 06787
860-283-8144

Tolland, CT

Del-Aire Campground
704 Shenipsit Lake Road
Tolland, CT 06084
860-875-8325

Voluntown, CT

Countryside Campground
75 Cook Hill Road
Voluntown, CT 06384
860-376-0029

Nature's Campsites
Route 49N
Voluntown, CT 06384
860-376-4203

Willington, CT

Moosemeadow Camping Resort
Moosemeadow Road
Willington, CT 06279
860-429-7451

Rainbow Acres Family Campground
150 Village Hill Road
Willington, CT 06279
860-684-5704

Winsted, CT

White Pines Campsites
232 Old North Road
Winsted, CT 06098
860-379-0124

Woodstock, CT

Beaver Pines Campgrounds
1728 Route 198
Woodstock, CT 06281
860-974-0110

Black Pond Campsites
Route 197
Woodstock, CT 06281
860-974-2065

Chamberlain Lake Campground
1397 Route 197
Woodstock, CT 06281
860-974-0567

Delaware

Bear, DE

Lums Pond State Park
1068 Howell School Road
Bear, DE 19701
302-368-6989

Dagsboro, DE

Jim's Hide A Way
Dagsboro, DE
302-539-6095

Tuckahoe Acres Camping Resort 19939
Dagsboro, DE
302-539-1841

Felton, DE

Killens Pond State Park
525 Killens Pond Road
Felton, DE 19943
302-284-3412

Fenwick Island, DE

Treasure Beach RV Park and Campground
Rt 54, Box 150A
Fenwick Island, DE 19975
302-436-8001

Houston, DE

The Houston G&R Campground
4075 Gun & Rod Club Road
Houston, DE 19954
302-398-8108

Laurel, DE

Trap Pond State Park
RD 2, Box 331
Laurel, DE 19956
302-875-2392

Lewes, DE

Cape Henlopen State Park
42 Cape Henlopen Drive
Lewes, DE 19958
320-645-2103

Tall Pines
221 Tall Pines
Lewes, DE 19958
302-684-0300

Millsboro, DE

Holly Lake Campsites

RD Box 141
Millsboro, DE 19966
800-227-7170

New Castle, DE

Delaware Motel and RV Park
235 South Dupont Hwy
New Castle, DE 19720
302-328-3114

Ocean View, DE

Pine Tree Campsites 19970
Ocean View, DE
302-539-7006

Sandy Cove Campsite
RD 1, Box 256
Ocean View, DE 19970
302-539-6245

Rehoboth Beach, DE

3 Seasons Camping Resort
727 Country Club Road
Rehoboth Beach, DE 19971
302-227-2564

Big Oaks Family Campgrounds
Box 53
Rehoboth Beach, DE 19971
302-645-6838

Delaware Seashore State Park
Inlet 850
Rehoboth Beach, DE 19971
302-539-7202

Sear Air Village
Hwy 1 and Sear Air Ave
Rehoboth Beach, DE 19971
302-227-8118

Florida

Alachua, FL

Traveler's Campground
17701 April Blvd.
Alachua, FL 32615
904-462-2505

Alligator Point, FL

Alligator Point Campground
Route 1, P.O. Box 3392
Alligator Point, FL 32346
850-349-2525

KOA
1320 Alligator Drive
Alligator Point, FL 32346
850-349-2525

Altamonte Springs, FL

Orlando Green Acres RV Resort
9701 Forest City Road
Altamonte Springs, FL 32714
800-894-8563

Apopka, FL

Orange Blossom RV Resort LLC
407-886-3260
3800 W. Orange Blossom Trl.
Apopka, FL

Sun Resort RV Park
407-889-3048
3000 Clarcona Road #99
Apopka, FL

Arcadia, FL

Arcadia Peace River Campground
2998 NW Highway 70
Arcadia, FL 34266
800-559-4011

Yogi Bear's Jellystone Park
9770 SW County Rd 769
Arcadia, FL 34266
800-795-9733

Astor, FL

Parramore's Campground
1675 S. Moon Road
Astor, FL 32102
800-516-2386

Auburndale, FL

Fish Haven Lodge
Box 1, Fish Haven Road
Auburndale, FL 33823
941-984-1183

Avon Park, FL

Lake Bonnet Village Campground
2900 E. Lake Bonnet Road
Avon Park, FL 33825
941-385-7010

Bagdad, FL

Sunny Acres RV Resort
P.O. Box 238
Bagdad, FL 32530
850-623-0576

Big Pine Key, FL

Breezy Pines RV Estates
P.O. Box 430191 Big Pin
Big Pine Key, FL 33043
305-872-9041

Bonita Springs, FL

Bonita Beach Trailer Park
27800 Meadow Lane
Bonita Springs, FL 33923
800-654-9907

Imperial Bonita Estates Cooperative
239-992-0511
27700 Bourbonniere Dr.
Bonita Springs, FL

Bradenton, FL

Arbor Terrace RV Resort
941-755-6494
405 - 57th Ave. W.
Bradenton, FL

Encore RV Resort - Sarasota North
941-745-2600
800 Kay Road NE
Bradenton, FL

Pleasant Lake RV Resort
941-756-5076
6633 S.R. 70 E.
Bradenton, FL

Winter Quarters RV Resort
800 Kay Road
Bradenton, FL 34202
800-678-2131

Bunnell, FL

Thunder Gulch Campground
386-437-3135
2129 N. U.S. Hwy. 1
Bunnell, FL

Bushnell, FL

Breezy Oaks RV Park
352-569-0300
9683 C.R. 671
Bushnell, FL

Duvals RV Park
352-793-5179
7961 C.R. 647
Bushnell, FL

Sumter Oaks RV Park
4602 County Route 673
Bushnell, FL 33513
352-793-1333

Cape Canaveral, FL

Mango-Oak Manor
190 Oak Manor Drive
Cape Canaveral, FL 32920
321-799-0741

Carrabelle, FL

Ho-Hum RV Park
850-697-3926
2132 Hwy. 98 E.
Carrabelle, FL

Cedar Key, FL

Cedar Key RV Park
P.O. Box 268
Cedar Key, FL 32625
352-543-5150

Rainbow Country RV Campground
11951 SW Shiloh Road
Cedar Key, FL 32625
352-543-6268

Century,FL

Lake Stone Campground
850-256-5555
801 Hwy. 4
Century,FL

Chattahoochee, FL

Chattahoochee KOA
850-442-6657
2309 Flat Creek Road
Chattahoochee, FL

Chipley, FL

NW Florida Campground & Music
677 Griffin Road
Chipley, FL 32428
850-638-0362

Chokoloskee, FL

Chokoloskee Island Park
75 Hamilton Lane
Chókoloskee, FL 33925
239-695-2414

Clearwater, FL

Clearwater Travel Resort
2946 Gulf to Bay Blvd.
Clearwater, FL 34619
727-791-0550
800-831-1204

Travel Towne Travel Trailer Resort
29850 US Highway 19 N
Clearwater, FL 34621
813-784-2500

Clermont, FL

Encore RV Resort - Orlando
863-420-1300
9600 U.S. Hwy. 192 W
Clermont, FL

Outdoor Resorts at Orlando
9000 US Hwy 192
Clermont, FL 34711
800-531-3033

Thousand Trails
2110 Highway 27 S
Clermont, FL 34711
800-723-1217

Clewiston, FL

Big Cypress RV Resort
863-983-1330
HC 61 Box 54A
Clewiston, FL

Clewiston/Lake Okeechobee KOA Campground
863-983-7078
194 C.R. 720
Clewiston, FL

Crooked Hook RV Resort
863-983-7112
51700 U.S. Hwy. 27
Clewiston, FL

Okeechobee Landings, Inc. RV
420 Holiday Blvd.

Clewiston, FL 33440
800-322-5933

Cocoa Beach, FL

Oceanus Mobile Village & RV P
152 Crescent Beach Dr.,
Cocoa Beach, FL 32931
407-783-3871

Cortez, FL

Holiday Cove R.V. Resort
11900 Cortez Road, W.
Cortez, FL 34215
941-792-1111

Crescent Cit, FL
 Crescent City Campground
386-698-2020
2359 Hwy. 17 S.
Crescent City, FL

Leonard's Landing Lake Crescent Resort
386-698-2485
100 Grove Ave.
Crescent City, FL

Cross Creek, FL

win Lakes Fish Camp
352-466-3194
Cross Creek, FL 17105 S. C.R. 325

Crystal River, FL

Encore SuperPark Crystal River
352-795-3774
11419 W. Fort Island Trl.
Crystal River, FL

Lake Rousseau RV and Fishing Resort
352-795-6336
10811 N. Coveview Ter.
Crystal River, FL

Nature Coast Landings RV Resort
352-447-2299
10173 N. Suncoast Blvd.
Crystal River, FL

Dade City, FL

Sawmill Camping Resort
352-583-0664
Dade City, FL 21710

Town & Country RV Resort
352-567-7707
18005 N. Hwy. 301
Dade City, FL

Travelers Rest Resort, Inc.
352-588-2013
29129 Johnston Road
Dade City, FL

Davenport, FL

21 Palms RV Resort
407-397-9110
6951 Osceola Polk Line Road
Davenport, FL

Deer Creek RV Golf & Tennis Resort
863-424-3153
42749 Hwy. 27 N.
Davenport, FL

Lakewood RV Resort
863-424-2669
7700 Osceola Polk Line Road
Davenport, FL

Mouse Mountain RV Resort
7500 Osceola Polk Line Road
Davenport, FL 33837
941-424-2791

Daytona Beach, FL

Daytona Beach Campground
4601 Clyde Morris Blvd.
Daytona Beach, FL 32119
386-761-2663

Nova Family Campground
1190 Herbert St.
Daytona Beach, FL 32119
904-767-0095

DeBary, FL

Highbanks Marina & CampResort
386-668-4491
488 W. Highbanks Road
DeBary, FL

DeFuniak Springs, FL

Sunset King Lake Resort
850-892-7229
366 Paradise Island Dr.
DeFuniak Springs, FL

Destin, FL

Camping on the Gulf Holiday
10005 W. Emerald Coast
Destin, FL 32541
850-837-6334

Destin RV Park
150 Regions Way
Destin, FL 32541
850-837-6215

RV Park
362 Miramar Beach Dr.
Destin, FL 32550
850-837-3529

Dover, FL

Citrus Hills RV Park
5311 E. State Route 60
Dover, FL 33527
813-737-4770

Tampa East Green Acres Travel
4630 McIntosh Road
Dover, FL 33527
800-45-GREEN

Dundee,FL

Greenfield Village RV Park
863-439-7409
1015 S.R. 542 W.
Dundee,FL

Dunedin, FL

Dunedin Beach Campground
2920 Alt 19 N
Dunedin, FL 34698
800-345-7504

E. Bradenton, FL

Horseshoe Cove RV Resort
5100 60th St.
E. Bradenton, FL 34203
800-291-3446

Pleasant Lake RV Resort
6633 53rd Ave.
34203
800-283-5076

E. Carrabell, FL

Ho-Hum RV Resort Park
2132 Highway 98
E. Carrabell, FL 32322
888-88HOHUM

E. Lakeland, FL

Morgan's RV Park
4411 State Route 542
E. Lakeland, FL 33801
941-665-9631

E. Marianna, FL

Arrowhead Campsites
4820 Highway 90
E. Marianna, FL 32446
850-482-5583

E. Nokomis, FL

Royal Coachmen Resort
1070 Laurel Road
E. Nokomis, FL 34275
800-548-8678

East Palatka, FL

St. John's Campground
386-328-4470
436 S. U.S. Hwy. 17
East Palatka, FL

Eustis, FL

Southern Palms RV Resort
352-357-8882
One Avocado Ln.
Eustis, FL

Flagler Beach, FL

Bulow RV Resort
P.O. Box 1328
Flagler Beach, FL 32136
800-RV-BULOW

Flagler By The Sea
2981 N. Oceanshore Blvd
Flagler Beach, FL 32136
800-434-2124

Picnickers Campground-Shelltown
2455 N. Oceanshore Blvd
Flagler Beach, FL 32136
800-553-2381

Singing Surf Campground
386-439-5473
2424 N. Oceanshore Blvd. (A1A)
Flagler Beach, FL

Florida City, FL

Southern Comfort RV Resort
345 E. Palm Dr.
Florida City, FL 33034
305-248-6909

Frostproof, FL

Lily Lake Golf Resort
500 US Highway 27
Frostproof, FL 33843
941-635-3685

Ft. Lauderdale, FL

Buglewood RV Resort
2121 NW 29th Ct.
Ft. Lauderdale, FL 33311
800-487-7395

Candlelight Park
5731 S. State Route 7
Ft. Lauderdale, FL 33314
954-791-5023

Kozy Kampers RV Park
3631 W. Commerical Blvd
Ft. Lauderdale, FL 33309
954-731-8570

Twin Lakes Travel Park
3055 Burris Road
Ft. Lauderdale, FL 33314
800-327-8182

Yacht Haven Park & Marina
2323 State Route 84
Ft. Lauderdale, FL 33312
800-581-2322

Ft. McCoy, FL

Ocklawaha Canoe Outpost RV Park
15260 NE 152nd Place
Ft. McCoy, FL 32134
352-236-4606

Fort Meade, FL

Hammock Lake Estates
863-285-9560
1800 Hammock Lake Dr
Fort Meade, FL

Ft. Myers, FL

Cypress Woods RV Resort
5551 Luckett Road
Ft. Myers, FL 33905
800-414-9879

Fort Myers Beach RV Resort
16299 San Carlos Blvd.
941-466-7171
Ft. Myers, FL

Fort Myers Beach RV Resort
16299 San Carlos Blvd.
Ft. Myers, FL 33908
800-553-7484

Garden RV Park
2830 Garden St.
Ft. Myers, FL 33917

941-995-7417

Gulf Air Travel Park
17279 San Carlos Blvd.
Ft. Myers, FL 33931
941-466-8100

Mar-Good RV Park, Cottages, Marina
Ft. Myers, FL
941-392-6383

Seminole Campground
8991 Triplett Road
Ft. Myers, FL 33917
941-543-2919

Seminole Campground
Ft. Myers, FL
941-543-2919

Shady Acres RV Travel Park
941-267-8448
19370 S. Tamiami Trl.
Ft. Myers, FL

Shady Acres Travel Park
19370 S. Tamiami Tr.
Ft. Myers, FL 33908
941-267-8448

Swan Lake Village & RV Resort
2400 N. Tamiami Tr.
Ft. Myers, FL 33903
941-995-3397

The Groves RV Campground
16175 John Morris Road
Ft. Myers, FL 33908
941-466-5909

The Groves RV Resort
Ft. Myers, FL
941-466-4300

The Plantation RV Resort
Ft. Myers, FL
941-275-1575

The Plantation, an RV Condo Resort
P.O. Box 60686
Ft. Myers, FL 33906
800-710-8819

Upriver Campground Resort
17021 Upriver Dr.
Ft. Myers, FL 33917

800-848-1652

Woodsmoke Camping Resort
19551 US Highway 41
Ft. Myers, FL 33908
800-231-5053

Ft. Myers Beach, FL

Ebb Tide RV Park
1725 Main Street
Ft. Myers Beach, FL 33931
941-463-5444

Gulf Air Travel Park
Ft. Myers Beach, FL
941-466-8100

San Carlos RV Park
Ft. Myers Beach, FL
941-466-3133

Ft. Pierce, FL

Easy Livin RV Park of White City
772-460-2424
4611 S. U.S. 1
Ft. Pierce, FL

Road Runner Travel Resort
5500 St. Lucie Blvd
Ft. Pierce, FL 34946
772-464-0969
800-833-7108

Ft. Walton Beach, FL

Playground RV Park
777 Beal Pkwy.
Ft. Walton Beach, FL 32547
850-862-3513

Georgetown, FL

Port Cove RV Park & Marina
110 Georgetown Landing
Georgetown, FL 32139
800-980-5263

Riverwood RV Village
386-467-7144
1389 C.R. 309
Georgetown, FL

Goodland, FL

Mar-Good RV Park Cottages & Marina
321 Pear Tree Ave.
Goodland, FL 34140
239-394-6383

Central Park of Haines City

863-422-5322
1501 W. Commerce Ave
Goodland, FL

Oak Harbor RV Park
863-956-1341
100 Oak Harbor
Goodland, FL

Paradise Island RV Resort
2900 S. US Highway 27
Goodland, FL 33844
800-831-2207

Hallandale, FL

Holiday Park
954-981-4414
3140 W. Hallandale Beach
Hallandale, FL

Hawthorne, FL

Ranch Motel & Campground
352-481-3851
8010 S.E. U.S. 301
Hawthorne, FL

High Springs, FL

High Springs Campground
24004 NW Old Bellamy Road
High Springs, FL 32643
904-454-1688

Hollywood, FL

Grice RV Park
954-983-8225
5931 Polk St.
Hollywood, FL

Trinity Towers/Lake Trinity Estates
954-962-7400
3300 Pembroke Road
Hollywood, FL

Holt, FL

Eagle's Landing RV Park
4504 Log Lake Road
Holt, FL 32564
850-537-9657

River's Edge RV Campground
P.O. Box 189
Holt, FL 32564
800-339-CAMP

Homestead, FL

GoldCoaster RV Resort
305-248-5462

34850 S.W. 187th Ave
Homestead, FL

Miami-Homestead KOA
20675 SW 162nd Ave.
Homestead, FL 33187
800-562-7732

The Boardwalk
100 NE 6th Ave.
Homestead, FL 33030
305-248-2487

Homosassa, FL
Camp N Water
11465 W. Priest Ln.
Homosassa, FL 34448
352-628-2000

Citrus Cnty Chassahowitzka River Campground
8600 W. Miss Maggie Dr.
Homosassa, FL 34446
352-382-2200

Homosassa Springs, FL
Covered Wagon Campground
352-628-4669
6049 S. Suncoast Blvd.
Homosassa Springs, FL

Hudson, FL
Gulf Coast Nudist Resort
13220 Houston Ave.
Hudson, FL 34667
813-868-1061

Indian Rocks, FL
Indian Rocks Beach RV Resort
601 Gulf Blvd.
Indian Rocks, FL 34635
800-354-7559

Inverness, FL
Shawnee Trail Campground
2000-C Bishop's Point
Inverness, FL 34450
800-834-7595

Jacksonville, FL
Flamingo Lake RV Resort
3640 Newcomb Road
Jacksonville, FL 32218
800-782-4323

Huguenot Memorial Park
904-251-3335

10980 Heckscher Dr.
Jacksonville, FL

KOA
PO Box 18244
Jacksonville, FL 32229
912-729-3232

Kathryn Abbey Hanna Park
500 Wonderwood Drive
Jacksonville, FL 32233
904-249-4700

Jennings, FL
Jennings Outdoor Resort Campg
Route 1, Box 221
Jennings, FL 32053
386-938-3321

Jensen Beach, FL
Nettles Island/VNI Realty
772-229-1300
9801 S. Ocean Dr.
Jensen Beach, FL

Jupiter, FL
West Jupiter Camping Resort
17801 N. 130th Ave.
Jupiter, FL 33478
888-746-6073

Key Largo, FL
America Outdoors
305-852-8054
97450 Overseas Hwy.
Key Largo, FL

Calusa Camp Resort
325 Calusa Road
Key Largo, FL 33037
305-451-0232

Key Largo Kampground & Marina
305-451-1431
101551 Overseas Hwy.
Key Largo, FL

Kings Kamp/RV Park & Marina
305-451-0010
103620 Overseas Hwy.
Key Largo, FL

Florida Keys RV Resort
100003 Overseas Hwy.
Key Largo, FL 33037
305-451-6090

113

Rock Harbor Marina
36 E. 2nd St
Key Largo, FL 33037
305-852-2025

Key West, FL

Boyd's Key West Campground
305-294-1465
6401 Maloney Ave.
Key West, FL

Elmar RV Resort
305-294-0857
6700 Maloney Ave.
Key West, FL

Jabour's Trailer Court
223 Elizabeth St.
Key West, FL 33040
305-294-5723

Sugarloaf Key KOA
Box 469
Key West, FL 33042
305-745-3549

Kissimmee, FL

Aloha RV Park
407-933-5730
4648 S. Orange Blossom Trail 17/92
Kissimmee, FL

Cypress Cove Nudist Resort & Spa
407-933-5870
4425 Pleasant Hill Road
Kissimmee, FL

Kissimmee Campground
2643 Alligator Lane
Kissimmee, FL 34746
407-396-6851

Orange Grove Campground
2425 Old Fineland Road
Kissimmee, FL 34746
800-3CAMPIN

Orlando-Kissimmee KOA
4771 W. Irlo Bronson Hw
Kissimmee, FL 34746
800-562-7791

Ponderosa Park Campground
1983 Boggy Creek Road
Kissimmee, FL 34744
407-847-6002

Sherwood Forest RV Park
5300 W. Irlo Bronson Hw
Kissimmee, FL 34746
407-396-7431
800-548-9981

Tropical Palms FunResort & Campground
2650 Holiday Trl
Kissimmee, FL 34746
800-64-PALMS

Yogi Bear's Jellystone Park
8555 W. Irlo Bronson, U
Kissimmee, FL 34747
800-776-YOGI

LaBelle, FL

Whisper Creek RV Resort
863-675-6888
1980 Hickory Dr.
LaBelle, FL

Lady Lake, FL

Recreation Plantation RV Resort
352-753-7222
609 Hwy. 466
Lady Lake, FL

Lake Buena Vista, FL

Disney's For Wilderness Camping
P.O. Box 10000
Lake Buena Vista, FL 32830
407/WDISNEY

Fort Summit Camping Resort
P.O. Box 22182
Lake Buena Vista, FL 32830
800-424-1880

Lake City, FL

E-Z Stop RV Park
386-752-2279
181 S.W. Howell St.
Lake City, FL

KOA
Lake City North KOA
386-752-9131
4743 N. U.S. Hwy. 441
Lake City, FL

Oaks 'N Pines RV Park
386-752-0830
3864 N. U.S. Hwy. 441
Lake City, FL

Wagon Wheel RV Resort
Route 3, Box 176
Lake City, FL 32024
904-752-2279

Wayne's RV Resort
Route 17, Box 501
Lake City, FL 32024
904-752-5721

Lake Panasoffkee, FL

Idlewild Lodge & RV Park
4110 County Road 400
Lake Panasoffkee, FL 33538
352-793-7057

Lake Place, FL

Camp Florida Resort
1525 US HIghway 27 S
Lake Place, FL 33852
941-699-1991
Lake Placid, FL

Cypress Isle RV Park & Marina
2 Cypress Isle Lane
Lake Placid, FL 33852
863-465-5241

Lake Wales, FL

The Harbor RV Resort and Marina
863-696-1194
10511 Monroe Ct.
Lake Wales, FL

Lake Worth, FL

Camping Resort of the Palm Beaches
5332 Lake Worth Road
Lake Worth, FL 33463
800-247-9650

Lakeland, FL

Lakeland RV Resort
863-687-6146
900 Old Combee Road
Lakeland, FL

Sanlan Ranch Campground
863-665-1726
3929 U.S. Hwy. 98 S.
Lakeland, FL

Tiki Village Campground
863-858-5364
905 Crevasse St.
Lakeland, FL

Valencia Estates & RV Park
3325 Barstow Hwy., SR 98 S
Lakeland, FL 33803
800-645-9033

Lakeport, FL

Aruba RV Camp Resort
863-946-1324
1825 Old Lakeport Road
Lakeport, FL

Lakeport RV Resort
863-946-1415
2800 Milum Dr. N.W.
Lakeport, FL

Lamont, FL

A Camper's World
Route 1, Box 164B
Lamont, FL 32336
850-997-3300

Land O' Lakes, FL

Riverboat Nudist Resort
813-996-6008
6901 Caliente Blvd.
Land O' Lakes, FL

Lantana, FL

Palm Beach Traveler Park
561-967-3139
6159 Lawrence Road
Lantana, FL

Largo, FL

Briarwood Travel Villa
27-581-6694
098 Seminole Blvd.
Largo, FL

Lee's Travel Park
1610 Belcher Road
Largo, FL 33771
888-510-8900

Leesburg, FL

Fiesta Key Resort KOA & Motel
305-664-4922
MM 70 on U.S. 1
Leesburg, FL

Holiday Travel Resort
28229 County Road 33
Leesburg, FL 34748
800-428-5334

Lillian, FL

Perdido Bay KOA
33951 Spinnaker
Lillian, FL 36549
334-961-1717

Live Oak, FL

The Spirit of Suwannee Music Park
3076 95th Dr.
Live Oak, FL 32060
904-364-1683

Loxahatchee, FL

Lion Country Safari KOA
2000 Lion Country Safari Road
Loxahatchee, FL 33470
561-793-9797

Sunsport Gardens Nudist Retreat
14125 North Road
Loxahatchee, FL 33470
800-551-7117

Lutz, FL

Encore RV Resort - Tampa North
813-949-6551
21632 S.R. 54
Lutz, FL

MacClenny, FL

Hidden River Ranch
P.O. Box 345
MacClenny, FL 32063
912-843-2603

Madison, FL

Madison Campground
850-973-2504
Route 1, Box 3095
Madison, FL

Yogi Bear's Jellystone Park
850-973-8269
1051 S.W. Old St. Augustine Road
Madison, FL

Marathon, FL

Jolly Roger Travel Park
59275 Overseas Hwy.
Marathon, FL 33050
800-995-1525

Pelican Motel & Trailer Park
59151 Overseas Hwy.
Marathon, FL 33050
305-289-0011

Marianna, FL

Arrowhead Campsites, Inc. & RV Sales
850-482-5583
4820 Hwy. 90
Marianna, FL

Dove Rest RV Park & Campground
850-482-5313
1973 Dove Rest Dr.
Marianna, FL

Marineland, FL

Marineland Camping Resort
9741 Ocean Shore Blvd.
Marineland, FL 32086
904-471-4700

May, FL

Jim Hollis' River Rendezvous
Route 2, Box 635
May, FL 32066
800-533-5276

McIntosh, FL

Sportsman Cove
P.O. Box 107
McIntosh, FL 32664
352-591-1435

Melbourne, FL

Palm Shores RV Park
321-254-4388
5090 N. Harbour City Blvd
Melbourne, FL

Mexico Beach, FL

Rustic Sands Resort Campground
HC03 800 N. 15th St.
Mexico Beach, FL 32456
850-648-5229

Miami, FL

Gator Park
24050 SW 8th St.
Miami, FL 33187
305-559-2255
800-559-2205

KOA
20675 SW 162 Ave.
Miami, FL 33187
305-233-5300

Kobe Trailer Park
11900 NE 16th Ave.
Miami, FL 33161

305-893-5121

Miami Everglades Campground
305-233-5300
20675 S.W. 162nd Ave.
Miami, FL

Milton, FL

By-the-Bay RV Park & Campground
850-623-0262
5550 Michael Dr.
Milton, FL

Cedar Pines Campground
6436 Robie Road
Milton, FL 32570
850-623-8869

Milton/Gulf Pines KOA
850-623-0808
8700 Gulf Pines Dr.
Milton, FL

Pelican Palms R.V. Park
850-623-0576
3700 Garcon Point Road
Milton, FL

Mims, FL

KOA
4513 W. Main St.
Mims, FL 32754
407-269-7361

Northgate Travel Park
3277 First Avenue
Mims, FL 32754
321-267-0144

Molino, FL

Lakeside at Barth
855 Barth Road
Molino, FL 32577
850-587-2322

Monticello, FL

KOA
Rt 2, Box 5160
Monticello, FL 32344
850-997-3890

Montverde, FL

Woodlands Camp
15749 County Road 455
Montverde, FL 34756
407-469-2792

Moore Haven, FL

The Glades Resort
863-902-7034
4380 Indian Hills Dr.
Moore Haven, FL

Meadowlark Campground
12525 Williams Road SW
Moore Haven, FL 33471
941-675-2243

Naples, FL

Club Naples
3180 Beck Blvd.
Naples, FL 34114
888-795-2780

Crystal Lake RV Resort
160 County Road 951 N
Naples, FL 34119
800-322-4525

Endless Summer RV Estates
2 Tina Lane, Radio Road
Naples, FL 33942
941-643-1511

KOA
1700 Barefoot Williams Road
Naples, FL 34113
941-774-5455

Kountree Kampinn RV Resort
5200 County Rd 951
Naples, FL 34114
941-775-4340

Lake San Marino RV Park
239-597-4202
1000 Wiggins Pass Road
Naples, FL

Naples KOA
1700 Barefoot Williams Road
Naples, FL 33962
941-774-5455

Port of the Islands RV Resort
12425 Union Road
Naples, FL 34114
800-319-4447

Silver Lakes RV Resort
1001 Silver Lakes Blvd.
Naples, FL 33961
800-843-2836

Navarre, FL

Emerald Beach RV Park
8899 Navarre Pkwy.
Navarre, FL 32566
850-939-3431

Navarre Beach Campground
9201 Navarre Pkwy. (Hwy
Emerald Beach RV Park
Navarre, FL 32566
850-939-2188

New Smyrna Beach, FL

Indian Mound Fish Camp
386-345-9845
295 Indian Creek Road
New Smyrna Beach, FL

KOA
1300 Old Mission Road
New Smyrna Beach, FL 32168
904-427-3581

Nokomis, FL

Encore RV Resort - Sarasota South
941-488-9674
1070 Laurel Road
Nokomis, FL

Lake Awesome
899 Knights Tr.
Nokomis, FL 34275
800-437-9397

North Ft. Myers, FL
New Garden RV Park, Inc.
239-995-7417
2830 Garden St.

Raintree RV Resort
239-731-1441
Nokomis, FL 19250 N. Tamiami Trl.

Seminole Campground
239-543-2919
8991 Triplett Road
Nokomis, FL

North Fort Myers

Sunseeker's RV Park
239-731-1303
19701 N. Tamiami Trl.
North Fort Myers

Swan Lake Village & RV Resort
239-995-3397

2400 N. Tamiami Trl.
North Fort Myers

Tamiami RV Park
239-997-2697
16555-A N. Cleveland Ave.
North Fort Myers

Oak Hill, FL

Riverwood Park Campground
386-345-3922
298 H.H. Burch Road
Oak Hill, FL

Ocala, FL

Grand Lake R.V. & Golf Resort
352-591-3474
4555 W. Hwy. 318
Ocala, FL

Holiday Trav-L-Park
352-622-5330
4001 W. Silver Springs Blvd.
Ocala, FL

Ocala Ranch RV Park
352-307-1100
2559 S.W. Hwy. 484
Ocala, FL

Ocala/Silver Springs KOA
352-237-2138
3200 S.W. 38th Ave.
Ocala, FL

Ocklawaha, FL

Lake Bryant MH & RV Park
352-625-2376
5000 S.E. 183rd Ave. Road
Ocklawaha, FL

Lake In the Forest Estates/RV Resort
352-625-6275
19115 S.E. 44th St.
Ocklawaha, FL

Okeechobee, FL

Bob's Big Bass RV Park
12766 Highway 441 SE
Okeechobee, FL 34974
941-763-2638

Elite Resorts at Okeechobee (Big "O") RV Resort
863-467-5515
7950 Hwy. 78 W.
Okeechobee, FL

Fijian RV Park
863-763-6200
6500 U.S. Hwy. 441 S.E.
Okeechobee, FL

Okeechobee Resort KOA
863-763-0231
4276 Hwy. 441 S.

Okee-Tantie Campground & Marina
863-763-2622
10430 Hwy. 78 W.
Okeechobee, FL

Stephens Winter Resort
863-763-4747
9750 Hwy. 78 W
Okeechobee, FL

Zachary Taylor Camping Resort
2995 US Highway 441 SE
Okeechobee, FL 34974
888-282-6523

Fijian RV Park
6500 SE Highway 441
Okeechobee, FL 34974
888-646-2267

Okeechobee KOA
4276 Hwy 441 S.
Okeechobee, FL 34974
941-763-0231

Old Town, FL

Joa Navatto Old Town Campground
Hwy 349, Box 522
Old Town, FL 32680
352-542-9500

Suwannee River KOA
P.O. Box 460
Old Town, FL 32680
800-562-7635

Orange City, FL

KOA
1440 E. Minnesota Ave.
Orange City, FL 32763
904-775-3996

Village Park Luxury RV Park
2300 E. Graves Ave.
Orange City, FL 32763
904-775-2545

Orange Park, FL

Whiteys Fish Camp
2032 County Road 220
Orange Park, FL 32073
904-269-4198

Orlando, FL

KOA
12345 Narcoossee Road
Orlando, FL 32827
407-277-5075

Ormond Beach, FL
Encore RV Resort - Daytona North
386-672-3045
1701 N. U.S. Hwy. 1
Orlando, FL

Harris Village and RV Park LLC
386-673-0494
1080 N. U.S. Hwy. 1
Orlando, FL

Ocean Village Camper Resort
2162 Ocean Shore Blvd.
Orlando, FL 32176
904-441-1808

On Ocean Seaside RV & Trailer
1047 Ocean Shore Blvd.
Orlando, FL 32176
904-441-0900

Sunshine Holiday Camper Resort
1701 N. US Highway 1
Orlando, FL 32174
904-672-3045

Pace, FL

The Farmers' Opry House Campgrounds
850-994-6000
8897 Byrom Campbell Road
Pace, FL

Pahokee, FL

Everglades Adventure RV & Sailing Resort
561-924-7832
190 N. Lake Ave.
Pahokee, FL

The Park Place RV Resort
561-924-2511
297 W. Main St.
Pahokee, FL

Palatka, FL

St. John's Campground
US Highway 17, Route 3
Palatka, FL 32131
904-328-4470

Palm Harbor, FL

Bay Aire RV Park
2242 US Highway Alt 19 N
Palm Harbor, FL 34683
813-784-4082

Caladesi Travle Trailer Park
205 Dempsey Road
Palm Harbor, FL 34683
813-784--362

KOA
37061 US 19 N.
Palm Harbor, FL 34684
727-937-8412

Palm Harbor Resort
2119 Alt 19 N
Palm Harbor, FL 34683
813-785-3401

Sherwood Forest RV Resort
251 US Highway Alt 19
Palm Harbor, FL 34683
800-413-9762

Palmetto, FL

Fiesta Grove RV Resort
8615 Bayshore Road
Palmetto, FL 34221
941-722-7661

Fisherman's Cove RV Resort
100 Palmview Road
Palmetto, FL 34221
941-729-3685

Frog Creek Campground
8515 Bayshore Road
Palmetto, FL 34221
800-771-3764

Winterset Travel Trailer RV Park
8515 US Highway 41 N
Palmetto, FL
800-263-3984

Panacea, FL

Holiday Park & Campground
14 Coastal Hwy.
Panacea, FL 32346
850-984-5757

Panama City, FL

Campers Inn, Inc.
850-234-5731
8800 Thomas Dr.
Panama City, FL

Emerald Coast RV Beach Resort
850-235-0924
1957 Allison Ave.
Panama City, FL

Ocean Park RV Resort
23026 Panama City Beach
Panama City, FL 32413
850-235-0306

Panama City Beach KOA
8800 Thomas Dr.
Panama City, FL 32408
800-562-2483

Pine Glen Motor Coach & RV Pa
11930 Panama City Beach
Panama City, FL 32407
230-8353

Panama City Beach, FL

KOA
8800 Thomas Drive
Panama City Beach, FL 32408
850-234-5731

Pensacola, FL

All Star RV Campground
13621 Perdino Key Drive
Pensacola, FL 32507
800-245-3602

Playa del Rio RV Park
850-492-0904
16990 Perdido Key Dr.
Pensacola, FL

Perry, FL

Southern Oaks
3641 Highway 19 S
Perry, FL 32347
800-339-5421

Polk City, FL

Lelynn RV Resort
863-984-1495
1513 S. R. 559
Polk City, FL

Port Charlotte, FL

Encore RV Resort - Port Charlotte
941-624-4511
3737 El Jobean Road
Port Charlotte, FL

Port Orange, FL

Nova Family Campground
386-767-0095
1190 Herbert St.
Port Orange, FL

Orange Isles Campground
386-767-9170
3520 S. Nova Road
Port Orange, FL

Port St. Joe, FL

Cape San Blas Camping Resort
PO Box 645
Port St. Joe, FL 32457
850-229-6800

Port St. Lucie, FL

Port St. Lucie RV Resort
772-337-3340
3703 S.E. Jennings Road
Port St. Lucie, FL

Punta Gorda, FL

Gulf View RV Resort
10205 Burnt Store Road
Punta Gorda, FL 33950
941-639-3978

KOA
6800 Golf Course Blvd.
Punta Gorda, FL 33982
941-637-1188

Punta Gorda RV Resort
3701 Baynard Dr.
Punta Gorda, FL 33950
941-639-2010

Sun-N-Shade Campground
14880 Tamiami Tr.
Punta Gorda, FL 33955
941-639-5388

Quincy, FL

Whippoorwill Sportsmans Lodge
3129 Cooks Landing Road
Quincy, FL 32351
850-875-2605

Riverview, FL

Alafia River RV Resort
9812 Gilbsonton Drive
Riverview, FL 33569
813-677-1997

Rockledge, FL

Space Coast RV Resort
820 Barnes Blvd.
Rockledge, FL 32955
407-636-2873

Ruskin, FL

Hide-A-Way RV Resort
2206 Chaney Dr.
Ruskin, FL 33570
800-607-2532

Lone Pine RV Park
201 11th Ave NW
Ruskin, FL 33570
813-645-6532

River Oaks RV Resort
201 Stephens Road
Ruskin, FL 33561
800-645-6311

Sun Lake RV Resort
813-645-7860
3006 - 14th Ave. S.E.
Ruskin, FL

Salt Springs, FL

Elite Resorts at Salt Springs RV Resort
352-685-1900
14100 N. Hwy. 19
Salt Springs, FL

Sanford, FL

Twelve Oaks RV Resort
6300 State Route 46 W
Sanford, FL 32771
800-633-9529

Santa Rosa, FL

Emerald Coast RV Resort
7525 W. Scenic Hwy, 30-
Santa Rosa, FL 32459
800-BEACH-RV

Peach Creek RV Park
850-231-1948
4401 E. Hwy. 98
Santa Rosa, FL

Sarasota, FL

Sun-N-Fun Resort
941-371-2505
7125 Fruitville Road
Sarasota, FL

Scottsmoor, FL

Crystal Lake RV Park
P.O. Box 362
Scottsmoor, FL 32775
407-268-8555

Sebastian, FL

Pelican's Landing of Sebastian
772-589-5188
11330 S. Indian River Dr.
Sebastian, FL

Vero Beach Kamp, Inc.
772-589-5643
8850 N. U.S. 1
Sebastian, FL

Sebring, FL

Buttonwood Bay RV Resort
10001 US Highway 27 S
Sebring, FL 33870
800-289-2522

Sebring Grove RV Resort
4105 US Highway 27
Sebring, FL 33870
941-382-1660

Tanglewood RV Resort
4545 US Highway 27 N
Sebring, FL 33870
800-386-4545

Seffner, FL

Lazy Days Campground Resort
6130 Lazy Days Blvd.
Seffner, FL 33584
800-626-7800

Seminole, FL

Holiday Campground
10000 Park Blvd.
Seminole, FL 34647
800-354-7559

Silver Springs, FL

Lake Waldena Resort
352-625-2851
13582 E. Hwy. 40
Silver Springs, FL

Silver Springs Campers Garden

3151 NE 56th Ave.
Silver Springs, FL 34488
800-640-3733

South Bay, FL

South Bay RV Campground
561-992-9045
100 Levee Road
South Bay, FL

Southport, FL

Deer Haven RV Park
2812 Highway 2321
Southport, FL 32409
850-265-6205

Spring Hill, FL

Big Oaks RV & Mobile Home Community
352-799-5533
16654 U.S. Hwy. 41
Spring Hill, FL

Chief Aripeka Travel Park
352-686-3329
1582 Osowaw Blvd.
Spring Hill, FL

St. Augustine, FL

Bryn Mawr Ocean Resort
4850 Highway A1A
St. Augustine, FL 32084
904-471-3353

Cooksey's Camping Resort
2795 State Road 3
St. Augustine, FL 32084
904-471-3171

Indian Forest Campground
1555 State Route 207
St. Augustine, FL 32086
800-233-4324

KOA
9950 KOA Road
St. Augustine, FL 32095
904-824-8309

North Beach Camp Resort
4125 Coastal Hwy.
St. Augustine, FL 32095
800-542-8316

Ocean Grove RV Resort
4225 Highway A1
St. Augustine, FL 32084
800-342-4007

Peppertree Beach Club
4825 Highway A1A
St. Augustine, FL 32084
800-325-2267

St. Augustine Beach KOA
525 W. Pope Road
St. Augustine, FL 32084
800-562-4022

Stagecoach RV Park, Inc.
2711 County Road 208
St. Augustine, FL 32092
904-824-2319

State Park Campground of America
1425 State Road 16
St. Augustine, FL 32095
904-824-4016

St. Augustine Beach

Ocean Grove Camp Resort
904-471-3414
4225 S. A1A Hwy.
St. Augustine Beach

St. Augustine Beach KOA
904-471-3113
525 W. Pope Road
St. Augustine Beach

St. Cloud, FL

Gator RV Resort
5755 E. Irlo Bronson Hw
St. Cloud, FL 34771
888-252-0020

St. James City, FL
Cherry Estates
239-283-1144
3039 York Road
St. Cloud, FL

For Myers-Pine Island KOA
5120 Stringfellow Road
St. Cloud, FL 33956
800-562-8505

St. Petersburg, FL

St. Petersburg KOA
5400 95th St. N.
St. Petersburg, FL 33708
727-392-2233

Starke, FL

KOA
1475 South Walnut St.
Starke, FL 32091
904-964-8484

Stock Island, FL

Boyd's Key West Campground
6401 Maloney Ave.
Stock Island, FL 33040
305-294-1465

Sugarloaf Key, FL

Bluewater Key RV Resort
P.O. Box 409
Sugarloaf Key, FL 33044
800-237-2266

Lazy Lakes Campground
P.O . Box 440179
Sugarloaf Key, FL 33044
800-354-5524

Tallahassee, FL

Big Oak RV Park
850-562-4660
4024 N. Monroe St.
Tallahassee, FL

Tallahassee RV Park
6504 Mahan Drive
Tallahassee, FL 32308
850-878-7641

Tampa, FL

Abbey's Wig Wam RV Park
813-935-1118
9102 Williams Road
Tampa, FL

Alafia River RV Resort
813-677-1997
9812 Gibsonton Dr.
Tampa, FL

Bay Bayou Traveler
12622 Memorial Hwy
Tampa, FL 33635
813-855-1000

Camp Nebraska RV Park
10314 N. Nebraska Ave.
Tampa, FL 33612
813-971-3460

Happy Traveler RV Park
813-986-3094

9401 E. Fowler Ave.
Tampa, FL

Tarpon Springs, FL

Bayshore Cove Mobile Home & RV Park
727-937-1661
403 Riverside Dr.
Tarpon Springs, FL

Hickory Point Mobile Home & RV
727-938-7989
1181 Anclote Road
Tarpon Springs, FL

Titusville, FL

Great Outdoors RV-Golf Resort
135 Plantation Drive
Titusville, FL 32780
800-621-2267

Umatilla, FL

Olde Mill Stream RV Resort
352-669-3141
1000 N. Central Ave.
Umatilla, FL

Venice, FL

Ramblers Rest Resort
941-493-4354
1300 N. River Road
Venice, FL

Venice Campground
941-488-0850
4085 E. Venice Ave.
Venice, FL

Venus, FL

Oak Acres Campground
326 Goff Road
Venus, FL 33960
941-465-2795

Vero Beach, FL

Encore RV Resort - Vero Beach
772-589-7828
9455 - 108th Ave.
Vero Beach, FL

Wabasso, FL

KOA
8850 North US 1, Box 337
Wabasso, FL 32970
561-589-5682

Wauchula, FL

Crystal Lake Village

237 Maxwell Road
Wauchula, FL 33873
800-661-3582

Little Charlie Creek RV Park
1850 Heard Bridge Road
Wauchula, FL 33873
941-773-0088

West Palm Beach, FL

Palm Beach RV Park
561-659-2817
1444 Old Okeechobee Road
West Palm Beach, FL

Trailer Gardens
1444 Old Okeechobee Road
West Palm Beach, FL 33401
561-659-2817

White Spring, FL

Kelly's RV-MH Park
RR1, Box 370
White Spring, FL 32096
904-397-2616

Wildwood, FL

KOA
882 E. SR 44
Wildwood, FL 34785
352-748-2774

Wayside RV Park
1201 S. Main St.
Wildwood, FL 34785
800-241-4133

Winter Garden, FL

Orlando Winter Garden Campgro
13905 W. Colonia Dr.
Winter Garden, FL 34787
407-656-1415

State Stop Campground
700 W. Hwy. 50 (AKA 144
Winter Garden, FL 34787
407-656-8000

Zephyrhills, FL

Hunters Run RV Estates
37041 Chancey Road
Zephyrhills, FL 33541
813-783-1133

Jim's RV Park
35120 Highway 54 W
Zephyrhills, FL 33541

813-782-5610

Leisure Days RV Resort
34533 Leisure Days Dr.
Zephyrhills, FL 33541
813-788-2631

Smitty's Country Style RV Campground
30846 State Route 54 W
Zephyrhills, FL 33543
813-973-4301

Georgia

Americus, GA

Brickyard Plantation Golf Club
121 Parker's Crossing
Americus, GA 31709
Voice: (229) 874-1234
Fax: (229) 874-6521
bpgcdeb@sowega.net
Outside Link: www.brickyardgolfclub.com

Bishop, GA

Pine Lake RV Campground
5540 High Shoals Road
Bishop, GA 30621
706-769-5486

Blairsville, GA

Lake Nottely RV Park
350 Haley Circle
Blairsville, GA 30512
Voice: (706) 745-4523
Fax: (706) 745-8806
lnrv@alltel.net
Outside Link: www.lakenottelyrv.com

Trackrock Campground
4887 Trackrock Camp Road
Blairsville, GA 30512
Voice: (706) 745-2420
Fax: (706) 745 0741
trackroc@alltel.net

Blue Ridge, GA

Lake Blue Ridge Campground
6050 Appalachian Hwy
Blue Ridge, GA 30513
706-632-3031

Buford, GA

Shoal Creek
6300 Shadburn Ferry Road
Buford, GA 30518
877-444-6777

Calhoun, GA

KOA
2523 Redbud Road NE
Calhoun, GA 30701
706-629-7511

Cartersville, GA

KOA
800 Cass-White Road NW
Cartersville, GA 30121
770-382-7330

Chatsworth, GA

Woodring Branch Campground
5026 Woodring Branch Road
Chatsworth, GA 30540
877-444-6777

Cleveland, GA

Leisure Acres Campground
3840 Westmoreland Road
Cleveland, GA 30528
Voice: (706) 865-6466 / (888) 748-6344
Fax: (706) 865-9544
info@leisureacrescampground.com

Commerce, GA

KOA
5473 Mt. Olive
Commerce, GA 30529
706-335-5535

Cordele, GA

Georgia Veterans Memorial State Park
2459-A US 280
West Cordele, GA 31015
229-276-2371

KOA
373 Rockhouse Road
Cordele, GA 31015
912-273-5454

Fargo, GA

Stephen Foster State Park
Rte 1 Box 131
Fargo, GA 31631
912-637-5274

Forsyth, GA

KOA
PO Box 967
Forsyth, GA 31029
912-994-2019

Hartwell, GA

Hart State Park
330 Hart State Park Road
Hartwell, GA 30643
800-864-7275

Paynes Creek
PO Box 248
Hartwell, GA 30645
877-444-6777

Helen, GA

Unicoi State Park
1788 Hwy. 356
Helen, GA 30545
706-878-3982

Jackson, GA

Indian Springs State Park
678 Lake Clark Road
Jackson, GA 30216
770-504-2277

Kennesaw, GA

KOA
2000 Old US 41 Hwy
Kennesaw, GA 30152
770-427-2046

Marietta, GA

Brookwood RV Resort Park
1031 Wylie Road
Marietta, GA 30067
Phone: (770)427-6853
info@bkwdrv.com
McDonough, GA

KOA
291 Mt. Olive Road
Marietta, GA 30253
770-957-2610

Nicholls, GA

General Coffee State Park
46 John Coffee Road
Nicholls, GA 31554
800-864-7275

Pine Mountain, GA

F.D. Roosevelt State Park
2970 Hwy
Pine Mountain, GA 31822
706-663-4858

Pine Mountain Campground
8804 Hamilton Road, Hwy. 27
Pine Mountain, GA 31822
Voice: (706) 663-4329
Fax: (706) 663-9837
jenningspmcg@aol.com

Richmond Hill, GA

KOA
Box 309
Richmond Hill, GA 31324
912-756-3396

Ringgold, GA

Chattanooga South/Lookout Mtn. KOA
199 KOA Blvd.
Ringgold, GA 30736
800-562-4167

Rutledge, GA

Hard Labor Creek State Park
PO Box 247
Rutledge, GA 30663
706-557-3001

St. Mary's, GA

Crooked River State Park
6222 Charlie Smith Sr Hwy
St. mary's, GA 31558
800-864-7275

Trenton, GA

Lookout Mtn./Chattanooga West KOA
930 Mountain Shadows Dr.
Trenton, GA 30752
706-657-6815

Tybee Island, GA

Rivers End Campground and RV Park
915 Polk St.
Tybee Island, GA 31328-0988
Voice: (912) 786-5518 / (800) 786-1016
Fax: (912) 786-4126
riversend1@aol.com

Idaho

American Falls, ID

Indian Springs
3249 Indian Springs Road
American Falls, ID 83211
202-226-2174

Arco, ID

Carroll's Travel Plaza
Rt.1, Box 20A
Arco, ID
208-527-3504

Ashton, ID

Aspen Acres Golf Club & RV Park
4179 E., 1100 N
Ashton, ID
208-652-3524

Boise, ID

Fiesta RV Park
11101 Fairview Ave.
Boise, ID 83713
Voice: (208) 375-8207 / (888) RV-IDAHO
Fax: (208) 322-2499
info@fiestarv.com

Cave Falls, ID

Jessen's RV and Bed & Breakfast
Box 11, 1146 S
Cave Falls, ID
208-652-3356

Pole Bridge Campground
Forest Road
Cave Falls, ID
208-652-7742

Riverside Campground
Forest Road
Cave Falls, ID
208-652-7442

Warm River Campground
Cave Falls, ID
208-652-7442

Athol, ID

Silverwood RV Park
N. 26225 Hwy. 95
Athol, ID
208-583-3400

Avery, ID

Swiftwater Motel
645 Old River Road
Avery, ID 83802
208-245-2845

Banks, ID

Big Eddy Campground
Banks, ID
208-365-7000

Canyon Campground
Banks, ID
208-365-7000

Cold Springs Campground
Banks, ID
208-365-7000

Swinging Bridge Campground
Banks, ID
208-365-7000

Bayview, ID

Mac Donald's Hudson Bay Resort
P.O. Box 38
Bayview, ID
208-683-2211

Scenic Bay Marina
P.O. Box 36
Bayview, ID
208-683-2243

Bellevue, ID

Riverside RV & Campground
Box 432
Bellevue, ID
208-788-2020

Boise, ID

Boise KOA
7300 Federal Way
Boise, ID 83706
208-345-7673

Hi Valley RV Park
10555 Hwy. 55
Boise, ID 83703
208-939-8080

Mountain View RV Park
2040 Airport Way
Boise, ID 83705
208-345-4141

On the River RV Park

6000 Glenwood
Boise, ID 83714
208-375-7432

Shafer Butte
Boise, ID 83714
208-364-4242

Willow Creek
Boise, ID 83714
208-364-4242

Bonners Ferry, ID

Bonners Ferry Resort
Rt. 4. Box 4700, 6438 S. Main
Bonners Ferry, ID
208-267-2422

Deep Creek Resort
Rt. 4, Box 628
Bonners Ferry, ID
208-267-2729

Idyl Acres RV Park
HCR 61, Box 170
Bonners Ferry, ID 83805
208-267-3629

Meadow Creek
208-267-5561

Town and Country Motel & RV Park
Route 4, Box 4664
Bonners Ferry, ID
208-267-7915

Buhl, ID

Banbury Hot Springs
Route 3, Box 408
Buhl, ID 83316
208-543-2098

Miracle Hot Springs
P.O. Box 171
Buhl, ID
208-543-6002

Calder, ID

Huckleberry Campground
1808 North 3rd Street
Calder, ID 83814
208-769-5000

Cambridge, ID

Brownlee Campground
Cambridge, ID
208-549-2420

Frontier Motel & RV Park
P.O. Box 178, 240 S. Superior St.
Cambridge, ID
208-257-3851

Woodhead Park
Cambridge, ID
800-422-3143

Carey, ID

Littlewood Reservoir
Carey, ID
208-436-4187

Cascade, ID

Arrowhead RV Park on the River
P.O. Box 337
Cascade, ID 83611
208-382-4534

Aurora Motel - RV Park & Storage
P.O. Box 799
Cascade, ID 83611
208-382-4948

Big Sage Campground
Cascade, ID 83611
208-382-4258

Buttercup Campground
Cascade, ID 83611
208-382-4258

Cabarton 1 Campground
Cascade, ID 83611
208-382-4258

Crown Point Campground
Cascade, ID 83611
208-382-4258

Curlew Campground
Cascade, ID 83611
208-382-4258

Herb's RV Park
P.O. Box 976
Cascade, ID 83611
208-382-3451

Huckleberry Campground
Cascade, ID 83611
208-382-4258

Poison Creek Campground
Cascade, ID 83611

208-382-4258

Sugarloaf
Cascade, ID 83611
208-382-4258

Van Wyck Park 1
Cascade, ID 83611
208-382-4258

Water's Edge RV Resort
P.O. Box 1018, Hwy. 55
Cascade, ID 83611
800-574-2038

West Mountain
Cascade, ID 83611
208-382-4258

Westside RV Park
P.O. Box 648
Cascade, ID 83611
208-325-4100

Challis, ID

Bayhorse Lake
Challis, ID 83226
208-838-2201

Challis All Valley RV Park
P.O. Box 928
Challis, ID 83226
208-879-2393

Challis Hot Springs
HC 63, P.O. Box 1779
Challis, ID 83226
208-879-4442

Clark Fork, ID

River Delta Resort
Star Rt., Box 128
Clark Fork, ID 83811
208-266-1335

River Lake RV Resort
P.O. Box 219
Clark Fork, ID 83811
208-266-1115

Whiskey Rock Bay
Clark Fork, ID 83811
208-263-5111

Cocolalla, ID

Sandy Beach Resort

4405 Loop Road
Cocolalla, ID
208-263-4328

Coeur D'Alene, ID

Boulevard Motel & RV Park
2400 Seltice Way
Coeur D'Alene, ID 83814
208-664-4978

Cedar Motel & RV Park
319 Coeur d'Alane Lake Dr.
Coeur D'Alene, ID 83814
208-664-2278

Idaho Pahandle National Forest
3815 Screiber Way
Coeur D'Alene, ID 83815
208-765-7223

Killarney Lake
I-90 E. Hwy. 3
Coeur D'Alene, ID 83814
208-769-5000

Monte Vista Motel & RV Park
320 S. Coeur d'Alene Lake Drive
Coeur D'Alene, ID 83814
208-664-8201

Robin Hood RV Park & Campground
703 Lincoln Way
Coeur D'Alene, ID 83814
208-664-2306

Rockford Bay Resort & Marina
West 8700 Rockford Bay
Coeur D'Alene, ID 83814
208-664-6931

Shady Acres Campground
N. 3630 Government Way
Coeur D'Alene, ID 83814
208-664-3087

Wolf Lodge Campground
12425 E. I-90
Coeur D'Alene, ID 83814
208-664-2812

Council, ID

Cabin Creek
Council, ID
208-253-4215

Evergreen

Council, ID
208-253-4215

Huckleberry
Council, ID
208-253-4215

Lafferty
Council, ID
208-253-4215

Darby, ID

Indian Creek
Darby, ID
406-821-3269

Paradise
Darby, ID
406-821-3269

Deary, ID

Little Boulder Creek
Deary, ID
208-875-1131

Declo, ID

Snake River RV Park
Rt. 1. Box 33
Declo, ID 83323
208-654-2133

Dixie, ID

Lodgepole Pine Inn
P.O. Box 71
Dixie, ID
208-842-2343

Donnelly, ID

Kenally Creek
Donnelly, ID
208-634-1453

Southwestern Idaho Sr. Citizens Recreation
Assoc.
P.O. Box 625
Donnelly, ID
208-325-9518

Downey, ID

Downata Hot Springs
P.O. Box 185
Downey, ID 25900
208-897-5736

Flag's West Truck Stop
Downey, ID 25900
208-897-5238

Driggs, ID

Reunion Flat Group Area
Driggs, ID 83422
208-354-2312

Reunion Flat
Driggs, ID 83422
208-354-2312

Teton Canyon
Driggs, ID 83422
208-354-2312

Eden, ID

Anderson Camp
Rt. 1
Eden, ID 83325
208-825-9800

Elk River, ID

Huckle Berry Heaven
P.O. Box 165
Elk River, ID
208-826-3405

Emmett, ID

Capital Mobile Park
1508 E. Main
Emmett, ID 83617
208-365-3889

Holiday Motel & RV
111 S. Washington Ave.
Emmett, ID 83617

Fairfield, ID

Bowns
Fairfield, ID, 83372
208-764-2202

Canyon Transfer Camp
Fairfield, ID, 83372
208-764-2202

Soldier Creek RV Park
Rt. 1, Box 1271
Fairfield, ID 83372
208-764-2684

Filer, ID

Curry Trailer Park
21323 Hw. 30
Filer, ID 83328
208-733-3961

Fruitland, ID

Neat Retreat
2701 Hwy. 95
Fruitland, ID 83619
208-452-4324

Garden Valley, ID

Boiling Springs
Garden Valley, ID
208-365-7000

Hardscrabble
Garden Valley, ID
208-365-7000

Rattlesnake
Garden Valley, ID
208-365-7000

Silver Creek Plunge
HC 76, Box 2377, Unit 1942
Garden Valley, ID
208-344-8688

Silver Creek
Garden Valley, ID
208-365-7000

Trail Creek
Garden Valley, ID
208-365-7000

Gibbonsville, ID

Broken Arrow
P.O. Box 26
Gibbonsville, ID 83463
208-856-2241

Grandjean, ID

Grandjean, ID
208-726-7672

Grangeville, ID

Junction Lodge
HC 67, Box 98
Grangeville, ID 83530
208-842-2459

Hagerman, ID

Sugar's 1000 Springs Resort
5 Gillhooley Lane
Hagerman, ID
208-837-4987

Harrison, ID

Albertini's Carlin Bay Resort
HCR 2, Box 45, I-97

Harrison, ID
208-689-3295

Bell Bay
Harrison, ID
208-769-3000

Squaw Bay Camping Resort
Rt. 2, Box 130
Harrison, ID 83833
208-664-6782

Harvard, ID

Giant White Pine
Harvard, ID
208-875-1131

Laird Park
Harvard, ID
208-875-1131

Pines RV Campground
4510 Hwy.
Harvard, ID
208-875-0831

Hayden, ID

Alpine Country Store & RV Park
17400 N 95 Hwy.
Hayden, ID 83835
208-772-4305

Coeur D'Alene North/Hayden Lake KOA
4850 E. Garwood Road
Hayden, ID 83835
208-772-4557

Hazelton, ID

R&E Greenwood Store
1015 Ridgeway Road
Hazelton, ID 83335
208-829-5735

Henry, ID

White Locks Marina & RV Park
3429 Hwy. 34
Henry, ID 83230
208-574-2208

Hope, ID

Beyond Hope Resort
248 Beyond Hope Hwy. 200E
Hope, ID
208-264-5251

Idaho Country Resort

141 Idaho Country Road
Hope, ID
208-264-5505

Island View RV Park
300 Island View
Hope, ID
208-264-5509

Jeb & Margaret's Trailer Haven
298 Trailer Haven
Hope, ID
208-264-5406

Island Park, ID

Aspen Lodge
HC 66, Box 269
Island Park, ID
208-558-7406

Island Park Kampground
HC 66, Box 447
Island Park, ID
208-558-7112

Pond's Lodge
P.O . Box 258
Island Park, ID
208-558-7221

Redrock RV & Camping Park
HC 66, Box 256
Island Park, ID
208-558-7442

Staley Springs Lodge
HC 66, Box 102
Island Park, ID
208-558-7471

Valley View General Store and RV Park
HC 66, Box 26
Island Park, ID
208-558-7443

Wild Rose Ranch
340 W. 7th S, HC 66, Box 140
Island Park, ID
208-558-7201

Jerome, ID

KOA
5431 US 93
Jerome, ID 83338
208-324-4169

Ketchum, ID

Boulder View
300 First Ave.W
Ketchum, ID
208-726-7672

Sawtooth National Recreation Area
HC 64 Box 8291
Ketchum, ID 83340
800-260-5970

Kooskia, ID

Apgar
208-926-42₇₅

Three Rivers Resort
HC 75, Box 61
Kooskia, ID 83539
208-926-4430

Wild Goose
Kooskia, ID 83539
208-926-4275

Wilderness Gateway
Kooskia, ID 83539
208-926-4275

Lava Hot Springs, ID

Cottonwood Family Campground
P.O. Box 307
Lava Hot Springs, ID 83246
208-776-5295

Lava Ranch Inn Motel & RV Campground
9611 Hwy. 30
Lava Hot Springs, ID 83246
208-776-9917

Mountain View Trailer Park, Inc.
P.O. Box 687
Lava Hot Springs, ID 83246
208-776-5611

Leadore, ID

Lema's Store & RV Park
P.O. Box 204
Leadore, ID 60096
208-768-2647

Lewiston, ID

Hells Gate State Park
Lewiston, ID
208-799-5015

Lowell, ID

Ryan's Wilderness Inn
HC 75, Box 60-A2

Lowell, ID 83539
208-926-4706

Lowman, ID

Barney's
Lowman, ID
208-259-3361

Bear Valley
Lowman, ID
208-259-3361

Bonneville
Lowman, ID
208-259-3361

Bull Trout Lake
Lowman, ID
208-259-3361

Cozy Cove
Lowman, ID
208-259-3361

Helende
Lowman, ID
208-259-3361

Hower's
Lowman, ID
208-259-3361

Mountain View
Lowman, ID
208-259-3361

Park Creek
Lowman, ID
208-259-3361

Riverside
Lowman, ID
208-259-3361

Sourdough Lodge & RV Resort
HC 77, Box 3109, Hwy. 21
Lowman, ID
208-259-3326

Lucille, ID

Prospector's Gold RV & Campground
P.O. Box 313
Lucille, ID 83542
208-628-3773

River Front Gardens RV Park

HCO 1, Box 15
Lucille, ID 83542
208-628-3777

Mack's Inn, ID

Mack's Inn Resort
P.O. Box 10
Mack's Inn, ID 83433
208-558-7272

Mackay, ID

Iron Bog
Mackay, ID 83521
208-588-2224

Mackay Reservoir
Mackay, ID 83521
208-756-5400

River Park Golf Course & RV Campground
717 Capital Ave., P.O. Box 252
Mackay, ID 83521
208-588-2296

Star Hope
Mackay, ID 83521
208-588-2224

Timber Creek
Mackay, ID 83521
208-588-2224

Wagon Wheel Motel & RV Park
P.O. Box 22
Mackay, ID 83521
208-588-3331

White Knob Motel & RV Park
Box 180
Mackay, ID 83521
208-588-2622

Wildhorse
Mackay, ID 83521
208-588-2224

Big Springs
208-558-7301

Flat Rock
208-558-7301

Upper Coffee Pot
208-558-7301

May, ID

River Haven RV Park
208-588-2224

McCall, ID

Buckhorn Bar
May, ID 83638
208-634-0600

Lake Fork
May, ID 83638
208-634-1453

Lakeview Village
1 Pearl St., Box 8
May, ID 83638
208-634-5280

Payette National Forest
800 West Lakeside Ave.'
McCall, ID 83638
208-634--0700

Ponderosa
May, ID 83638
208-634-1465

Upper Payette Lake
May, ID 83638
208-634-1453

Melba, ID

Given's Hot Springs
HC 79, Box 103
Melba, ID 83641
208-495-2000

Montpelier, ID

Rendezvous Village RV Park
577 N. 4th St.
Montpelier, ID
208-847-1100

Mountain Home, ID

The Wagon Wheel
1880 e 5th N, #3,
Mountain Home, ID
208-587-5994

Moyle Springs, ID

Twin Rivers Canyon Resort
HCR 62, Box 25
Moyle Springs, ID 83845
208-267-5932

Mt. Lolo, ID

Jerry Johnson Campground
Mt. Lolo, ID

406-942-3113

Powell Campground
Mt. Lolo, ID
406-942-3113

Wendover Campground
Mt. Lolo, ID
406-942-3113

White Sand Campground
Mt. Lolo, ID
406-942-3113

Whitehouse Campground
Mt. Lolo, ID
406-942-3113

Nampa, ID

Mason Creek RV Park
807 Franklin Road
Nampa, ID
208-465-7199

Naples, ID

Blue Lake Campground & RV Park
HCR 01, P.O. Box 277
Naples, ID 83847
208-267-2029

New Meadows, ID

Goose Creek Campground
HC 75, Box 3270
New Meadows, ID 50091
208-347-2116

Grouse Creek Campground
New Meadows, ID 50091
208-347-2141

Meadows RV Park
P.O. Box 60
New Meadows, ID 50091
208-347-2325

Zim's Hot Springs
P.O. Box 314
New Meadows, ID 50091
208-347-2686

North Fork, ID

Cummings Lake Lodge
P.O. Box 8
North Fork, ID
208-865-2424

Rivers Fork Inn

PO Box 68
North Fork, ID 83466
208-865-2301

Wagonhammer Springs Campground
P.O. Box 102
North Fork, ID
208-865-2246

Ola, ID

Antelope Campground
Ola, ID
208-365-7000

Eastside Campground
Ola, ID
208-365-7000

Hollywood Point Campground
Ola, ID
208-365-7000

Sagehen Creek Campground
Ola, ID
208-365-7000

Orangeville, ID

Mtn. View MH & RV Park
P.O. Box 25
Orangeville, ID 83530
208-983-2328

Orofino, ID

Hidden Village
14615 Hwy. 12
Orofino, ID
208-476-3416

Vacation Land Motel & RV
14115 Highway 12
Orofino, ID
208-476-4012

Osburn, ID

Blue Anchor Motel & RV
P.O. Box 645
Osburn, ID 83849
208-752-3443

Payette, ID

Lazy River RV Park
11575 N. River Road
Payette, ID
208-642-9667

Pierce, ID

Aquarius
Pierce, ID
208-476-3775

Hidden Creek
Pierce, ID
208-476-3775

Kelly Forks
Pierce, ID
208-476-3775

Noe Creek
Pierce, ID
208-476-3775

Washington Creek
Pierce, ID
208-476-3775

Pine, ID

Nester's Riverside Campground
HC 87, Box 210
Pine, ID 83647
208-653-2222

Pine Resort
HC 87, Box 200
Pine, ID 83647
208-653-2323

Pinehurst, ID

Kellogg/Silver Valley KOA
Box 949
Pinehurst, ID 83850
208-682-3612

Plummer, ID

Heyburn State Park
1291 Chatcolet Road
Plummer, ID
208-686-1308

Pocatello, ID

Cowboy RV Park
845 Barton Road
Pinehurst, ID
208-232-4587

Post Falls, ID

Coeur D'Alene RV Resort
2600 E. Mullan Ave.
Post Falls, ID 83854
208-773-3527

Suntree RV Park

401 Idahline
Post Falls, ID 83854
208-773-9982

Preston, ID

Deer Cliff Store, Cafe and RV
1942 N. Deer Cliff Road
Preston, ID 30006
208-852-3320

Priest Lake, ID

Priest Lake RV Resort and Marina
HCR 5, Box 172
Priest Lake, ID
208-443-2405

Priest Lake State Park, 3 Units
208-443-2200

Rathdrum, ID

Twin Lakes Mobile Home Park
Rt. 4, Box 235
Rathdrum, ID
208-687-1242

Rexburg, ID

Rainbow Lake & Campground
2245 S. 2000W
Rexburg, ID
208-356-3681

Riggins, ID

River Village RV Park
P.O. Box 2
Riggins, ID
208-628-3441

Riverside RV Park
P.O. Box 1270
Riggins, ID
208-628-3390

Seven Devils
208-628-3916

Sleepy Hollow RV Park
P.O. Box 1159
Riggins, ID
208-628-3401

Windy Saddle
208-628-3916

Ririe, ID

7N Ranch
5156 E. Heise Road
Ririe, ID 83443

208-538-5097

Ririe Reservoir
208-538-7871

Rogerson, ID

Desert Hot Springs
208-857-2233

Murphy Hot Springs Lodge
208-857-2238

Rupert, ID

Walcott Park
Rt. 4, Box 292
Rupert, ID
208-436-6117

Sagle, ID

Fox Farm RV Resort
3160 Dufort Road
Sagle, ID 83860
208-263-8896

Garfield Bay Resort
6890 W. Garfield Bay Road
Sagle, ID 83860
208-263-1078

Salmon, ID

Century II Campground
603 Hwy. 93N
Salmon, ID
208-756-2063

Heald's Haven
HC 61, Box 15
Salmon, ID
208-756-3929

Salmon Meadows
P.O. Box 705
Salmon, ID
208-756-2640

Williams Lake Resort
P.O. Box 1150
Salmon, ID
208-756-2007

Sandpoint, ID

Bottle Bay Resort
1360 Bottle Bay Road
Sandpoint, ID
208-263-5916

Sandpoint KOA Kampground

100 Sagle Road
Sandpoint, ID
208-263-4824

Sandy Beach Resort
4405 Loop Road
Sandpoint, ID
208-263-4328

Travel America Plaza
P.O. Box 199
Sandpoint, ID
208-263-6522

Silverton, ID

Silver Leaf Motel & RV Park
P.O. Box 151
Silverton, ID 83867
208-752-0222

Smelterville, ID

White's Buffalo RV Park
Box 579
Smelterville, ID 83868
208-786-9551

Spirit Lake, ID

Silver Beach Resort
8350 W. Spirit Lake Road
Spirit Lake, ID
208-623-4842

St. Charles, ID

Cedars & Shade Campground
P.O. Box 219
St. Charles, ID
208-945-2608

Minnetonka RV & Campground
P.O. Box 6, 220 N. Main
St. Charles, ID
208-945-2941

St. Maries, ID

Ed's R&R Shady River RV Park
1211 Lincoln
St. Maries, ID
208-245-3549

Misty Meadows RV Park & Camping
HC 03, Box 52
St. Maries, ID
208-245-2639

Stanley, ID

Beaver Creek

Stanley, ID
208-838-2201

Blind Creek
Stanley, ID
208-838-2201

Bonanza
Stanley, ID
208-838-2201

Boundary Creek
Stanley, ID
208-879-5204

Chinook Bay
Stanley, ID
208-726-7672

Custer #1
Stanley, ID
208-838-2201

Dagger Falls #1
Stanley, ID
208-879-5204

Summer Home Trailer Park
HC 64, Box 9916
Stanley, ID
208-774-3310

Sun Valley, ID

Park Creek
208-588-2224

Phi Kappa
208-588-2224

The Meadows RV Park
P.O. Box 1440
Sun Valley, ID
208-726-5445

Wildhorse
208-588-2224

Swan Valley, ID

South Fork Lodge
P.O. Box 22
Swan Valley, ID
208-483-2112

Twin Falls, ID

Blue Lakes RV Park
1122 North Blue Lakes Blvd.

Twin Falls, ID 83301
208-734-5782

Burren West LLC RV/Trailer Resort
255 Los Lagos
Twin Falls, ID 83301
208-487-2571

Nat-Soo-Pah Hot Springs & RV Park
2738 E. 2400 N
Twin Falls, ID 83301
208-655-4337

Oregon Trail Campground & Family Fun Center
2733 Kimberly Road
Twin Falls, ID 83301
208-733-0853

Victor, ID

Mike Harris Campground
Victor, ID
208-354-2321

Pine Creek Campground
Victor, ID
208-354-2321

Teton Valley Campground
P.O. Box 49, 128 Hwy 31
Victor, ID
208-787-2647

Trail Creek Campground
Victor, ID
208-354-2312

Virginia, ID

Hawkins Reservoir
208-766-4766

Wallace, ID

Lookout RV Park and Campground
Lookout Pass
Wallace, ID 208-744-1392

Weiser, ID

Gateway RV Park
229 E. 7th St.
Weiser, ID
208-549-2539

Indian Hot Springs
914 Hot Springs Road
Weiser, ID
208-549-0070

Indianhead Motel & RV Park

747 US hwy. 95
Weiser, ID
208-549-0331

Mann Creek Campground
208-365-2682

Monroe Creek Campground
822 US Hwy. 95
Weiser, ID
208-549-2026

Paradise/Justrite Campground
208-549-2420

Spring Creek Campground
208-549-2420

White Bird, ID

Slate Creek Campground
208-962-3245

Swiftwater RV Park and Store
HC 01 Box 24
White Bird, ID 83554
88-291-5065

Illinois

Amboy, IL

Green River Oaks Camping Resort
1442 Sleepy Hollow Road
Amboy, IL 61310
815-857-2815

Mendota Hills Camping Resort
642 US Rt. 52
Amboy, IL 61310
815-849-5930

O'Connells Yogi Bear Jellystone Park
970 Green Wing Road
Amboy, IL 61310
800-FOR-YOGI

Antioch, IL

Fox River Recreation
27884 West Rt. 173
Antioch, IL 60001
847-395-6090

Belvidere, IL

Outdoor World - Pine Country
5710 Shattuck Road
Belvidere, IL 61008
815-547-5517

Benton, IL

KOA
RR 1, N. DuQuoin St.
Benton, IL 62812
618-439-4860

Byron, IL

Lake Louise Campground
PO Box 451
Byron, IL 61010
815-234-8483

Cambridge, IL

Gibson's RV Park & Campground
10768 E 1600 St.
Cambridge, IL 61238
Voice: (309) 937-2314
Fax: (309) 937-1200
gibsonrv@theinter.com

Casey, IL

KOA
PO Box 56
Casey, IL 62420

800-554-9206

Chatham, IL

Springfield Best Holiday
9683 Palm Road
Chatham, IL 62629
217-483-9998

Chebanse, IL

KOA
425 E. 6000 Road
Chebanse, IL 60922
815-939-4603

Earlville, IL

Smith's Stone House Park
3719 Suydam Road
Earlville, IL 60518
815-246-9732

East St. Louis, IL

Casino Queen RV Park
200 S. Front St.
East St. Louis, IL 62201
618-874-5000

Edwardsville, IL

Red Barn Rendezvous
3955 Blackburn Road
Edwardsville, IL 62025
618-692-9015

Effingham, IL

Camp Lakewood Campground
1217 W Rickelman Ave.
Effingham, IL 62401
Voice: (217) 342-6233
camp@camplakewoodcampground.com
Outside Link:
www.camplakewoodcampground.com

Gages Lake, IL

Gages Lake Camping
18887 W. Gages Lake Road
Gages Lake, IL 60030
847-223-5541

Galena, IL

Palace Campground
11357 Rt. 20 W
Galena, IL 61036
Voice: (815) 777-2466
palace@galenalink.net

Garden Prairie, IL

Jellystone Park of Belvidere

7050 Epworth
Garden Prairie, IL 61038
815-547-7846

Paradise RV Park
PO Box 96
Garden Prairie, IL 61038
815-597-1671

Geneseo, IL

Geneseo Campground
22978 Illinois Hwy 82
Geneseo, IL 61254
309-944-6465

Goodfield, IL

Goodfield's Yogi Bear's Jellystone Park Camp
Resort
PO Box 92
Goodfield, IL 61742
309-965-2224

Granite City, IL

Northeast/I-270/Granite City KOA
3157 West Chain of Rocks Road
Granite City, IL 62040
800-562-5861

Joliet, IL

Martin Campground
725 Cherry Hill Road
Joliet, IL 60433
Voice: (815) 726-3173
Fax: (815) 726-8166

Knoxville, IL

Galesburg East Best Holiday
1081 US Hwy 150 East
Knoxville, IL 61448
309-389-2267

Leland, IL

Hi-Tide Recreation
4611 East 22nd Road
Leland, IL 60531
815-495-9032

Lena, IL

KOA
10982 US Hwy 20 W.
Lena, IL 61048
815-369-2612

Mahomet, IL

Tincup Camper's Park
PO Box 486
Mahomet, IL 61853

217-586-3011

Marengo, IL

Lehman's Lakeside RV Resort
19709 Harmony Road
Marengo, IL 60152
815-923-4533

Marseilles, IL

Whispering Pines Campground
2776 E. 2625 Road
Marseilles, IL 61341
815-795-5720

Marshall, IL

Lincoln Trail State Park
RR 1, Box 117
Marshall, IL 62441
217-826-2222

Millbrook, IL

Fitzpatrick's Yogi Bear
8574 Millbrook Road
Millbrook, IL 60536
630-553-5172

Mt. Vernon, IL

Quality Times RV Park
9746 E. IL Hwy. 15
Mt. Vernon, IL 62864
618-244-0399

Nauvoo, IL

Nauvoo RV Campground
PO Box 89
Nauvoo, IL 62354
217-453-2253

New Windsor, IL

Shady Lakes Campground
3355 75th Ave.
New Windsor, 61465
309-667-2709

Oakland, IL

Hebron Hill Camping
14349 N. Country Road
Oakland, IL 61943
217-346-3385

Oregon, IL

River Road Camping & Marina
3922 River Road
Oregon, IL 61061
815-234-5383

Pearl City, IL

Emerald Acres Campground
3351 S. Mill Grove Road
Pearl City, 61062
815-443-2550

Peoria, IL

Mt. Hawley RV Park
8327 N. Knoxville Ave.
Peoria, IL 61615
309-692-2223

Percy, IL

Lake Camp-A-Lot
PO Box 357
Percy, IL 62272
618-497-2942

Pittsfield, IL

Pine Lakes Resort
RR 3, Box 3077
Pittsfield, IL 62363
217-285-6719

Pocahontas, IL

Tomahawk RV Park
119 Tomahawk Road
Pocahontas, IL 62275
618-669-2781

Putnam, IL

Condit's Ranch
RR 1, Box 13
Putnam, IL 61560
815-437-2226

Quincy, IL

Valley View Campground
2300 Bonansinga
Quincy, IL 62301
217-222-7229

Rochester, IL

KOA
4320 KOA Road
Rochester, IL 62563
217-498-7002

Rock Island, IL

Rock Island / Quad Cities KOA at Camelot
2311 78th Ave., W
Rock Island, IL 61201
Voice: (309) 787-0665 / (800) 787-0605
Fax: (309) 787-1320
koa@riqckoa.com
Outside Link: www.riqckoa.com

Rockford, IL

Blackhawk Valley Campground
6540 Valley Trail Road
Rockford, IL 61109
815-874-9767

Savanna, IL

Mississippi Palisades State Park
16327 A IL Rte 84
Savanna, IL 61074
815-273-2731

Sheridan, IL

Mallard Bend Campground & RV Park
2838 N. 431st Road
Sheridan, IL 60551
816-496-2496

Rolling Oaks Campground
Rt. 1
Sheridan, IL 60551
815-496-2334

South Beloit, IL

Pearl Lake
1220 Dearborn Ave.
South Beloit, IL 61080
815-389-1479

Springfield, IL

Double J Campground
9683 Stanton St
Springfield, IL 62703
800-657-1414

Mr. Lincoln's Campground & RV Center
3045 Stanton Ave.
Springfield, IL 62703
217-529-8206

St. Elmo, IL

Bail's Timberline Lake Campground
PO Box 15
St. Elmo, IL 62458
618-829-3383

Sterling, IL

Crow Valley Campground
23807 Moline Road
Sterling, IL 61081
815-626-5376

Sycamore, IL

Sycamore RV Resort
PO Box 15
Sycamore, IL 60178
815-895-5590

143

Tinley Park, IL

Windy City Campground
18701 S. 80th Ave.
Tinley Park, IL 60477
708-720-0030

Topeka, IL

Evening Star Camping Resort
16474 Walker Road
Topeka, IL 61567
309-562-7590

Union, IL

KOA
8404 S. Union Road
Union, IL 60180
815-923-4206

Vandalia, IL

Okaw Valley Campground
RR 2 Box 55A
Vandalia, IL 62418
888-470-3968

West York, IL

Hickory Holler Campground
9876 E. 2000th Ave.
West York, IL 62478
618-563-4779

Whittington, IL

Benton Best Holiday
12997 State Highway 37
Whittington, IL 62807
618-435-3401

Wilmington, IL

Fossil Rock Campground
24615 W. Strip Mine Road
Wilmington, IL 60481
815-476-6785

Indiana

Angola, IN

Oakhill Family Campground & Retreat
4450 N 50 W
Angola, IN 46703
Voice: (260) 668-7041 / (800) 359-0405
Fax: (260) 665-7092
truejestic@aol.com

Auburn, IN

KOA
5612 CR 11A
Auburn, IN 46706
219-925-6747

Batesville, IN

Thousand Trails NACO Indian Lakes
7234 Hwy 46
Batesville, IN 47006
800-427-3392

Bedford, IN

Free Spirit RV Resort
4140 Erie Church Road
Bedford, IN 47421
Voice: (812) 834-6164
Fax: (812) 834-6164
freespiritcamping@yahoo.com

Bloomington, IL

Lake Monroe Village Recreation Resort
8107 South Fairfax Road
Bloomington, IN 47401
812-824-CAMP

Bristol, IL

Eby;s Pines Campground
14583 SR 120
Bristol, IN 46507
574-848-4583

Cloverdale, IN

Cloverdale RV Park
2789 East CR 800 S
Cloverdale, IN 46120
Voice: (765) 795-3294 / (888) 298-0035
Fax: (765) 795-3075
cdalerv@ccrtc.com

Columbus, IN

Columbus Woods-N-Water
8855 S 300 W
Columbus, IN 47201-8869

Voice: (812) 342-1619
Fax: (812) 342-0895

Crawfordsville, IN

KOA
1600 Lafayette Road
Crawfordsville, IN 47933
765-362-4190

Elkhart, IN

Elkhart Campground
25608 County Road 4 E
Elkhart, IN 46514
Voice: (574) 264-2914
Fax: (574) 264-2914

Howe, IN

Twin Mills Resort Inc.
1675 W SR 120
Howe, IN 46746
Voice: (219) 562-3212
Fax: (219) 562-3212
twinmill@howenet.com

Monticello, IN

Indiana Beach Camp Resort
5224 E Indiana Beach Road
Monticello, IN 47960
Voice: (800) 583-5306 / (800) 583-5306
Fax: (219) 583-6473
tim@monti.net

Yogi Bear's Jellystone Park / Indiana Beach
2882 NW Shafer Dr.
Monticello, IN 46217
Voice: (574) 583-8646 / (888) 811-9644
Fax: (574) 583-6473
booboo@monti.net

Nashville, IN

The Last Resort RV Park and Campground
2248 State Road 46 E
Nashville, IN 47448
Voice: (812) 988-4675
Fax: (812) 988-4475
tlrofbc@aol.com
Outside Link: www.lastresortrvpark.com

Westward Ho Campground
4557 E State Road 46
Nashville, IN 47448
Voice: (812) 988-0008

New Castle, IN

Walnut Ridge Resort Campground / Family
Trailer Sales

408 N County Road 300 W
New Castle, IN 47362
Voice: (765) 533-2288
Fax: (765) 533-2312
info@walnutridgerv.com

7638 W 300 N
Warsaw, IN 46582-9528
Voice: (574) 858-9628
Fax: (574) 858-9628

Peru, IN

Honey Bear Hollow Campground
4252 West North 200
North Peru 46970
765-473-4342

Plymouth, IN

Jellystone Camp Resort
7719 Redwood Road
Plymouth, IN 46563-8816
Voice: (574) 936-7851
Fax: (574) 936-6426

Richmond, IN

Grandpa's Farm RV Park Inc.
4244 SR 227 N
Richmond, IN 47374
Voice: (765) 962-7907 / (888) 756-4490
gpasfarm@aol.com

Rochester, IN

Lakeview Campground
7781 East 300
Rochester, IN 46975
574-353-8114

Terre Haute, IN

Lake Rudolph Campground & RV Resort
78 N Holiday Blvd. (PO Box 98)
Santa Claus, IN 47579
Voice: (812) 937-4458 / (877) 478-3657
Fax: (812) 937-4470
info@lakerudolph.com

Shipshewana, IN

Shipshewana Campground / South Location
1105 S Van Buren St. SR 5 (PO Box 172)
Shipshewana, IN 46565
Voice: (260) 768-4669
info@amish.org

Thorntown, IN

Old Mill Run Park
8544 W 690 N
Thorntown, IN 46071
Voice: (765) 436-7190
Fax: (765) 436-2506
oldmill@frontiernet.net

Warsaw, IN

Hoffman Lake Camp

Iowa

Adel, IA
Des Moines West KOA
Adel, IA
(515) 834-2729

Amana, IA
Amana Colonies RV Park
(319) 622-3344

Cedar Falls, IA
Black Hawk Park
2410 West Lone Tree Road
Cedar Falls, IA 50613
319-266-6813

Clear Lake, IA
Oakwood RV Park
(515) 357-4019

Clermont, IA
Skip-A-Way RV Park & Campground
(319) 423-7338

Johnston, IA
Saylorville, Lake
5600 NW 78th Ave
Johnston, IA 50131
515-276-4656

Kellogg, IA
Kellogg RV Park
1570 Hwy 224 S
Kellogg IA 50135
641-526-8535

Liberty, IA
KOA
1961 Garfield Ave. West
Liberty, IA 52776
319-627-2676

Newton, IA
Rolling Acres Family Campground
(515) 792-2428

Onawa, IA
KOA
21788 Dogwood Ave.
Onawa, IA 51040
712-423-1633

Lewis and Clark State Park

21914 Park Loop
Onowa, IA 51040
712-423-2829

Oxford, IA
Sleepy Hollow RV Park & Campground
Oxford, IA
(319) 628-4900

Waukee, IA
Timberline Best Holiday Trav-L-Park
3165 Ashworth Road
Waukee, 50263
515-987-1714

West Des Moines, IA
Timberline Campground
3165 Ashworth Road
West Des Moines, IA 50262
515-987-1714

West Liberty, IA
West Liberty KOA
(319) 627-2676

Kansas

Abilene, KS

Four Seasons RV Acres
2502 Mink Road
Abilene, KS 67410
Toll Free: (800)658-4667
Phone: (785)598-2221
Fax: (785)598-2223
4season@access-one.com

Caney, KS

Cheyenne Ridge RV Park
Rt. 1, Box 285
Abilene, KS 67333
620-879-2425

Council Grove, KS

Council Grove Lake
Rte 2 Box 110
Council Grove, KS 66846
877-444-6777

Dodge City, KS

Gunsmoke Trav-L-Park
11070 108th Road
Dodge City, KS 67801
Voice: (620) 227-8247 / (800) 789-8247
Fax: (620) 227-0826
gunsmokecampground@yahoo.com

Water Sports Campground and RV Park
500 Cherry Street
Dodge City, KS 67801
Phone: (620)225-8044
Fax: (620)225-4407
watersportscampground@cox.net

Elkhart, KS

Prairie RV Park
Box 699, 48 Hwy 56
Elkhart, KS 67950
620-697-4124

Farlington, KS

Crawford State Park
1 Lake Road
Farlington, KS 66734
620-362-3671

Garden City, KS

KOA
4100 E. Hwy 50
Garden City, KS 67846

316-276-8741

Goodland, KS

Goodland KOA Kampground
1114 E Hwy. 24
Goodland, KS 67735
Voice: (785) 890-5701
goodlandkoa@st-tel.net

Mid-America Camp Inn
2802 Commerce Road
Goodland, KS 67735
Voice: (785) 899-5431
midamerica@st-tel.net

Grantville, KS

KOA
3366 KOA Road
Grantville, KS 66429
785-246-3419

Hutchinson, KS

Melody Acres Campground
1009 East Blanchard
Hutchinson, KS 67501
620-665-5048

Lawrence, KS

KOA
1473 Hwy 40
Lawrence, KS 66044
913-842-3877

Norton, KS

Prairie Dog State Park
Rr 431
Norton, KS 67654
785-877-2953

Oakley, KS

High Plains Camping
462 US Highway 83
Oakley, KS 67748
Toll Free: (888)446-3507
Phone: (785)672-3538
Fax: (785)672-3092
office@highplainscamping.com
Salina, KS

Wakeeney, KS

KOA
Box 235
Wakeeney, KS 67672
785-743-5612

Wellington, KS

KOA
RR 1, Box 227
Wellington, KS 67152
316-326-6114

Wichita, KS

USI RV Park
2920 E. 33rd St North
Wichita, KS 67219
Toll Free: (800)782-1531
Phone: (316)838-8699
usirvpark@aol.com

Kentucky

Bardstown, KY

Holt's Campground
Bardstown, KY
(502) 348-6717

My Old Kentucky Home State Park
PO Box 323
Bardstown, KY 40004
502-348-3502

White Acres Campground
Bardstown, KY
(502) 348-9677

Berea, KY

Oh Kentucky Campground
(606) 986-1150

Walnut Meadow Campground
(606) 986-6180

Bow, KY

Dale Hollow Lake State Resort Park
502-433-7431

Bowling Green, KY

KOA
1960 Three Springs Road
Bowling Green, KY 42104
502-843-1919

Breaks, KY

Breaks Interstate Park

800-98205122

Burnside, KY

General Burnside State Park

606-561-4104

Cadiz, KY

Lake Barkley State Resort Park
Box 790
Cadiz, KY 42211
270-924-1131

Prizer Point Marina & Resort
(502) 522-3762

Calvert City, KY

Cypress Lakes RV Park

(502) 395-4267

KOA I-24 / Kentucky Lake Dam
(502) 395-5841

Cave City, KY

Jellystone Park Camp Resort
1002 Mammoth Cave Road
Cave City, KY 42127
(270) 773-3840

Campbellsville, KY

Green River Lake State Park
502-465-8255

Carrollton, KY

General Butler State Resort Park
502-732-4384

Clarksville, KY

KOA
900 Marriott Drive
Clarksville, KY 47129
812-282-4474

Columbus, KY

Columbus Belmont State Park
502-677-2327

Corbin, KY

Cumberland Falls State Resort Park
606-528-4121

KOA
171 E. City Dam Road
Corbin, KY 40701
606-528-1534

Crittenden, KY

Cincinnati South KOA
Box 339
Crittenden, KY 41030
859-428-2000

Eddyville, KY

Indian Point RV Park
1136 Indian Hills Tr;
Eddyville, KY 42038
(502) 388-7230

Lake Barkley RV Resort
(502) 388-4752

Elizabethtown, KY

KOA
209 Tunnel Hill Road

Elizabethtown, KY 42701
502-737-7600

Falls of Rough
Elizabethtown, KY

Rough River Dam State Resort Park
502-257-2311

Falmouth, KY
Kincaid Lake State Park
606-654-3531

Frankfort, KY
Elkhorn Campground
(502) 695-9154

Franklin, KY
KOA
PO Box 346
Franklin, 42135
502-586-5622

Gilbertsville, KY
Kentucky Dam Village State Resort Park
502-362-4271

Greenup, KY
Greenbo Lake State Resort Park
606-473-7324

Hardin, KY
Kenlake State Resort Park
542 Kenlake Road
Hardin, KY 42048
270-474-2211

Henderson, KY
John James Audubon State Park
PO Box 576
Henderson, KY 42419
270-826-2247

Horse Cave, KY
KOA
Box 87
Horse Cave, 42749
502-786-2819

Jamestown, KY
Lake Cumberland State Resort Park
502-343-3111

Lexington, KY
Lexington Horse Park Campground
4089 Iron Works Parkway
Lexington, KY 40511

859-259-4257

London, KY
Levi Jackson Wilderness Road State Park
998 Levi Jackson Mill Road
London, KY 40744
606-878-8000

Lucas, KY
Barren River Lake State Resort Park
502-646-2151

Mammoth Cave, KY
Mammoth Cave National Park
PO Box 7
Mammoth Cave, KY 42259
270-758-2180

Mount Oliver, KY
Blue Licks Battlefield State Park
606-289-5507

Olive Hill, KY
Carter Caves State Resort Park
606-286-4411

Grayson Lake State Park
314 Grayson Lake park Road
Olive Hill, KY 41164
606-474-9727

Parkers Lake, KY
Eagle Falls Resort
11251 Hwy 90
Parkers Lake, KY 42623
888-318-2658

Pineville, KY
Pine Mountain State Resort Park
606-337-3066

Prestonburg, KY
Jenny Wiley State Resort Park
606-886-2711

Renfro Valley, KY
KOA
Red Foley Road, Box 54
Renfro Valley, KY 40473
606-256-2474

Renfro Valley RV Park
(800) 765-7464

Richmond, KY
Fort Boonesborough State Park
4375 Boonesboro Road

Richmond, KY 40475
606-527-3131

Russell Springs, KY

KOA
1440 Hwy 1383
Russell Springs, KY 42642
502-866-5616

Sassafras, KY

Carr Creek State Park
PO Box 249
Sassafras, KY 41759
606-642-4050

Shepherdsville, KY

KOA
2433 Hwy 44E
Shepherdsville, KY 40165
502-543-2041

Slade, KY

Natural Bridge State Resort Park
606-663-2214

Taylorsville, KY

Taylorsville Lake State Park
502-477-8313

Walton, KY

Oak Creek Campground
(606) 485-9131

Louisiana

Abbeville, LA
Abbeville RV Park
1501 West Port Street
Abbeville, LA
318-898-4042

Ajax, LA
Country Livin' RV Park
1115 Hwy 174
Ajax, LA
318-796-2543

Bastrop, LA
Chemin-A-Haut State Park
14656 State Park Road
Bastrop, LA 71220
318-283-0812

Baton Rouge, LA
Night RV Park
14740 Florida Blvd.
Baton Rouge, LA 70819
225-275-0679

Bossier City, LA
Maplewood RV Park
452 Maplewood Drive
Bossier City, LA 71111
318-742-5497

Boyce, LA
KOA
64 Kisatchie Lane
Boyce, LA 71409
318-445-5227

Braithwaite, LA
St. Bernard State Park
PO box 534
Braithwaite, LA 70092
888-677-7823

Broussard, LA
Maxie's Campground
PO Box 181
Broussard, LA 70518
318-837-6200

Carencro, LA
Bayou Wilderness RV Resort
201 St Clair Road
Carencro, LA 70520

Voice: (318) 896-0598

Chatham, LA
Caney Creek Lake State Park
State Road #1209
Chatham, LA 71226
318-249-2595

Chauvin, LA
Coco Marina
106 Pier 56
Chauvin, LA 70344
504-594-6626

Covington, LA
Land-O-Pines Campground
17145 Million Dollar Road
Covington, LA 70435
504-892-6023

Denham Springs, LA
KOA Baton Rouge, East
7628 Vincent Road
Denham Springs, LA 70726-5621
Voice: (504) 664-7281 / (800) 562-5673
Fax: (504) 664-0564

Doyline, LA
Lake Bistineau State Park
PO Box 589
Doyline, LA 71023
318-745-3503

Farmerville, LA
Lake D'Arbonne
PO Box 236
Farmerville, LA 71241
318-368-2086

Gardner, LA
Kincaid Lake Recreation Area
Kisatchie National Forest
9912 HWY 28 West
Gardner, LA 71409
318-793-9427

Gibson, LA
Hideway Ponds Recreational Resort
6367 Bayou Black Drive
Gibson, LA 70356
504-575-9928

Grand Isle, LA
Grand Isle State Park
PO Box 741
Grand Isle, LA 70358

504-787-2559

Hammond, LA

Hidden Oaks Family Campground
669 Robert Lane
Hammond, LA 70466
504-345-9244

KOA New Orleans-Hammond
14154 Club Deluxe Road
Hammond, LA 70403
504-542-8094

Homer, LA

Lake Claiborne State Park
PO Box 246
Homer, LA 71040
318-927-2976

Houma, LA

Capri Court Campground
101 Capri Court
Houma, LA 70364
800-428-8026

Independence, LA

Indian Creek Campground & RV Park
53013 W Fontana Road
Independence, LA 70443
Voice: (504) 878-6567 / (888) 716-4687
Fax: (504) 878-6517
indiancreek@l-55.com

Kinder, LA

Grand Casino Coushatta's RV Resort
711 Pow Wow Parkway
Kinder, LA
888-867-8727

Quiet Oaks RV Park
18159 TV Tower Road
Kinder, LA
888-755-2230

Lake Charles, LA

Sam Houston Jones State Park
101 Southerland Road
Lake Charles, LA 70611
318-855-2665

Madisonville, LA

Fairview-Riverside State Park
PO Box 856
Madisonville, LA 70447
504-845-3318

Mandeville, LA

Fontainebleau State Park
PO Box 8925
Mandeville, LA 70470
504-624-4443

Minden, LA

Caney Lakes Recreation ASrea
3288 HWY 795
Minden, LA 71040
318-927-2061

New Orleans, LA

Jude Travel Park & Guest House
7400 Chef Mneteur
New Orleans, LA 70126
504-241-0632

New Orleans West KOA Campground
11129 Jefferson Highway
New Orleans, LA 70123
504-467-1792

New Orleans-East KOA
56009 Hwy 433
New Orleans, LA 70461
504-643-3850

Patterson, LA

Kemper Williams Park
Box 599
Patterson, LA 70392
504-395-2298

Port Allen, LA

Cajun Country Campground
4667 Rebelle Lane
Port Allen, LA 70767
Voice: (800) 264-8554

Port Barre, LA

Bayou Teche RV Park
PO Box 219
Port Barre, LA
318-585-7646

River Ridge, LA

KOA New Orleans West
11129 Jefferson Hwy
River Ridge, LA 70123
504-467-1792

Robert, LA

Yogi Bear's Jellystone Park
PO Box 519
Robert, LA 70455
504-542-1507

Scott, LA

KOA Lafayette
537 Apollo Road
Scott, LA 70583
318-235-2739

Shreveport, LA

KOA Shreveport-Bossier
6510 West 79th St.
Shreveport, LA 71129
318-687-1010

Springfield, LA

Tickfaw State Park
27225 Patterson Road
Springfield. LA 70462
225-294-5020

St. Joseph, LA

Lake Bruin State Park
Rt. 1, Box 183
St. Joseph, LA 71366
318-766-3530

St. Martinville, LA

Lake Fausse Pointe State Park
5400 Levee Road
St. Martinville, LA 70582
318-229-4764

Sulphur, LA

Hidden Ponds RV Park
1201 Ravia Road
Sulphur, LA 70665
318-583-4709

Vidalia, LA

Riverview RV Park & Resort
100 Riverview Parkway
Vidalia, LA 71373
Voice: (318) 336-1400
Fax: (318) 336-1401
rv@vidalialanding.com

Ville Platte, LA

Chicot State Park
Rt. 3, Box 494
Ville Platte, LA 70586
318-363-2403

Vinton, LA

Lake Charles / Vinton RV Park
1514 Azema St.
Vinton, LA 70668
Voice: (337) 589-2300 / (866) 589-2300

Fax: (337) 589-5615
vintonrv@aol.com
Outside Link: www.vintonrv.com

Violet, LA

St. Bernard State Park
PO Box 534
Violet, LA 70092
504-682-2101

West Monroe, LA

Pavilion RV Park
309 Well Road
West Monroe, LA 71292
Voice: (318) 322-4216
Fax: (318) 322-8598
kmk@centurytel.net

Westwego, LA

Bayou Segnette State Park
7777 Westbank Expressway
Westwego, LA 70094
504-736-7140

Zwolle, LA

North Toledo Bend State Park
2907 North Toledo Park Road
Zwolle, LA 71486
888-677-6400

Maine

Alfred, ME

Walnut Grove Campground
599 Gore Road
Alfred, ME 04002
207-324-1207

Andover, ME

South Arm Campground
Box 310
Andover, ME 04216
207-364-5155

Appleton, ME

Sennebec Lake Campground
Rt. 131, Box 602
Appleton, ME 04862
207-785-4250

Bangor, ME

Paul Bunyan Campground
1862 Union Street
Bangor, ME 04401
207-941-1177

Pleasant Hill Campground
RFD 3, Box 180, Union St.
Bangor, ME 04401
207-848-5127

Wheeler Stream Camping Area
RR 2, Box 2800
Bangor, ME 04401
207-848-3713

Bar Harbor, ME

Bar Harbor Campground
RFD, Box 1125
Bar Harbor, ME 04609
207-288-5185

Barcadia Campground
RR 1, Box 2165
Bar Harbor, ME 04609
207-288-3520

Hadley's Point Campground
33 Hadley Point Road
Bar Harbor, ME 04609
207-288-4808

Mt. Desert Narrows Camping
RR 1, Box 2045

Bar Harbor, ME 04609
207-288-4782

Seawall Campground
PO Box 177
Bar Harbor, ME 04609
207-244-3600

Spruce Valley Campground
RR 1, Box 2420, Rt. 102
Bar Harbor, ME 04609
207-288-5139

Bass Harbor, ME

Quietside Campground & Cabins
PO Box 10
Bass Harbor, ME 04653
207-244-5992

Bath, ME

Meadowbrook Camping
33 Meadowbrook Road
Bath, ME 04562
800-370-CAMP

Belfast, ME

Moorings Oceanfront Campground
Rt. 1, Box 69M
Belfast, ME 04915
207-338-6860

Northport Travel Park Campground
207-338-2077

Berwick, ME

Beaver Dam Campground
551 School Street
Berwick, ME 03901
207-698-2267

Bethel, ME

Bethel Outdoor Adventures & Campground
800-533-3607

Stony Brook Recreation
Rt. 2, 42 Powell Place
Bethel, ME 04237
207-824-2836

Biddeford, ME

Shamrock RV Park, Inc.
391 West St.
Biddeford, ME 04005
207-284-4282

Boothbay, ME

Camper's Cove Campground
Box 136
Boothbay, ME 04537
207-633-5013

Little Ponderosa
159 Wiscasset Road
Boothbay, ME
207-633-2700

Shore Hills Campground and RV Park
553 Wiscasset Road
Boothbay, Maine 04537
(207) 633-4782

Boothbay Harbor, ME

Gray Homestead Oceanfront Campground
Box 334 HC66
Boothbay Harbor, ME 04576
207-633-4612

Shore Hills Campground
RR 1, Box 448M, Route 27
Boothbay Harbor, ME 04537
207-633-4782

Bridgton, ME

Bridgton Pines Cabins & Campground
207-647-8227

Lakeside Pines Campground
Box 182
Bridgton, ME 04057
207-647-3935

Vicki-Lin Camping Area
207-647-8489

Brownfield, ME

River Run Canoe & Camp
PO Box 90'
Brownfield, ME 04010
207-452-2500

Woodland Acres Camp 'N' Canoe
207-935-2529

Brunswick, ME

White's Beach & Campground
207-729-0415

Thomas Point Beach & Campground
29 Meadow Road
Brunswick, ME 04011
207-725-6009

Bucksport, ME

Flying Dutchman Campground
PO Box 1639
Bucksport, ME 04416
207-469-3256

Shady Oaks Campground and Cabins
207-469-7739

Byron, ME

Coos Canyon Campground
207-364-388-

Calais, ME

Pleasant Lake Camping Area
207-454-7467

Camden, ME

Camden Hills State Park
280 Belfast Road
Camden, ME 04843
207-236-3109

Megunticook By The Sea
US Route 1, P.O. Box 375
Camden, ME 04856
207-594-2428

Canaan, ME

Skowhegan/Canaan KOA
P.O. Box 87
Canaan, ME 04924
800-562-7571

Carmel, ME

Shady Acres RV & Campground
207-848-5515

Casco, ME

Point Sebago Resort
261 Point Sebago Road
Casco, ME 04015
800-655-1232

Damariscotta, ME

Lake Pemaquid Camping
207-563-5202

Danforth, ME

Greenland Cove Campground
207-448-2863

Deer Isle, ME

Sunshine Campground
207-348-6681

Denmark, ME

Granger Pond Camping Area

207-452-2342

Pleasant Mt. Camping Area
207-452-2170

Dixfield, ME

Mountain View Campground
208 Weld St.
Dixfield, ME 04224
207-562-8285

Eagle Lake, ME

Birch Haven Campground
207-444-5102

East Machias, ME

River's Edge Campground
207-255-4523

East Orland, ME

Balsam Cove Campground
PO Box C
East Orland, ME 04431
207-469-7771

Whispering Pines Campground
US Route 1
East Orland, ME 04431
207-469-3443

Eastport, ME

The Seaview
16 Norwood Road
Eastport, ME 04631
207-853-4471

Eddington, ME

Greenwood Acres Campground
RR 2, Box 2210, Rte. 178
Eddington, ME 04428
207-989-8898

Ellsworth, ME

Branch Lake Camping Area
RFD #5
Ellsworth, ME
207-667-5174

Enfield, ME

Lakeside Camping & Cabins
207-732-4241

Timberland Acres RV Park
207-667-3600

Eustis, ME

Cathedral Pines Campground
Rte 27
Eustis, ME 04936
207-246-3491

Farmingdale, ME

Foggy-Bottom RV Campground
207-582-0075

Freeport, ME

Blueberry Pond Campground
218 Poland Range Road
Freeport, ME 04069
207-688-4421

Cedar Haven
39 Baker Road
Freeport, ME
207-865-6254

Desert Dunes of Main Campground
US Route 1 & 95 Desert Road
Freeport, ME 04032
207-865-6962

Flying Point Campground
10 Lower Flying Point Road
Freeport, ME 04032
207-865-4569

Recompence Shore Campsites
8 Burnett Road
Freeport, ME 04032
207-865-9307

Gardiner, ME

Augusta/Gardiner KOA
RFD 1, Box 2410M
Gardiner, ME 04357
207-582-5086

Georgetown, ME

Camp Seguin Ocean Camping
Reid State Park Road
Georgetown, ME 04548
207-371-2777

Sagadahoc Bay Campground
207-371-2014

Gray, ME

Twin Brooks Camping Area
P.O. Box 194
Gray, ME 04039
207-428-3832

Greenville, ME

Casey's Spencer Bay Camps
PO Box 1190
Greenville, ME 04441
207-695-2801

Moosehead Family Campground
207-695-2210

Hanover, ME

Stony Brook Recreation
207-824-2836

Harrison, ME

Vacationland Campsites
207-583-4953

Hebron, ME

Hebron Pines Campground
207-966-2179

Holden, ME

Red Barn Campground
207-843-6011

Houlton, ME

My Brothers Place
207-532-6739

Island Falls, ME

Birch Point
Box 120
Island Falls, ME 04747
207-463-2515

Jackman, ME

Jackman Landing Campground
207-668-3301

John's Four Season Accommodations
207-668-7683

Loon Echo Family Campground
P.O. Box 711
Jackman, ME 04945
207-668-4829

Moose Alley Campground
Route 201, Box 298
Jackman, ME 04945
207-668-2781

The Last Resort Campground & Cabins
207-668-5091

Kennebunkport, ME

Kennebunkport Camping
117 Old Cape Road
Kennebunkport, ME 04046
207-967-2732

Red Apple Campground
207-967-4927

Kingfield, ME

Deer Farm Campground
207-265-4599

Lebanon, ME

Kings & Queens Court Resort
Flat Rock Ridge Road, RFD 1, Box 763
Lebanon, ME 04027
207-339-9465

Potter's Place Adult Park
RR 2, Box 490
Lebanon, ME 04027
207-457-1341

Leeds, ME

Riverbend Campground
Rt. 106, RR 2, Box 5050M
Leeds, ME 04263
207-524-5711

Lewiston, ME

Lew/Aub No. Allen Pond Campground
207-946-7439

Litchfield, ME

Birches Family Campground
207-268-4330

Livermore, ME

Rol-Lin Hills
207-897-6394

Locke Mills, ME

Littlefield Beaches Campground
RR 1, Box 4300
Locke Mills, ME 04255
207-875-3290

Lovell, ME

Kezar Lake Camping Area
RR 1, Box 246M
Lovell, ME 04051
207-925-1631

Lubec, ME

South Bay Campground
RR 1, Box 6565
Lubec, ME 04652

162

207-733-1037

Sunset Point Trailer Park
Rt. 189
Lubec, ME 04652
207-733-2150

Madison, ME
Abnaki Family Camping Center
207-474-2070

Yonder Hill Campground
207-474-7353

Medway, ME
Katahdin Shadows Campground
PO Box HM
Medway, ME 04460
800-794-5267

Pine Grove Campground & Cottages
207-746-5172

Millinocket, ME
Frost Pond Campground
36C Minuteman Drive
Millinocket, ME 04462
207-695-2821

Hidden Springs Campground
888-685-2288

Jo-Mary Lake Campground
800-494-0031

Nesowadnehunk Campground
207-458-1551

Monticello, ME
Wilde Pines Campground
207-538-9004

Moose River, ME
Moose River Campground
P.O. Box 98
04945
207-668-3341

Mount Desert, ME
Somes Sound View Campground
Hall Quarry Road
Mount Desert, ME 04660
207-244-3890

N. Monmouth, ME
Beaver Brook Campground

RR 1, Box 1835M
N. Monmouth, ME 04265
207-933-2108

N. New Portland, ME
Happy Horseshoe Campground
207-628-3471

N. Waterford, ME
Papoose Pond Resort & Campground
207-583-4470

Naples, ME
Bay of Naples Family Camping
Route 11/114, Box 240M
Naples, ME 04055
800-348-9750

Brandy Pond Park
207-693-3129

Colonial Mast Campground
Kansas Road, P.O. Box 95
Naples, ME 04055
207-693-6652

Four Seasons Camping Area
P.o. Box 927
Naples, ME 04055
207-693-6797

Loon's Haven Family Campground
P.O. Box 557
Naples, ME 04055
207-693-6881

Newport, ME
Christies Campground
Rt. 1, Box 565
Newport, ME 04953
207-368-4645

Palmyra Gold & RV Resort
207-938-5677

Tent Village Travel Trailer Park
RR 2, Box 580
Newport, ME 04953
207-368-5047

Nobleboro, ME
Duck Puddle Campground
P.O. Box 176M
Nobleboro, ME 04555
207-563-5608

Town Line Campsites

163

483 East Pond Road
Nobleboro, ME 04348
207-832-7055

Norridgewock, ME

Main Roads Camping
207-634-4952

Ogunquit, ME

Pinederosa Campground
128 North Village Road
Ogunquit, ME 04090
207-646-2492

Orland, ME

Shady Oaks Campground & Cabins
32 Leaches Point
Orland, ME 04472
207-469-7739

Old Orchard Beach, ME

Hid'n Pines Campground
Route 98, Cascade Road, P.O. Box 647
Old Orchard Beach, ME 04064
207-934-2352

Ne're Beach Family Campground
38 Saco Ave., Route 5
Old Orchard Beach, ME 04064
207-934-7614

Old Orchard Beach Campground
Route 5/27 Ocean Park Road
Old Orchard Beach, ME 04064
207-934-4477

Paradise Park Resort Campground
207-934-4633

Powder Horn Family Camping
P.O. Box 366M, Route 98
Old Orchard Beach, ME 04064
207-934-4733

Wagon Wheel Campground & Cabins
3 Old Orchard Road, Dept. M
Old Orchard Beach, ME 04064
207-934-2160

Wild Acres Family Camping
179M Saco Ave.
Old Orchard Beach, ME 04064
207-934-2535

Oquossoc, ME

Stephen Phillips Preserve
207-864-2003

Orr's Island, ME

Orr's Island Campground
207-833-5595

Oxford, ME

Mirror Pond Campground
207-539-4888

Two Lakes Camping Area
Rt. 26, Box 206
Oxford, ME 04270
207-539-4851

Matagamon Wilderness
Shin Pond Village Campground
RR 1, Box 280M
Oxford, ME 04765
207-528-2900

Pemaquid, ME

Sherwood Forest Campsite
Pemaquid Trail, P.O. Box 189
Pemaquid, ME 04554
800-274-1593

Peru, ME

Honey Run Beach & Campgrounds
456 East Shore Road
Peru, ME 04290
207-562-4913

Phippsburg, ME

Ocean View Park Campground & Camps
Route 209
Phippsburg, ME 04562
207-389-2564

Perry, ME

Knowlton's Campground
207-726-4756

Poland, ME

Range Pond Campground
94 Plains Road
Poland, ME 04274
207-998-2624

Poland Spring, ME

Poland Spring Campground
Route 26, P.O. Box 409M
Poland Spring, ME 04274
207-998-2151

Presque Isle, ME

Neil E. Michaud Campground
US No. 1 Hwy

Presque Isle, ME
207-769-1951

Rangeley, ME

Cupsuptic Campground
207-864-5249

Raymond, ME

Kokatosi Campground
635M Webbs Mills Road
Raymond, ME 04071
207-627-4642

Richmond, ME

Augusta/Gardiner KOA
Route 1, Box 2410
Richmond, ME 04357
800-562-1496

Rockport, ME

Camden Hills RV Resort
888-842-0592

Camden Rockport Camping
P.O. Box 170, Rt. 90
Rockport, ME 04865
888-842-0592

Rockwood, ME

Old Mill Campground & Cabins
207-534-7333

Woody's Campground & Cottages
207-534-7752

Roxbury, ME

Silver Lake Campground
207-545-0416

Rumford, ME

Madison's Wilderness Camping
Rt. 2
Rumford, ME
800-258-6234

Saco, ME

Homestead by the River Campground
Route 5, Box 107
Saco, ME 04072
207-282-6445

Saco Portland South KOA
814A Portland Road
Saco, ME 04072
207-282-0502

Silver Springs Campground
705 Portland Road
Saco, ME 04072
207-283-3880

Sanford, ME

Jellystone Park Camp Resort
1175 Main St., Route 109
Sanford, ME 04073
207-324-7782

Scarborough, ME

Bayley's Camping Resort
Box M9, 27 Ross Road
Scarborough, ME 04074
207-883-6043

Wild Duck Campground
39 Dunstan Landing Road
Scarborough, ME 04074
207-883-4432

Searsmont, ME

Aldus Shores Lakeside Campground
Rt. 131, P.O. Box 38
Searsmont, ME 04973
207-342-5618

Searsport, ME

Searsport Shores Camping
Coastal US Route 1
Searsport, ME 04970
207-548-6059

Sebago Lake, ME

Sebago Lake Family Campground
1550 Richville Road
Sebago Lake, ME 04084
207-787-3671

Skowhegan, ME

Eaton Mountain Ski & Campground
207-474-2666

Skowhegan/Canaan KOA
207-474-2858

Two Rivers Campground
HCR 71, Box 14
Skowhegan, ME 04976
207-474-6482

Small Point, ME

Hermit Island Campground
42T Front St.
Small Point, ME 04530

165

207-443-2101

Solon, ME
The Evergreens Campground
Route 201A
Solon, ME 04979
207-643-2324

South Hiram, ME
Locklin Camping Area
207-625-8622

Southwest Harbor, ME
Smuggler's Den Campground
PO Box 787, Rout 102
Southwest Harbor, ME 04679
207-244-3944

White Birches Campground
Sal Cover Road, Box 421
Southwest Harbor, ME 04679
207-244-3797

St. Agatha, ME
Lakeview Camping Resort
207-543-6331

Standish, ME
Family -N- Friends Campground
140 Richville Road, Route 114
Standish, ME 04084
207-642-2200

Steep Falls, ME
Acres of Wildlife Campground
Route 113/11, P.O. Box 2
Steep Falls, ME 04085
207-675-CAMP

Stetson, ME
Stetson Shores Campground
Rt. 143, PO Box 86
Stetson, ME 04488
207-296-2041

Steuben, ME
Mainayr Campground
207-546-2690

Stonington, ME
Greenlaw's RV Tent & Rental
207-367-5049

Sullivan, ME
Mountainview Campground
207-422-6215

Surry, ME
The Gatherings Family Campground
RR 1, Box 4069
Surry, ME 04684
207-667-8826

The Forks, ME
Indian Pond Campground
800-371-7774

Thomaston, ME
Saltwater Farm Campground
207-354-6735

Topsfield, ME
Maine Wilderness Camps
HC 82, Box 1085
Topsfield, ME 04490
207-738-5052

Trenton, ME
Narrows Too Camping Resort
RR 1, Box 193
Trenton, ME 04605
207-667-4300

Vassalboro, ME
Green Valley Campground
207-923-3000

Warren, ME
Loon's Cry Campground
US Route 1
Warren, ME 04864
800-493-2324

Sandy Shores RV Resort
207-273-2073

Waterford, ME
Bear Mt. Village Cabins & Sites
RR 2, Box 745
Waterford, ME 04088
207-583-2541

Waterville, ME
Countryside Campground
207-873-4603

Weld, ME
Dummer's Beach Campground
207-585-2200

Wells, ME
Riverside Campground
2295 Post Road

Wells, ME 04090
207-646-3145

Sea Breeze Campground
2073 Post Road
Wells, ME 04090
207-646-4301

Sea-vu Campground
US Route 1, P.O. Box 67
Wells, ME 04090
207-646-7732

Wells Beach Resort
1000M Post Road, US Route 1
Wells, ME 04090
207-646-7570

West Bethel, ME

Pleasant River Campground
P.O. Box 92
West Bethel, ME 04286
207-836-2000

West Poland, ME

Mac's Campground
207-998-4238

Wilson Mills, ME

Aziscoos Valley Camping Area
207-486-3271

Winslow, ME

Glordano's Campground & Recreation
207-873-2408

Winterville, ME

Winterville Lakeview Camps & Campground
207-444-4581

Winthrop, ME

Augusta-West Resort
207-377-9993

Wiscasset, ME

Chewonki Campground
P.O. Box 261
Wiscasset, ME 04578
207-882-7426

Down East Family Camping
207-882-5431

Woodland, ME

Sunset Acres Campground
207-454-1440

York Beach, ME

York Beach Camper Park
11 Cappy's Ln, Box 127
York Beach, ME
207-363-1343

York Harbor, ME

Camp Eaton
P.O. Box 626, Route 1A
York Harbor, ME
207-363-3424

Libby's Oceanside Camp
Box 40, Dept. M-99, US Route 1A
York Harbor, ME
207-363-4171

Maryland

Abingdon, MD

Bar Harbor RV Park and Marina
4228 Birch Ave.
Abingdon, MD 21009
Voice: (410) 679-0880 / (800) 351-2267
Fax: (410) 671-7278

Berlin, MD

Bayside Campground and Oceanside
Campground
Assateague Island National Seashore
7206 National Seashore Road
Berlin, Md 21811
410-641-3030

Clarksburg, MD

Little Bennet Regional Campground
23701 Frederick Road
Clarksburg, Md 20871
301-972-9222

College Park, MD

Cherry Hill Park Holiday Trav-L-Park
9800 Cherry Hill Road
College Park, MD 20740
301-937-7116

Crisfield, MD

James Island State Park
26280 Alfred Dawson Road
Crisfield, Md 21817
410-968-1565

Ellicott City, MD

Patapsco Valley State Park
8020 Baltimore National Pike
Ellicott City, MD 21043
410-461-5005

Frederick, MD

Gambrill State Park
6430 Gambrill State Park Road
Frederick, MD 21702
301-271-7574

Freeland, MD

Morris Meadows Recreation Farm
1523 Freeland Road
Freeland, MD 21053
Voice: (410) 329-6636
Fax: (410) 357-4089
mm@bcpl.net

Grantville, MD

Big Run State Park
349 Headquarters Ln
Grantville, MD 21536
301-895-5453

Hagerstown, MD

Yogi Bear's Jellystone Park
16519 Lappans Road
Hagerstown, MD 21795
800-421-7116

Millersville, MD

Washington DC, NE KOA
768 Cecil Avenue N.
Millersville, MD 21108
800-562-0248

Newburg, MD

Aqualand on the Potomac Campground & Marina
9700 Orland Park Road
Newburg, MD 20664
Voice: (301) 259-2575
Fax: (301) 259-2575

Quantico, MD

Sandy Hill Family Camp
5752 Sandy Hill Road
Quantico, MD 21856
Voice: (410) 873-2471
sandyhill@sandyhillfamilycamp.com

Whaleyville, MD

Fort Whaley Campground
11224 Dale Road
Whaleyville, MD 21872
Voice: (410) 641-9785
Fax: (410) 641-2876
info@fortwhaley.com

Williamsport, MD

Hagerstown/Snug Harbor KOA
11759 Snug Harbor Lane
Williamsport, MD 21795
800-562-7607

Yogi Bears Jellystone Park Hagerstown
16519 Lappans Road
Williamsport, MD 21795
Toll Free: (800)421-7116
Phone: (301)223-7117
camp@jellystonemaryland.com

Massachusetts

Ashburnham, MA

Howe's Camping
133 Sherbert Road
Ashburnham, MA 01430
978-827-4558

Ashby, MA

The Pines
39 Davis Road
Ashby, MA 01431
978-386-7702

Assonet, MA

Forge Pond Campground
62 Forge Road
Assonet, MA 02702
508-644-5701

Baldwinville, MA

Otter River State Forest
Route 202
Baldwinville, MA 01436
978-939-8962

Bass River, MA

Bass River Trailer Park
Rte. 28
Bass River, MA 02664
508-398-2011

Bellingham, MA

Circle C.G. Adult Family Campground & RV Park
131 N. Main St.
Bellingham, MA 02019
508-966-1136

Circle C.G. Farm Campground
131 North Main St.
Bellingham, MA 02019
508-966-1136

Bernardston, MA

Travelr's Woods of New england
Box 88
Bernardston, MA 01337
413-48-9105

Bolton, MA

Crystal Springs Campground
PO Box 279
Bolton, MA 01740
978-799-2711

Bourne, MA

Bay View Campgrounds
260 MacArthur Blvd.
Bourne, MA 02532
508-759-7610

Brewster, MA

Nickerson State Park
Rte 6A
Brewster, MA 02631
508-896-3491

Sweetwater Forest
PO Box 1797
Brewster, MA 02631
508-896-3773

Brimfield, MA

Quinebaug Cover Campsite
49 East Brimfield-Holland rd.
Brimfield, MA 01010
413-245-9525

Village Green Family Campground
228 Sturbridge Road
Brimfield, MA 01010
413-245-3504

Brookfield, MA

Lakeside Resort
12 Hobbs Ave.
Brookfield, MA 01506
508-867-2737

Charlemont, MA

Country Aire Campground
Box 286
Charlemont, MA 01339
413-625-2996

Mohawk Trail State Forest
PO Box 7, Route 2
Charlemont, MA 01339
413-339-5504

Chester, MA

Bonny Rigg Camping Club
Box 14
Chester, MA 01011
413-623-5366

Chester Blandford State Forest
Rte. 20
Chester, MA 01050
413-354-6347

Walker Island Camping
#27 Route 20
Chester, MA 01011
413-354-2295

Clarksburg, MA

Clarksburg State Park
1199 Middle Road
Clarksburg, MA 01247
413-664-8345

Dennisport, MA

Campers Haven RV Resort
184 Old Wharf Road
Dennisport, MA 02639
Voice: (508) 398-2811
Fax: (508) 398-3661
camphavn@capecod.net

E. Douglas, MA

Lake Manchaug Camping
76 Oak St.
E. Douglas, MA 01516
508-476-2471

E. Falmouth, MA

Cape Cod Campresort
176 Thomas Landers Road
E. Falmouth, MA 02536
508-548-1458

E. Wareham, MA

Maple Park Family Campground
RFD 2
E. Wareham, MA 02538
508-295-4945

East Otis, MA

Laurel Ridge Camping Area
Box 519
East Otis, MA 01029
413-269-4804

Eastham, MA

Atlantic Oaks Campground
3700 Rte. 6, RR2
Eastham, MA 02642
508-255-1437

Erving, MA

Erving State Forest
RFD 1, Route 2A
Erving, MA 01364
978-544-3939

Falmouth, MA

Otis Trailer Village-Johns Pond Campground

Box 586 (Mashpee)
Falmouth, MA 02541
508-349-3007

Sippewissett Campground and Cabins
836 Palmer Ave
Falmouth, MA 02540
508-548-2542

Florida, MA

Savoy Mountain State Forest
260 Central Shaft Road
Florida, MA
413-663-8469

Foxboro, MA

Normandy Farms Campground
72 West St.
Foxboro, MA 02035
508-543-7600

Normandy Farms Campground
72 West St.
Foxboro, MA 02035
508-543-7600

Gloucester, MA

Annisquam Campground
Stanwood Pt.
Gloucester, MA 01930
978-283-2992

Cape Ann Camp Site
80 Atlantic St
Gloucester, MA 01930
978-283-8683

Goshen, MA

D.A.R. State Forest
Route 112
Goshen, MA 01096
413-268-7098

Granville, MA

Granville State Forest
323 West Hartland Road, Route 57
Granville, MA 01034
413-357-6611

Prospect Mountain Campground
1349 Main Road
Granville, MA 01034
413-357-6494

Hingham, MA

Wompatuck State Park
 Union St

172

Hingham, MA 02043
781-749-7160

Lanesboro, MA

Hidden Valley Campground
15 Scott Road
Lanesboro, MA 01237-0700
Voice: (413) 447-9419 / (413) 447-9419
Fax: (413) 447-3775
hdnvaly@bcn.net

Lee, MA

October Mountain State Forest
Woodland Road
Lee, MA 01238
413-243-1778

Littleton, MA

Minuteman Campground
(PO Box 2122) 264 Ayer Road Rte. 2A
Littleton, MA 01460
Voice: (978) 772-0042 / (877) 677-0042
Fax: (978) 772-9332
info@minutemancampground.com

Mansfield, MA

Canoe River Campground
137 Mill St., East
Mansfield, MA 02031
508-339-6462

Mashpee, MA

John's Pond Campground
Rte. 151
Mashpee, MA 02649
508-477-0444

Otis Trailer Village
Rte. 151
Mashpee, MA 02649
508-477-0444

Middleboro, MA

Plymouth Rock KOA
438 Plymouth St., Box 616
Middleboro, MA 02346
508-947-6435

Monson, MA

Partridge Hollow
PO Box 41, Munn Road
Monson, MA 01057
413-267-5122

Sunsetview Farm Camping Area
57 Town Farm Road

Monson, MA 01057
413-267-9269

Monterey, MA

Beartown State Forest
PO Box 97, Blue Hill Road
Monterey, MA 01245
413-528-0904

N. Egremont, MA

Prospect Lake Park
50 Prospect Lake Road
N. Egremont, MA 02152
413-528-4158

N. Rutland, MA

Pout & Trout Family Campground
94 River Road
N. Rutland, MA 01543
508-886-6677

North Andover, MA

Harold Parker State Forest
1951 Turnpike Road
North Andover, MA 01845
978-686-3391

North Truro, MA

North Truro Camping Area
Highland Road
02652
508-487-1847

Northfield, MA

Barton Cover Campground
99 Millers Falls Road
Northfield, MA 01360
413-863-9300

Oakham, MA

Pine Acres Family Camping Resort
203 Bechan Road
Oakham, MA 01068
508-882-9509

Otis, MA

Camp Overflow
Box 645
Otis, MA 01253
413-269-4036

Mountain View Campground
P.O Route 8
Otis, MA 01253
413-269-8928

173

Phillipston, MA

Lamb City Campground
85 Royalston Road
Phillipston, MA 01331
978-249-2049

Pittsfield, MA

Bonnie Brae Cabins & Campsites
108 Broadway St.
Pittsfield, MA 01201
413-442-3754

Pittsfield State Forest
1041Cascade Street
Pittsfield, MA 01201
413-442-8992

Plainfield, MA

Peppermint Park Camping Resort
169 Grant St, Box 52
Plainfield, MA 01070
413-634-5385

Plymouth, MA

Ellis Haven Family Campground
531 Federal Furnace Road
Plymouth, MA 02360
508-746-0803

Indianhead Resort
Rte. 3A, State Road
Plymouth, MA 02360
508-888-3688

Pinewood Lodge Campground
190 Pinewood Road
Plymouth, MA 02360
508-746-3548

Sandy Pond Campground
834 Bourne Road
South Plymouth, MA 02360
Phone: (508)759-9336
info@sandypond.com

Provincetown, MA

Coastal Acres Camping Court
PO Box 593
Provincetown, MA 02657
508-487-1700

Dunes' Edge Campground
Box 875, 386 Rt. 6
Provincetown, MA 02657
508-487-9815

Rochester, MA

Outdoor World
90 Stevens Road
Rochester, MA 02770
508-763-5911

S. Carver, MA

Shady Acres
PO Box 128
S. Carver, MA 02366
508-866-4040

Salisbury, MA

Black Bear Campground
54 Main St.
Salisbury, MA 01952
978-462-3183

Rusnik Campground
Box 5441
Salisbury, MA 01952
978-462-9551

Salisbury Beach State Reservation
Beach Road, Route 1A
Salisbury, MA 01952
978-462-4481

Sandwich, MA

Dunroamin' Trailer Park
5 John Ewer Road, RR3
Sandwich, MA 02563
508-477-0541

Peters Pond Park
185 Cotuit Road
Sandwich, MA 02563
508-477-1775

Shawme-Crowell State Forest
42 Main St
Sandwich, MA 02563
508-888-0351

Savoy, MA

Shady Pines Campground
547 Loop Road
Savoy, MA 01256
413-743-2694

Shelburne, MA

Springbrook Family Camping Area
RFD 1, 32 Tower Road
Shelburne, MA 01370
413-625-6618

Southwick, MA

Sodom Mountain Campground
227 s. Loomis St., Box 702
Southwick, MA 01077
413-569-3930

Southwick Acres Campground
PO Box 984, College Hwy
Southwick, MA 01077
413-569-6339

Sturbridge, MA

Outdoor World Resort
19 Mashapaug Road
Sturbridge, MA 01566
508-347-7156

Wells State Park
Rte. 39
Sturbridge, MA 01566
508-347-9257

Yogi Bear's Sturbridge Jellystone Park
Box 600
Sturbridge, MA 01566
508-347-2336

W. Brookfield, MA

The Old Sawmill Campground
Box 377, Long Hill Road
W. Brookfield, MA 01585
508-867-2427

W. Gloucester, MA

Cape Ann Campsite
80 Atlantic St.
W. Gloucester, MA 01930
978-283-8683

W. Granville, MA

Prospect Mountain
Route 57
W. Granville, MA 01034
413-357-6494

W. Sutton, MA

Sutton Falls Camping Area
Manchaug Road
W. Sutton, MA 01590
508-865-3898

The Old Holbrook Place
114 Manchaug Road
W. Sutton, MA 01590
508-865-5050

Wales, MA

Oak Haven Family Campground
Route 19
Wales, MA 01081
413-245-7148

Warwick, MA

Wagon Wheel Camping Area
909 Wendell Road
Warwick, MA 01378
978-544-3425

Winchendon, MA

Lake Dennison State Recreational Area
Rte. 202
Winchendon, MA 01475
978-939-8962

Windsor, MA

Windsor State Forest
River Road
Windsor, MA 01270
413-684-0948

Worthington, MA

Berkshire Park Camping Area
Box 531, Harvey Road
Worthington, MA 01098
413-238-5918

Michigan

Allegan, MI

Tri-Ponds Family Camp Resort
3687 Dumont Road
Allegan, MI 49010
269-673-4740

Alpena, MI

Campers Cove RV Park & Canoe Livery
5005 Long Rapids Road
Alpena, MI 49707
888-306-3708

Bellaire, MI

Chain O'Lakes Campground
7231 S. M-88
Bellaire, MI 49615
231-533-8432

Belmont, MI

Grand Rogue Campgrounds, Canoe
6400 West River Dr.
Belmont, MI 49306
616-361-1053

Benzonia, MI

Vacation Trailer Park
2080 Benzie Hwy
Benzonia, MI 49616
231-882-5101

Buchanan, MI

Fuller's Resort and Campground on Clear Lake
1622 East Clear Lake Road
Buchanan, MI 49107
269-695-3785

Buckley, MI

Traverse City KOA
9700 M 37
Buckley, MI,49620
800-562-0280

Cadillac, MI

Camp Cadillac
10621 East 34 Road
Cadillac, MI, 49601
231-775-9724

Cedar Springs, MI

Lakeside Camp Park
13677 White Creek Ave.
Cedar Springs, MI. 49319

616-696-1735

Cement City, MI

Irish Hills Kampground
16230 US-12
Cement City, MI, 49233
517-592-6751

Champion, MI

Michigamme Shores
Box 6 (US-41 and M-28)
Champion, MI, 49814
906-339-2116

Cheboygan, MI

Waterways Campground
P.O. Box 262
Cheboygan, MI, 49721
231-627-7066

Coldwater, MI

Waffle Farm Campgrounds
790 Union City Road
Coldwater, MI, 49036
517-278-4315

Decatur, MI

Leisure Valley RV Resort and Campground
40851 CR 669
Decatur, MI, 49045
269-423-7122

Oak Shores Campground
86882 CR 215
Decatur, MI 49045
269-423-7370

Durand, MI

Walnut Hills FamilyCampground and RV Resort
7685 Lehring Road
Durand, MI, 48429
1-866-634-9782

Elk Rapids, MI

Honcho Rest RV Resort
8988 Cairn Hwy.
Elk Rapids, MI 49629
231-264-8548

Empire, MI

Sleepy Bear Campground
6760 W. Empire Hwy. M-72
Empire, MI,.49630
231-326-5566

Fenwick, MI

Snow Lake Campground
644 East Snow Lake Road
Fenwick., MI 48834
989-248-3224

Frankenmuth, MI

Frankenmuth Jellystone Park
1339 West Street
Frankenmuth, MI 48734
989-652-6668

Pine Ridge RV Campground
11700 Gera Road
Frankenmuth., MI 48415
989-624-9029

Grand Junction, MI

Warner Camp
60 - 55th Street
Grand Junction, MI, 49056
269-434-6844

Grayling, MI

River Park Campground and Trout Pond
2607 Peters Road
Grayling, MI 49738
989-517-9092

Harrison, MI

Countryside Campground
805 Byfield Dr.
Harrison, MI, 48625
989-539-5468

Hastings, MI

Whispering Waters Campground
1805 North Irving Road
Hastings, MI 49058
800-985-7019

Holland, MI

Oak Grove Campground Resort
2011 Ottawa Beach Road
Holland, MI, 49424
616-399-9230
Iron Mountain, MI

Summer Breeze Campground
W8576 Twin Falls Road
Iron Mountain, MI, 49801
906-774-7701
Jackson, MI

Greenwood Acres
2401 Hilton Road
Jackson, MI, 49201
517-522-8600

Houghton Lake, MI

Houghton Lake Travel Park
370 Cloverleaf Lane
Houghton Lake, MI 48629
989-422-3931

Sandyoak RV Park
2757 Owens Road
Houghton Lake, MI 48629
989-366-5555

Wooded Acres Family Campground
997 Federal Ave
Houghton Lake, MI 48629
989-422-3413

Kimball, MI

Port Hurron KOA
5111 Lapeer,48074
800-562-0833

Laingsburg, MI

Moon Lake Community and Campground
12700 Colby Lake
Laingsburg, MI, 48848
517-675-7212

Linwood, MI

Hoyle's Marina and Campground
135 S. Linwood Beach Road
Linwood, MI, 48634
989-697-3153

Ludington, MI

Crystal Lake Best Holiday Trav-L Park
1884 West Hansen Road
Ludington, MI 49454
231-757-4510

Poncho's Pond
5335 West Wallace Road
Ludington, MI 49431
888-308-6602

Vacation Station RV Park
4895 West US 10
Ludington, MI 49431
877-856-0390

Mackinaw City, MI

Mackinaw City KOA
Box 616
Mackinaw City, MI, 49701
800-562-1738

Mill Creek Camping

Box 728 M 9730 US-23 and Lake Huron
Mackinaw City, MI, 49701
231-436-5584

Manistee, MI

Matson's Big Manistee River Campground
2680 Bialik Road
Manistee, MI, 49660
888-556-2424

Manistique, MI

Indian Lake Travel Resort
202 South CR 455
Manistique, MI 49854
906-341-2807

Marshall, MI

Tri-Lakes Trails Campground
219 Lyon Lake Road
Marshall, MI, 49068
616-781-2297

Middleville, MI

Indian Valley Campground and Canoe Livery
8200 108th St.
MIddleville, MI,49333
616-891-8579

Monroe, MI

Harbortown RV Resort
14931 LaPlaisance Road
Monroe, MI, 48161
734-384-4700

Muskegon, MI

Muskegon KOA
3500 N. Strand
Muskegon, MI 49445
800-562-3902

Newyago, MI

Little Switzerland Resort and Campground
254 Pickerel Lake Dr.
Newaygo, MI, 49337
231-652-7939

Newberry, MI

Newberry KOA
Route 4, Box 783
Newberry, MI 49868
800-562-5853

Niles, MI

Spaulding Lake Campground
2305 Bell Road
Niles, MI 49120

269-684-1393

North Branch, MI

Washakie Golf and RV Resort
3461 Burnside Road
North Branch, MI, 48461
810-688-3235

Oscoda, MI

Oscoda KOA
3591 Forest Road
Oscoda, MI 48750
800-562-9667

Petersburg, MI

Monroe Co/Toledo North KOA
US 23 at Exit 9
Petersburg, MI 49270
800-562-7646

Totem Pole Park
16333 Lulu Road
Petersburg, MI, 49270
734-279-2110

Petoskey, MI

Petoskey KOA
1800 North US 31
Petoskey, MI 49770
800-562-0253

Port Austin, MI

Port Austin KOA
8195 North Van Dyke
Port Austin, MI 48467
800-562-5211

Riverside, MI

Benton Harbor/St. Joseph KOA
3527 Coloma Road
Riverside, MI 49084
800-562-5341

Roscommon, MI

Higgins Hills RV Park
3800 West Federal Hwy.
Roscommon, MI, 48653
800-478-8151

Scottville, MI

Crystal Lake Campground
1884 W. Hansen Road
Scottville, MI 49454
616-757-4510

Smyrna, MI

Double R Ranch Camping Resort

4424 Whites Bridge Road
Smyrna, MI 48809
800-734-3575

6680 Bunton Road
Ypsilanti, MI 48197
800-562-7603

St. Ignace, MI

Castle Rock Mackinas\c Trail Campark
2811 Mackinac Trail
St. Ignace, MI 49781
800-333-8754

Lakeshore Park
416 Pte. LaBarbe Road
St. Ignace, MI, 49781
906-643-9522

St. Ignace/Mackinac Island KOA
1242 US 2 W
St. Ignace, MI 49781
800-562-0534

Sumner, MI

Leisure Lake FaMI
ly Campground
54 S. Warner Road
Sumner, MI, 48889
989-875-4689

Traverse City, MI

Timber Ridge Campground
4050 Hammond Road
Traverse City, MI,49686
231-947-2770

Holiday Park Campground
4860 US 31 South
Traverse City, MI 49864
231-943-4410

Timber Ridge Campground
4050 Hammond Road
Traverse City, MI 49686
800-909-2327

Tustin, MI

Cadillac KOA
23163 M-115
Tustin, MI 49688
800-562-4072

Zeeland, MI

Dutch Treat Camping and Recreation
10300 Gordon
Zeeland, MI, 49464
616-772-4303

Ypsilanti, MI

Detroit/Greenfield KOA

Minnesota

Aitkin, MN

Big "K" Campground
RR2, Box 965
Aitkin, MN 56431
218-927-6001

Buck's Resort
Rt. 1, Box 284
Aitkin, MN 56431
218-678-3787

Farm Island Lake Resort & Campground
Rt. 2, Box 225
Aitkin, MN 56431
218-927-3841

Akeley, MN

City of Akeley Park & Campground
P.O. Box 67
Akeley, MN 56433
218-652-2172

Albert Lea, MN

Hickory Hills Campground
15694 717th ave
Albert Lea, MN 56007
507-852-4555

Alexandria, MN

Eden Acres Resort
5181 Fish Hook Drive SW
Alexandria, MN 56308
320-763-7434

Greenwood Bay RV Park
754 W. Lake Cowdry Road NW
Alexandria, MN 56308
320-763-7391

Hillcrest RV Park & Campground
715 Birch Ave
Alexandria, MN 56308
320-763-6330

Sun Valley Resort & Campground
10045 State Hwy. 27
Alexandria, MN 56308
320-866-5417

Altura, MN

Lazy D Campground
Rt. 1, Box 252

Altura, MN 55910
507-932-3098

Andover, MN

Bunker Hills Campground
550 Bunker Lake Blvd.
Andover, MN 55304
612-757-3920

Annandale, MN

Schroeder County Park
9201 Ireland Ave.
Annandale, MN 55302
320-274-8870

Apple Valley, MN

Labanon Hills Regional Park Campground
12100 Johnny Cake Ridge Road
Apple Valley, MN 55124
612-454-9211

Ashby, MN

Ashby Resort & Campground
P.O. Box 57
Ashby, MN 56309
218-747-2959

Sundowner Campground & RV Park
RT. 1, Box 145
Ashby, MN 56309
218-747-2931

Austin, MN

Beaver Trails Campground
Rt. 5, Box 71J
Austin, MN 55912
507-584-6611

Riverbend Campground
Rt. 3, Box 122-A
Austin, MN 55912
507-325-4637

Alexandria, MN

Sun Valley Resort and Campground
10045 MN 27 West
Alexandria, MN 56308
320-886-5417

Altura, MN

Lazy D Campground
RR1 Box 252
Altura, MN 55910
507-932-3098

Whitewater State Park

Rte. ! Box 256
Altura, MN 55910
507-932-3007

Babbitt, MN

Birch Lake RV Park & Campgrounds
2015 Hwy. 623
Babbitt, MN 57706
218-827-2342

Backus, MN

Lindsey Lake Campground
RR 1, Box 383
Backus, MN 56435
218-947-4728

Pine Mountain Lake Seasonal Campground
Rt. 2, Box 51
Backus, MN 56435
218-587-4315

Bagley, MN

Bagley City Park Campground
P.O. Box 178
Bagley, MN 56621
218-694-2871

Long Lake Park & Campground
213 Main Ave. N
Bagley, MN 56621
218-657-2275

Barnum, MN

Bear Lake Park Campground
P.O. Box 101
Barnum, MN 55707
218-389-3162

Bent Trout Lake Campground
2928 Bent Trout Lake Road
Barnum, MN 55707
218-389-6322

Battle Lake, MN

Sunset Beach Resort & Campground
RR3, Box 181
Battle Lake, MN 56515
218-583-2750

Bemidji, MN

Big Wolf Lake Resort & Campground
12150 Walleye Lane
Bemidji, MN 56601
218-751-5749

Hamilton's Fox Lake Campground
2555 Island View Dr.

Bemidji, MN 56601
218-586-2231

Bena, MN

Nodak Lodge
15080 Nodak Drive
Bena, MN 56626
800-752-2758

Benson, MN

Ambush Park
W. Hwy. 9
Benson, MN 56215
320-843-4775

Swift Falls County Park
P.O. Box 241
Benson, MN 56215
320-843-4900

Big Falls, MN

Big Falls Campground
410 2nd St. NW
Big Falls, MN 56627
218-276-2282

Big Lake, MN

Shady River Campground
21353 Cty. Road 5
Big Lake, MN 55309
612-263-3705

Blackduck, MN

Bunk's Territory Resort & RV Park
HC 3, Box 183A
Blackduck, MN 56630
218-335-2324

Lost Acres Resort & Campground
HC 3, Box 162D, Kitchi Lake
Blackduck, MN 56630
800-835-6414

Blooming Prarie, MN

Brookside Campground
RR 1, Box 60A
Blooming Prarie, MN 55917
507-583-2979

Blue Earth, MN

Fairground Campsite
Fairbault County Fairground, N. Main & 11
Blue Earth, MN 56013
507-526-2916

Brainerd, MN

Don & Mayva's Crow Wing Lake Camp

8831 Crow Wing Camp Road SW
Brainerd, MN 56401
218-829-6468

Greer Lake Campground
1601 Minnesota Dr.
Brainerd, MN
218-828-2565

Gull & Love Lake Marina & Campground
5617 Love Lake Road, NW
Brainerd, MN 56401
218-829-8130

Rock Lake Campground
1601 Minnesota Dr.
Brainerd, MN 56401
218-828-2565

Shady Hollow Resort & Campground
P.O. Box 207
Brainerd, MN 56401
218-828-9308

Sullivan's Resort and Campground
7685 CR 127
Brainerd, MN 56401
888-829-5697

Twin Oaks Resort
1777 Nokay Lake Road
Brainerd, MN 56401
218-764-2965

Breckenridge, MN

Welles Memorial Park & Fairgrounds
420 Nebraska Ave.
Breckenridge, MN 56520
218-643-3455

Breezy Point, MN

Highview Campground & RV Park
HC 83, Box 1084
Breezy Point, MN 56472
218-543-4526

Caledonia, MN

Dunromin' Park Campground
Rt. 1, Box 146
Caledonia, MN 55921
800-822-2514

Canby, MN

Stonehill Park
Stonehill Park, Box 2
Canby, MN 56220

507-223-7586

Cannon Falls, MN

Lake Byllesby Reg'l Park Campground
7650 Echo Point Road
Cannon Falls, MN 55009
507-263-4447

Cass Lake, MN

Cass Lake Lodge Resort & RV Park
Rt. 2, Box 60
Cass Lake, MN 56633
218-335-6658

Marclay Point Campground, Inc.
Rt. 2, Box 80F
Cass Lake, MN 56633
218-335-6589

Stony Point Resort, Trailer Park & Campground
P.O. Box 518
Cass Lake, MN 56633
218-335-6311

Clearwater, MN

A-J Acres Campground
1300-195th St. E
Clearwater, MN 55320
320-558-2847

St. Cloud/Clearwater KOA
2454 Cty. Road 143
Clearwater, MN 55320
320-558-2876

St. Cloud/Clearwater/I-94 KOA
2454 CR 143
Clearwater, MN 55320
800-562-5025

Cleveland, MN

Beaver Dam Resort
German & Jefferson Lake, RR 1, Box 202
Cleveland, MN 56017
507-931-5650

Cloquet, MN

Cloquet/Duluth KOA
1479 Old Carlton Road
Cloquet, MN 55720
800-562-9506

Cohasset, MN

Sugar Bay Campgrounds/Resort
805 N. Sugar Bay Dr.
Cohasset, MN 55721

218-326-8493

Cokato, MN

Cokato Lake Country Campground
2945 Cty. Road 4 SW
Cokato, MN 55321
320-286-5779

Collinwood Regional Park
17251-70th St. SW
Cokato, MN 55320
320-286-2801

Coleraine, MN

Greenway Lions Beach & Campsite Area
P.O. Box 696
Coleraine, MN 55722
218-245-3382

Crane Lake, MN

Beddow's Campground
7516 Bayside Dr.
Crane Lake, MN 55725
218-993-2389

Cromwell, MN

Island Lake Campground
1391 Middle Road
Cromwell, MN 55726
218-644-3543

Crookston, MN

Crookston Central Park
Ash St. & Mitchell Lane
Crookston, MN 56716
218-281-1242

Currie, MN

Schreier's On Shetek Campground
35 Resort Road
Currie, MN 56123
507-763-3817

Cushing, MN

Fish Trap Campground
30894 Fish Trap Lake Dr.
Cushing, MN 56443
218-575-2603

Dassel, MN

Lake Dale Campground
24473 CSAH 4
Dassel, MN 55325
612-275-3387

Deer River, MN

Backwoods Resort & RV Park

Rt. 1, Box 299A
Deer River, MN 56636
218-246-2542

Moose Lake Campground
Box 157
Deer River, MN 56636
218-246-8343

Northern Acres Resort & Campground
HCR 3, Box 446
Deer River, MN 56636
218-798-2845

Deerwood, MN

Camp Holiday Resort & Campground
17467 Round Lake Road
Deerwood, MN 56444
218-678-2495

Dalois Campground
685 Katrine Dr. NE
Deerwood, MN 56444
218-678-2203

Detroit Lakes, MN

American Legion Campground
810 W. Lake Dr.
Detroit Lakes, MN 56501
218-847-3759

Country Campground
13639 260th ave
Detroit Lakes, MN 56501
800-898-7901

Forest Hills RV Resort & Golf Course
RR 1, Box 6
Detroit Lakes, MN 56501
218-439-6033

Long Lake Campsite
Rt. 3, Box 301
Detroit Lakes, MN 56501
218-847-8920

Duluth, MN

Buffalo Valley Camping
2590 Guss Road
Duluth, MN 55810
218-624-9901

Indian Post Campground
75th Ave. W & Grand Ave. (Hwy. 23)
Duluth, MN 55807
218-624-5637

Island Beach Campground
6640 Fredenberg Lake Road
Duluth, MN 55803
218-721-3292

East Grand Forks, MN

River's Edge Campground
P.O. Box 295
East Grand Forks, MN 56721
218-773-7481

Effie, MN

Larson Lake Campground
P.O. Box 95
Effie, MN 56639
218-743-3694

Lost Lake Campground
P.O. Box 95
Effie, MN 56639
218-743-3694

Owen Lake Campground
P.O. Box 95
Effie, MN 56639
218-743-3694

Elbow Lake, MN

Tipsinah Mounds Campground/Park
Rt. 2, Box 52A
Elbow Lake, MN 56531
218-685-5114

Ely, MN

Canoe Country Campground
Box 30
Ely, MN 55731
218-365-4046

Fall Lake Campground
5721A CBO Road
Ely, MN 55731
218-365-5638

Superior Forest Lodge
HC 1, Box 3199
Ely, MN 55731
218-365-4870

Timber Trail Resort & Campground
HC 1, Box 3111
Ely, MN 55731
218-365-4879

Timber Wolf Lodge
P.O. Box 147

Ely, MN 55731
218-827-3512

Fairbault, MN

Camp Faribo
21851 Bagley Ave
Fairbault, MN 55021
800-689-8453

Fairfax, MN

Valley View Campground
RR. 1, Box 111
Fairfax, MN 55322
507-426-7420

Fairmont, MN

Flying Goose Campground
Rt. 2, Box 274
Fairmont, MN 56031
507-235-3458

Faribault, MN

Camp Faribo Campground/RV Park
21851 Bagley Ave.
Faribault, MN 55021
507-332-8453

Maiden Rock Campgrounds
22661 Dodge Ct.
Faribault, MN 55021
507-685-4430

Roberds Lake Resort & Campground
18192 Roberd Lake Blvd.
Faribault, MN 55021
800-879-5091

Farwell, MN

Wildridge Lakeside Campground
2221 Reuben's Lane SW
Farwell, MN 56327
320-886-5370

Fergus Falls, MN

Elks Point
P.O. Box 502, Rt. 1
Fergus Falls, MN 56537
218-736-5244

Swan Lake Resort
Rt. 6, Box 426
Fergus Falls, MN 56537
218-736-4626

Finlayson, MN

Waldheim Resort

906 Waldheim Ln.
Finlayson, MN 55735
320-233-7405

Forest Lake, MN

Timm's Marina & Campground
9080 N. Jewel Lane
Forest Lake, MN 55025
612-464-3890

Fosston, MN

City of Fosston Campground
Fosston Fairgrounds
Fosston, MN 56542
218-435-1806

Frazee, MN

Birchmere Family Resort & Campground
Rt. 1, Box 159
Frazee, MN 56544
218-334-5741

Garden City, MN

Shady Oaks
340 Fairgrounds St.
Garden City, MN 56034
507-546-3986

Garfield, MN

Alexandria Oak Park Kampground
9561 Cty. Road 8 NW
Garfield, MN 56322
320-834-2345

Garrison, MN

Wigwam Inn
18271 460th St.
Garrison, MN 56450
320-692-4579

Gilbert, MN

Gilbert Sherwood Forest Campground
City Hall, Box 549, 16 S. Broadway St.
Gilbert, MN 55741
218-749-0703

Glenwood, MN

Barsness Park/Chalet
137 E. Minnesota Ave.
Glenwood, MN 56334
320-634-5433

El Reno Resort & Campground
Rt. 1, Box 80
Glenwood, MN 56334
320-283-5594

Woodlawn Resort & Campground
2370 N. Lakeshore Dr.
Glenwood, MN 56334
320-634-3619

Grand Marais, MN

Gunflint Pines Resort
217 S. Gunflint Lake
Grand Marais, MN 55604
218-388-4454

Grand Marais Recreation Area & RV Park
P.O. Box 820
Grand Marais, MN 55604
218-387-1712

Gunflint Pines
217 S. Gunflint Lake Road
Grand Marais, MN 55604
218-388-4454

Hungry Jack Lodge & Campground
475 Cunflint Trail
Grand Marais, MN 55604
218-388-2265

NOr'Wester Lodge
7778 Gunflint Trail
Grand Marais, MN 55604
218-388-2252

Grand Rapids, MN

Birch Cove Resort & Campground
431 Southwood Road
Grand Rapids, MN 55744
218-326-8754

Prairie Lake Campgrounds
400 Wabana Road
Grand Rapids, MN 55744
218-326-8486

Sugar Bay Campground/Resort
21812 Moose Point Road
Grand Rapids, MN 55721
218-326-8493

Hackensack, MN

Quietwoods Campground
HC 75, Box 568
Hackensack, MN 56452
218-675-6240

Ham Lake, MN

Ham Lake Campground
2400 Constance Blvd.
Ham Lake, MN 55304

612-434-5337

Harmony, MN

Amish Country Camping
RR 2, Box 418
Harmony, MN 55939
507-886-6731

Hastings, MN

Greenwood Campground
13797 190th St. E.
Hastings, MN 55033
612-437-5269

Hawick, MN

Old Wagon Campground
21611-132nd St. NE
Hawick, MN 56246
320-354-2165

Henderson, MN

Allanson's Park
900 S. St.
Henderson, MN 56044
507-248-3234

Henricks, MN

Lake Hendricks Campground
City Hall
Henricks, MN 56136
507-275-3192

Hibbing, MN

Bear Lake Campground
1208 E. Howard St.
Hibbing, MN 55746
218-262-6760

Button Box Lake Campground
1208 E. Howard St
Hibbing, MN 55746
218-262-6760

Forest Heights RV Park
2240 East 25th St
Hibbing, MN 55746
218-263-5782

Thistledew Lake Campground
1208 E. Howard St.
Hibbing, MN 55746
218-262-6760

Hill City, MN

Ann Lake Campground
P.O. Box 9

Hill City, MN 55748
218-697-2476

Hay Lake Campground
P.O. Box 9
Hill City, MN 55748
218-697-2476

Hinckley, MN

Boulder Campground
Rt. 2, Box 386B
Hinckley, MN 55037
612-384-6146

Grand Casino Hinckley RV Resort/Chalets
Rt. 3, Box 14
Hinckley, MN 55037
800-995-4726

Pathfinder Village
Hwy. 48, Rt. 3, Box 233
Hinckley, MN 55037
320-384-7726

Snake River Campground
Rt. 2, Box 386 B
Hinckley, MN 55037
320-384-6146

St. Croix Haven Campground
Rt. 3, Box 385
Hinckley, MN 55037
320-655-7989

St Croix State Park
30065 St. Croix Park Road
Hinckley, MN 55037

Houston, MN

Money Creek Haven
RR 1, Box 154
Houston, MN 55943
507-896-3544

Hoyt Lakes, MN

Fisherman's Point Campground
206 Kennedy Memorial Dr.
Hoyt Lakes, MN 55750
218-225-2344

Hutchinson, MN

Masonic/West River Park
900 Harrington
Hutchinson, MN 55350
320-587-2975

International Falls, MN
Arnold's Campground & RV Park
Hwy. 53 & 21st St.
International Falls, MN 56649
218-285-9100

Isanti, MN
Country Camping Tent & RV Park
750-273rd Aven. NW
Isanti, MN 55040
612-444-9626

Dickies Portside Resort
Mille Lacs Lake, 42089 Vista Road
Isanti, MN 56342
320-676-8795

Eastside Marina, Inc.
HC 69, Box 150
Isanti, MN 56342
320-676-8735

South Isle Family Campground
Rt. 1, Box 228
Isanti, MN 56342
320-676-8538

Jackson, MN
Loon Lake Campground
405-4th St.
Jackson, MN 56143
507-847-2240

Jordan, MN
MPLS SW/US 169/Jordan-Shakopee KOA
3315 W 166th St.
Jordan, MN 55352
800-562-6317

Kabetogama Lake, MN
Cedar Cove Campsites & Resort
9940 Gappa Road
Kabetogama Lake, MN 56669
218-875-3851

Kelliher, MN
Rogers' On Red Lake Campground/RV Park
49690 Rogers Rd NE
Kelliher, MN 56650
218-647-8262

Knife River, MN
Depot Campground & Cafe
P.O. Box 115,
Knife River, MN 55609
218-834-5044

Lake City, MN
Kruger Recreation Area
1801 S. Oak
Lake City, MN 55041
612-345-3216

Lake Pepin Campground & Trailer Court
1818 N. High St.
Lake City, MN 55041
612-345-2909

Lanesboro, MN
Eable Cliff Campground & Lodging
RR 1, Box 344
Lanesboro, MN 55949
507-467-2598

Laporte, MN
Pine Beach Resort & Campground
Rt. 1, Box 40
Laporte, MN 56461
218-224-2313

LeSueur, MN
Peaceful Valley Campsites
213 Peaceful Valley Road
LeSueur, MN 56058
507-665-2297

Lindstrom, MN
Hillcrest RV Park
32715 North Lakes Trail
Lindstrom, MN 55045
612-257-5352

Whispering Bay Resort
114430 291st St. N
Lindstrom, MN 55045
612-257-1784

Lino Lakes, MN
Rice Creek Campground
7401 Main St.
Lino Lakes, MN 55038
612-757-3920

Litchfield, MN
Lake Ripley Campground
East Shore/Lake Ripley, P.O. Box 820-C
Litchfield, MN 55355
320-693-8184

Little Falls, MN
Charles A. Lindbergh State Park
1615 Lindbergh S
Little Falls, MN 56345

320-616-2525

Fletcher Creek Campground
Rt. 5, Box 93A
Little Falls, MN 56345
320-632-9636

Littlefork, MN

Lofgren Park
413 Fourth Ave.
Littlefork, MN 56653
218-278-6710

Longville, MN

Holiday Haven Lakeview Resort
HC 2, Box 165, Mute Lake
Longville, MN 56655
218-363-2473

Longville Campground "Austin's Swamp"
P.O. Box 404
Longville, MN 56655
218-363-2610

Lonsdale, MN

Shields Lake Campground
14398 Irwin Path
Lonsdale, MN 55046
507-334-8526

Madelia, MN

Watona Park
116 W. Main
Madelia, MN 56062
507-642-3245

Madison Lake, MN

Point Pleasant Resort & Campground
400 Sheppard Circle
Madison Lake, MN 56063
507-243-3611

Sakatah Trail Campground
301 Main St., Box 191
Madison Lake, MN 56063
507-243-3886

Mahnomen, MN

Shooting Star Lodge Campgrounds
P.O. Box 418, Casino Dr.
Mahnomen, MN 56557
218-935-2701

Mankato, MN

Bray Park Blue Earth County Park
35 Map Dr.

Mankato, MN 56001
507-625-3281

Daly Park Blue Earth County Park
35 Map Dr.
Mankato, MN 56001
507-625-3281

Land of Memories Campground
P.O. Box 3368
Mankato, MN 56002
507-387-8649

Maple Lake, MN

Olson's Campgrounds
5669 123rd St. NW
Maple Lake, MN 55358
320-963-5175

Mazeppa, MN

Ponderosa Campground
RR 1, Box 209
Mazeppa, MN 55956
507-843-3611

Menahga, MN

Menahga Memorial Forest Park
825 Aspen Ave.
Menahga, MN 56464
218-564-4557

Montevideo, MN

Lagoon Park Campground
103 Canton Ave.
Montevideo, MN 56265
320-269-5527

Moorhead, MN

Moorhead/Fargo KOA
Route 4, Box 168
Moorhead, MN 56560
800-562-0217

Moose Lake, MN

Gavert Campground
Rt. 2, 701 Kenwood
Moose Lake, MN 55767
218-485-5400

Red Fox Campground & RV Park
P.O. Box 10
Moose Lake, MN 55767
218-569-4181

Willow River Campground
Rt. 2, 701S Kenwood

Moose Lake, MN 55767
218-485-5400

Mora, MN

Camperville
2351-310th Ave.
Mora, MN 55051
320-679-2336

Riverview Campground
764 Fish Lake Dr.
Mora, MN 55051
320-679-3275

Morris, MN

Pomme De Terre Campground
Cty. Road 10
Morris, MN 56267
320-589-3141

Morton, MN

Jackpot Junction Casino HOtel Campground
P.O. Box 400
Morton, MN 56270
507-644-2645

Mountain Iron, MN

West Two Rivers Reservoir Campground
Campground Road
Mountain Iron, MN 55768
218-735-8831

N. Jackson, MN

Jackson KOA
2035 Hwy. 71
N. Jackson, MN 56143
800-562-5670

Nisswa, MN

Fritz's Resort
P.O. Box 803
Nisswa, MN 56468
218-568-8988

Upper Cullen Campground
Upper Cullen Lake, Box 72
Nisswa, MN 56468
218-963-2249

Ogilvie, MN

Hilltop Family Campground
2186 Empire St.
Ogilvie, MN 56358
320-272-4300

Orr, MN

Ash River Campground

P.O. Box 306, 4656 Hwy. 53
Orr, MN 55771
218-757-3274

Cabin O'Pines Resort & Campground
Box CG, 4378 Pelican Road
Orr, MN 55771
800-757-3122

Hidden Hills Campground
10247 Ash River Trail
Orr, MN 55771
218-374-4412

Pine Acres Resort & Campground
4498C Pine Acres Road
Orr, MN 55771
218-757-3144

Sunset Resort & Campground
Ash River Trail
Orr, MN 55771
218-374-3161

Woodenfrog Campground
P.O. Box 306, 4656 Hwy. 52
Orr, MN 55771
218-757-3274

Ortonville, MN

Lakeshore RV Park & Fruit Farm
RT. 1, Box 95
Ortonville, MN 56278
320-839-3701

Osakis, MN

Blacks Crescent Beach Resort/Campground
Box 416EM, Lake Osakis
Osakis, MN 56360
320-859-2127

Owatonna, MN

Hope Oak Knoll Inc.
Rt. 2, Box 71
Owatonna, MN 55060
507-451-2998

Owatonna Campgrounds, Inc.
2554 SW 28th St.
55060
507-451-8050

Park Rapids, MN

Big Pines Tent & RV Park
501 S. Central Ave.
Park Rapids, MN 56470
218-732-4483

Breeze Camping Resort
HC 05, Box 210
Park Rapids, MN 56470
218-732-5888

Hungry Man Lake Campground
607 W. 1st St.
Park Rapids, MN 56470
218-732-3309

Itasca State Park
36750 Main Park Road
Park Rapids, MN 56470
218-266-2129

Mantrap Lake Campground
607 W. 1st St, Hwy. 34
Park Rapids, MN 56470
218-732-3309

Round Bay Resort & RV Park
Rt. 4, Box 133C
Park Rapids, MN 56470
218-732-4880

Sleeping Fawn Resort & Campground
Rt. 3, Box 271
Park Rapids, MN 56470
218-732-5356

Spruce Hill Campground
Rt. 4, Box 449
Park Rapids, MN 56470
218-732-3292

Vagabond Village Campground
HC 06, Box 381-A
Park Rapids, MN 56470
218-732-5234

Paynesville, MN

Koronis Regional Park
51625 CSAH 20
Paynesville, MN 56362
320-276-8843

Pelican Rapids, MN

Pelican Hills Park
Rt. 4, Box 218-B
Pelican Rapids, MN 56572
218-532-3726

Pennington, MN

Paradise Resort
HC 3, Box 204

Pennington, MN 56663
218-835-6514

Pequot Lakes, MN

Clint Converse Memorial Campground
Box 27
Pequot Lakes, MN 56472
218-568-4566

Rager's Acres
Rt. 2, Box 348
Pequot Lakes, MN 56472
218-568-8752

Pine City, MN

Pokegama Lake RV Park & Golf Course
RR 4, Box 54
Pequot Lakes, MN 55063
800-248-6552

Pine Island, MN

Wazionia Campground
6450-120th St. NW
Pine Island, MN 55963
507-356-8594

Pine River, MN

River View RV Park
3040 16th ave SW
Pine River, MN 56474
218-587-4112

Pipestone, MN

Pipestone RV Campground
919 N. Hiawatha Ave.
Pipestone, MN 56164
507-825-2455

Ponsford, MN

Tamarac Resort & Campground
Rt. 1, Box 351
Ponsford, MN 56575
218-575-3262

Preston, MN

Hidden Valley Campground
RTE 1
Preston, MN 55965
507-765-2467

The Old Barn Resort
Rt. 3, Box 57
55965
507-467-2512

Prior Lake, MN

Dakotah Meadows RV & Park Home
Campground
2341 Park Place
Prior Lake, MN 55372
612-445-8800

Fish Lake Acres Campground
3000-210th St. E.
Prior Lake, MN 55372
612-492-3393

Red Wing, MN

Hay Creek Valley Campground
31673 Hwy. 58 Blvd.
Red Wing, MN 55066
612-388-3998

Island Camping & Marina
2361 Hallquist Ave.
Red Wing, MN 55066
715-792-2502

Treasure Island RV Park
P.O. Box 75, 5734 Sturgeon Lk. Road
Red Wing, MN 55066
800-222-7077

Remer, MN

Big Springs Resort & Campground
HCR 3, Box 101
Remer, MN 56672
218-566-2322

Richmond, MN

Browns Lake Resort & Campground
18091 Browns Lake Road
Richmond, MN 56368
320-597-2611

El Rancho Manana Campground & Riding Stable
27301M Ranch Road
Richmond, MN 56368
320-597-2740

Yoru Haven Campground & Seasonal RV Park
18337 State Hwy. 22
Richmond, MN 56368
320-597-2450

Richville, MN

Head Lake Camp
P.O. Box 66
Richville, MN 56576
218-346-7200

Northern Lights Resort
Rt. 1, Box 147

Richville, MN 56576
218-758-2343

Rochester, MN

Brookside RV Park
516-17th Ave. NW
Rochester, MN 55901
507-288-1413

Rochester/Marion KOA
5232 65th Ave. SE
Rochester, MN 55904
800-562-5232

Rochester/Marion KOA
5232-65th Ave. SE
Rochester, MN 55904
507-288-0785

Rogers, MN

Minneapolis NW/Maple Grove KOA
Box 214
Rogers, MN 55374
800-562-0261

Royalton, MN

Two Rivers Park
P.O. Box 137
Royalton, MN 56373
320-584-5125

Rush City, MN

Rush Lake Resort
51170 Rush Lake Trail
Rush City, MN 55069
320-358-4427

Rutledge, MN

Pine River Campground
7201 Hwy. 61
Rutledge, MN 55795
320-233-7678

Savage, MN

Town & Country Campground
12630 Boone Ave. S
Savage, MN 55378
612-445-1756

Schroeder, MN

Lamb's Campgrounds & Cabins
North Shore, P.O. Box 415
Schroeder, MN 55613
218-663-7292

Sebeka, MN

Huntersville Forest Campground

Rt. 2, Box 330
Sebeka, MN 56477
218-472-3262

Shell City Campground
Rt. 2, Box 320
Sebeka, MN 56477
218-472-3262

Shakopee, MN

Shakopee Valley RV Park
1245 E. Bluff Ave.
Shakopee, MN 55379
612-445-7313

Side Lake, MN

CC Campground 717
7595 McCarthy Beach Road, P.O. Box 302
Side Lake, MN 55781
218-254-5301

Pine Beach Resort & Campground
7504 McCarthy Beach Road, P.O. Box 5
Side Lake, MN 55781
218-254-3144

Timberwoods Resort & Campground
10255 Nevens Ave. NW
Side Lake, MN 55382
320-274-5140

Spring Grove, MN

Supersaw Valley Campground
RR 2
Spring Grove, MN 55974
507-498-5880

Spring Lake, MN

Edgewater 4-Season Resort & RV Park
HCR 1, Box 240C
Spring Lake, MN 56680
218-798-2620

Ghost Bay Mobile Home & RV Resort
HCR1 Box 238
Spring Lake, MN 56680
218-798-2128

Springfield, MN

Riverside Park & Campground
2 E. Central
Springfield, MN 56087
507-723-4416

St. Anthony Villa, MN

Lowry Grove Campground

2501 Lowry Ave.NE
St. Anthony Villa, MN 55148
612-781-3148

St. Cloud, MN

St. Cloud Campground & RV Park
2491 2nd St. SE
St. Cloud, MN 56304
(612) 251-4463

St. Paul, MN

St. Paul East KOA
568 Cottage Grove Dr.
St. Paul, MN 55129
612-436-6436

Stanchfield, MN

Springvale Campground
36955 Palm St. NW
Stanchfield, MN 55080
612-689-3208

Staples, MN

Dower Lake Recreational Area
Staples, MN 56479
218-894-2550

Stillwater, MN

Golden Acres RV Park & Picnic Area
15150 Square Lake Trail N.
Stillwater, MN 55082
612-439-1147

Sturgeon Lake, MN

Edelweiss Resort & Campground
Rt. 2
Sturgeon Lake, MN 55783
218-372-3363

Timberline Best Holiday Trav-L-Park
Rt. 1, Box 20, Timberline Road
Sturgeon Lake, MN 55783
218-372-3272

Timberline Campground
Rt. 1, Box 20
Sturgeon Lake, MN 55783
218-372-3272

Taylors Falls, MN

Camp Waub-O-Jeeg
2185 Chicago St.
Taylors Falls, MN 55084
612-465-5721

Wildwood Campground

P.O. Box 235
Taylors Falls, MN 55084
612-465-6315

Tenstrike, MN

Gull Lake Campgriund
10647 Clydesdale Cir. NE
Tenstrike, MN 56683
218-586-2842

Theilman, MN

Whippoorwill Ranch Kampground
RR 1, Box 145
Theilman, MN 55978
507-534-3590

Thief River Falls, MN

Thief River Falls Tourist Park
Hw. 32 S. & Oakland Park Road
Thief River Falls, MN 56701
218-681-2519

Toomsuba, MN

Meridian East/Toomsuba KOA
3953 KOA Campground Road
Toomsuba, MN 39364
800-562-4202

Tower, MN

Hoodoo Point Campgrounds
P.O. Box 576
Tower, MN 55790
218-753-4070

Moccasin Point Resort
Box 4650 Moccasin Point
Tower, MN 55790
218-753-3309

Two Harbors, MN

Big Blaze Campground
Big Blaze Circle
Two Harbors, MN 55616
218-834-2512

Burlington Bay Campground
Hwy. 61
Two Harbors, MN 55616
218-834-2021

Eckbeck Camground
120 State Road
Two Harbors, MN 55616
218-834-6602

Finland Campground
120 State Road

Two Harbors, MN 55616
218-834-6602

Indian Lake Campground
120 State Road
Two Harbors, MN 55616
218-834-6602

Wagon Wheel Campground
W. Star Rt., Box 92
Two Harbors, MN 55616
218-834-4901

Wabasha, MN

Pioneer Camp
130 Pioneer Drive
Wabasha, MN 55981
612-565-2242

Wadena, MN

Sunnybrook Park Campground
P.O. Box 30
Wadena, MN 56482
218-631-2884

Walker, MN

Anderson's Cove Campground/Resort
HC 73, Box 508
Walker, MN 56484
218-547-2999

Anderson's Northland Lodge
HCR 84, Box 376
Walker, MN 56484
800-247-1719

Bayview Resort & Campground
P.O. Box 58
Walker, MN 56484
218-547-1595

Moonlight Bay Resort and Campground on
Leech Lake
6409 Wedgewood Rd NW
Walker, MN 56484
888-973-7078

Shores of Leech Lake Campground & Marina
P.O. Box 327
Walker, MN 56484
218-547-1819

Waters Edge RV Park
HCR 73, Box 530
Walker, MN 56484
218-547-3552

Waseca, MN

Kiesler's Campground on Clear Lake
P.O. Box 503
Waseca, MN 56093
507-835-3179

Waterville, MN

Kamp Dels
Rt. 2, Box 49
Waterville, MN 56096
507-362-8616

Watkins, MN

Clear Lake Campground
36649 657th Ave.
Watkins, MN 55389
320-764-2592

Waubun, MN

Elk Horn Resort & Campground
Rt 2., Box 323
Waubun, MN 56589
218-935-5437

Oxbow Resort & Campground
RR 2, Box 217
Waubun, MN 56589
218-734-2244

Welcome, MN

KC's Welcome Campground
RR 1, Box 127A
Welcome, MN 56181
507-728-8811

Williams, MN

Zippel Bay Resort
HC 2, Box 51
Williams, MN 56686
218-783-6235

Willow River, MN

Wilderness Campgrounds
Long Lake Road
Willow River, MN 55795
218-372-3993

Winona, MN

Winona KOA
Route 6, Box 18-I
Winona, MN 55987
800-562-0843

Woodbury, MN

St. Paul East KOA

568 Cottage Grove Dr.
Woodbury, MN 55129
800-562-3640

Worthington, MN

Olson Park Campground
P.O. Box 279
Worthington, MN 56187
507-372-8650

Young America, MN

Baylor Regional Park Campground
10775 Cty. Road 33
Young America, MN 55397
612-467-4200

Zimmerman, MN

Camp in the Woods
14791 289th Ave.
Zimmerman, MN 55398
612-389-2516

Zumbro Falls, MN

Bluff Valley Campground, Inc.
RR 1, Box 194
Zumbro Falls, MN 55991
507-753-2955

Shades of Sherwood Camping Area
14334 Sherwood Tr.
Zumbro Falls, MN 55992
507-732-5100

Zumbro Valley Sportsman's Park
P.O. Box 91
Zumbro Falls, MN 55991
507-753-2568

Mississippi

Aberdeen, MS

Blue Bluff
20051 Blue Bluff Road
Aberdeen, MN 39730
662-369-2832

Bay St. Louis, MS

Casino Magic RV Park
711 Casino Magic Drive
Bay St., MS 39520
800 5-magic-5

Biloxi, MS

Mazalea Travel Park
8220 West Oaklawn Road
Biloxi, MS 39532
228-392-8575

Parker's Landing
7577 East Oaklawn Road
Biloxi, MS 39532
228-392-7717

Collinsville, MS

Twitley Branch Camping Area
Okatibee Lake
9200 Hamrick Rd N
Collinsville, MS 39352
601-626-8431

Columbus, MS

DeWayne Hayes Campground
7934 Barton Ferry Road
Columbus, MS 39701
662-434-6939

Lake Lowndes State Park
3319 Lake Lowndes Road
Columbus, MS 39702
662-328-2110

Town Creek Campground
3606 West Plymouth Road
Columbus, MS 39773
662-327-2142

Dennis, MS

Piney Grove Campground
82 Bay Springs Resources Road
Dennis, MS 38859
662-728-1134

Whitten Park Campground
82 Bay Springs Resources Road
Dennis, MS 38859
662-862-7070

Enid, MS

Wallace Creek Campground
264 CR 39
Enid, MS 38927
877-444-6777

Gulfport, MS

Baywood Campground RV Park
1100 Cowan Road
Gulfport, MS 39507
228-896-4840

Gaywood Best Holiday Trav-L-Park
1100 Cowan Road
Gulfport, MS 39507
228-896-4840

Ocean Springs, MS

Ocean Springs/Biloxi KOA
7501 Hwy. 57
Ocean Springs, MS 39564
800-562-7028

Toomsuba, MS

Meridian East-Toomsuba KOA
3953 KOA Campground Road
Toomsuba, MS 39364
601-632-1684

Missouri

Arcadia, MO

Black Stallion Camp/RN Park
RR!, Box 184
Arcadia, MO 63621
573-546-0013

Barnhart, MO

St. Louis South KOA
8000 Metropolitan Blvd.
Barnhart, MO 63012
800-562-3049

Branson, MO

Acorn Acres RV Park & Campground
(417) 338-2500

America's Best Campground
(800) 671-4399

Blue Mountain Campground
(417) 338-2114

Branson KOA
1025 Headwaters Road
Branson, MO 65616
800-562-4177

Branson Shenanigans RV Park
(800) 338-7275

Branson View Campground
2362 Hwy 265
Branson, MO 65616
800-992-9055

Chastain's RV Park
(417) 334-4414

Compton Ridge Campground
(417) 338-2911

Cooper Creek Campground
(417) 334-5250

Glenwood Campground
1550 Fall Creek Road
Branson, MO 65616
417-334-7024

Musicland KOA
(417) 334-0848

Stormy Point Camp & Resort
(417) 338-2255

Tall Pines Best Holiday
HCR 9, Box 1175
Branson, MO 65616
417-338-2445

Cameron, MO

Down Under Camp Resort
8074 NE CR H
Cameron, MO 64493
816-632-3695

Carthage, MO

Ballard's Campground
13965 Ballard Loop
Carthage, MO 64836
417-359-0359

Charleston, MO

Boomland Campground
Beasly Park Road
Charleston, MO 63834
573-683-6108

Danville, MO

Kan-DO Kampground RV Park
99 Hwy TT
Danville, MO 63361
573-564-7993

Eagle Rock, MO

Paradise Cover Camping Resort
HC 1 Box 1067
Eagle Rock, MO 65641
417-271-4888

Eagleville, MO

Eagle Ridge RV Park
(816) 867-5518

Eminence, MO

Jacks Fork Campground
PO Box 188
Eminence, MO 65466
800-333-5628

Forsyth, MO

Forsyth KOA
11020 Hwy. 76
Eagle Rock, MO 65653
800-562-7560

Grain Valley, MO

Trailside Campers' Inn of Kansas City

1000 R.D. Mize Road
Grain Valley, MO 64029
800-748-7729

Higginsville, MO

Fairground Park
(816) 584-7313

Jonesburg, MO

Jonesburg/Warrenton KOA
P.O. Box H
Jonesburg, MO 63351
800-562-5634

Joplin, MO

Joplin KOA
4359 Hwy. 43
Joplin, MO 64804
800-562-5675

Kimberling, MO

Kimberling City KOA
HCR 5, Box 465
Kimberling, MO 65686
800-562-5685

Lake Ozark, MO

Osage Beach/Lake Ozark KOA
498 Hwy. 42
Lake Ozark, MO 65049
800-562-7554

Riverview Campground
(573) 365-1122

Lebanon, MO

Menagerie Campground
RR 16, Box 1010
Lebanon, MO 65536
417-588-3353

Lesterville, MO

Parks Bluff Campground
PO Box 24
Lesterville, MO 63654
573-637-2290

Macon, MO

Long Branch Lake State Park
28615 Visitors Center
Macon, MO 63552
660-773-5229

Monett, MO

Pine Trails RV Ranch
40 Hwy 60
Monett, MO 65708

417-235-8682

Oak Grove, MO

Kansas City East/Oak Grove KOA
303 NE 3rd.
Oak Grove, MO 64075
800-562-7507

Ozark, MO

Ozark RV Park
320 North 20th St
Ozark, MO 65721
417-581-3203

Stage Stop RV Park
5255 N. 17th St.
Ozark, MO 65721
417-581-6482

Perryville, MO

Perryville/Cape Girardeau KOA
89 KOA Lane
Perryville, MO 63775
800-562-5304

Phillipsburg, MO

Lebanon KOA
18376 Campground Road
Phillipsburg, MO 65722
800-562-3424

Platte City, MO

Basswood Country RV park
15880 Interurban Road
Platte City, MO 64079
816-858-5556

Poplar Bluff, MO

Camelot RV Campground
215 CR 527
Poplar Bluff, MO 63901
573-785-1016

Portageville, MO

Hayti/Portageville KOA
2824 MO St. East Outer Road
Portageville, MO 65873
800-562-1508

Rock Port, MO

Rock Port KOA
Route 4, Box 204
Rock Port, MO 64482
800-562-5415

Sarcoxie, MO

WAC Campground

Rt. 1, Box 1014
Sarcoxie, MO 64862
417-548-2258

Springfield, MO

Springfield KOA
5775 West Farm Road 140
Springfield, MO 65802
800-562-1228

Travelers Park Campground
425 South Trailview Road
Springfield, MO 65802
(417) 866-4226

Stanton, MO

Stanton/Meramec KOA
Box 177
Stanton, MO 63079
800-562-4386

Sullivan, MO

Sullivan/Meramec KOA
1451 E. Springfield
Sullivan, MO 63080
800-562-8730

Warsaw, MO
Deer Rest Camp Park
(816) 438-6005

Williamsville, MO

Lake Wappapello State Park
HC 2 Box 102
Williamsville, MO 63966
573-297-3232

Montana

Alder, MT

Alder/Virginia City KOA
Box 103
Alder, MT 59710
800-562-1898

Belt, MT

Fort Ponderosa Family Campground and RV
Park
568 Armington Road
Belt, MT 59412
406-277-3232

Big Timber, MT

Big Timber KOA
HC 88, Box 3634
Big Timber, MT 59011
800-562-5869

Billings, MT

Billings Metro KOA
547 Garden Ave.
Billings, MT 59101
800-562-8546

Yellowstone River Campground
407 Garden Avenue
Billings, MT 59101
Voice: (406) 259-0878
Fax: (406)259-1416

Bozeman, MT

Bozeman KOA
81123 Gallatin Road US 191
Bozeman, MT 59715
800-562-3036

Butte, MT

Butte KOA
1601 Kaw Avenue
Butte, MT 59701
800-562-8089

Cameron, MT

Madison River Cabins and RV
1403 Hwy 287 North
Cameron, MT 59720
406-682-4890

Cardwell, MT

Cardwell Store and RV Park
770 Hwy 2 East

Cardwell, MT 59721
406-287-5092

Choteau, MT

Choteau KOA
Hwy. 221
Choteau, MT 59422
800-562-4156

Darby, MT

Wilderness Motel, RV & Tent Park
308 South Main Street
Darby, MT 59829
406-821-3405

Deer Lodge, MT

Deer Lodge KOA
Park St.
Deer Lodge, MT 59722
800-562-1629

Dillon, MT

Dillon KOA
735 W. Park St.
Dillon, MT 59725
800-562-2751

Ennis, MT

Ennis RV Village
PO Box 1463
Ennis, MT 59729

Garryowen, MT

7th Ranch RV Camp
Reno Creek Road
Garryowen, MT 59031
Voice: (800) 371-7963
wattsln@mcn.net

Great Falls, MT

Great Falls KOA
1500 51st St. South
Great Falls, MT 59405
800-562-6584

Hardin, MT

Hardin KOA
RR 1
Hardin, MT 59034
800-562-1635

Helena, MT

Helena Campground and RV Park
5820 N Montana Avenue
Helena, MT 59602
Voice: (406) 458-4714

Fax: (406) 458-6001
info@helenacampgroundrvpark.com

Hungry Horse, MT

Canyon RV and Campground
9540 Hwy 2 East
Hungry Horse, MT 59919
406-387-9393

Mountain Meadow Campground
9125 Hwy 2 East
Hungry Horse, MT 59919
406-387-9125

Timber Wolf Resort
9105 Hwy 2 East
Hungry Horse, MT 59919
406-387-9653

Livingston, MT

Livingston/Paradise Valley KOA
163 Pine Creek Road
Livingston, MT 59047
800-562-2805

Yellowstone's Edge RV Park
3502 Hwy 89
Livingston, MT 59047
406-333-4036

Miles City, MT

Miles City KOA
1 Palmer St.
Miles City, MT 59301
800-562-3909

Missoula, MT

Yogi Bear's Jellystone Park
10955 Highway 93 North
Missoula, MT 59802
Voice: (406) 543-9400 / (800) 318-9644
Fax: (406) 543-9400
info@campjellystonemt.com

Polson, MT

Polson/Flathead Lake KOA
200 Irvine Flats Road
Polson, MT 59860
800-562-2130

Red Lodge, MT

Red Lodge KOA
HC 50, Box 5340
Red Lodge, MT 59068
800-562-7540

St. Mary, MT

St. Mary KOA
106 West Shore
St. Mary, MT 59417
800-562-1054

St. Regis, MT

St. Regis KOA
105 Old Hwy. 10 East, Box 187
St. Regis, MT 59866
800-562-4670

Sula, MT

Sula KOA
7060 Hwy. 93 S.
Sula, MT 59871
800-562-9867

Three Forks, MT

Three Forks KOA
15 KOA Road
Three Forks, MT 59752
800-562-9752

W. Yellowstone, MT

Yellowstone Grizzly RV Park
210 South Electric Avenue (PO Box 150)
West Yellowstone, MT 59758
Voice: (406) 646-4466
Fax: (406) 646-4335

Yellowstone Park/West Entrance KOA
Box 348
W. Yellowstone, MT 59758
800-562-7591

West Glacier, MT

Glacier Campground
PO Box 447
West Glacier, MT 59936
406-387-5689

West Glacier KOA
Box 215
West Glacier, MT 59936
800-562-3313

Whitefish, MT

Whitefish/Kalispell N KOA
5121 Hwy. 93S
Whitefish, MT 59937
800-562-8734

Nebraska

Crofton, NE

Lewis and Clark Recreation Area
54731 897 Road
Crofton, NE 68730
402-388-4169

Doniphan, NE

Grand Island KOA
904 South B Road
Doniphan, NE 68832
800-562-0850

Gothenburg, NE

Gothenburg KOA
I-80 & Hwy. 47S, Box 353
Gothenburg, NE 69138
800-562-1873

Gretna, NE

West Omaha KOA
14601 Hwy. 6
Gretna, NE 68028
800-562-1632

Hastings, NE

Hastings KOA
302 E. 26th
Hastings, NE 68901
800-562-2171

Henderson, NE

Henderson/York KOA
913 Road B
Henderson, NE 68371
800-562-4171

Prairie Oasis
913 Rd B
Henderson, NE 68371
402-723-4310

Kimball, NE

Kimball KOA
RR 1, Box 128 D
Kimball, NE 69145
800-562-4785

Lincoln, NE

Camp A Way Campground
200 Ogden Road
Lincoln, NE 68521
Voice: (402) 476-2282 / (866) 719-CAMP

Fax: (402) 476-5439
jqueen@neb.rr.com

North Platte, NE

Holiday Park
601 Halligan Drive
North Platte, NE 69101
Voice: (308) 534-2265 / (800) 424-4531

Ponca, NE

Ponca State Park
88090 Spur 26-E
Ponca, NE 68770
402-755-2284

Raymond, NE

Branched Oak State Recreation Area
13401 W Branched Oak Road
Raymond, NE 68428

Scottsbluff, NE

Scottsbluff/Chimney Rock KOA
180037 KOA Drive
Scottsbluff, NE 69361
800-562-0845

Valentine, NE

Fishberry Campground
HC 14, Box 1
Valentine, NE 69201
Voice: (402) 376-1858
rwjacobson@yahoo.com

Nevada

Amargosa Valley, NV
Longstreet Inn, Casino, and RV Park
HCR 70
PO Box 559
Amargosa Valley, NV 89020
702-372-1777

Austin, NV
Austin RV Park
702-964-1011

Baker, NV
Lower and Upper Lehman Creek Campgrounds
100 Great Basin National Park
Baker, NV 89311
775-234-7331

Beatty, NV
Baily's Hot Springs
US Hwy 95
Beatty, NV 89003
702-553-2395

Burro Inn
US Hwy 95
Beatty, NV 89003
702-553-2225

Death Valley National Park
State Rt. 374
Beatty, NV 89003
619-786-2331

Kay's Korral RV Park
US Hwy 95
Beatty, NV 89003
702-553-2732

Space Station RV Park
US Hwy 95
Beatty, NV 89003
702-533-9039

Boulder City, NV
Lake Mead National Recreation Area
601 Nevada Hwy
Boulder City, NV 89005
702-293-8906

Caliente, NV
Aqua Caliente Trailer Park
US Hwy 93 N.

Caliente, NV 89008
702-726-3399

Beaver Dam State Park
702-728-4467

Kershaw-Ryan State Park
702-726-3564

Young's RV Park
US Hwy 93
Caliente, NV 89008
702-726-3418

Carson City, NV
Comstock Country RV Resort
5400 s. Carson St.
Carson City, NV 89701
702-882-2445

Davis Creek Regional Park
25 Davis Creek Road
Carson City, NV 89704
775-849-0684

Washoe Lake State Recreation Area
4855 E. Lake Blvd.
Carson City, NV 89704
775-687-4319

Carson Valley, NV
Topaz Lake State Park
775-266-3343

Dayton, NV
Dayton State Park
U.S. Highway 50 East
Dayton, NV 89403
775-687-5678

Denio, NV
Denio Junction
PO Box 10
Denio, NV 89404
702-941-0371

Elko, NV
Double Dice RV Park
3730 E. Idaho Street
Elko, NV 89801
Toll Free: (888)738-3423
Phone: (775)738-5642
Fax: (775) 753-0055
rvtours@aol.com

Hidden Valley Guest & RV Resort

PO Box 1454
Elko, NV 89803
702-738-2347

Jarbidge Recreation Area
208-543-4129

Rydon Campground
PO Box 1656
Elko, NV 89801
702-738-3448

South Fork State Recreation Area
702-744-4346

Valley View RV Park
HC 34, Unit 1
Elko, NV 89801
702-753-9200

Wild Horse State Recreation Area
702-758-6493

Wildhorse Resort and Ranch
HC 31, Box 213
Elko, NV 89801
702-758-6471

Ely, NV

Cove Lake State Park
PO Box 761
Ely, NV 89301
775-728-4467

Eldorado Service
US Hwy 50 & Strawberry Junction
Ely, NV 89301
702-237-1002

Ely KOA
HC 10, Box 10800
Ely, NV 89301
800-562-3413

Holiday Inn-Prospector Casino RV Park
1501 Avenue F
Ely, NV 89301
702-289-8900

KOA of Ely
Pioche Hwy
Ely, NV 89301
702-289-3413

Rainbow RV Park
1011 Pioche hwy
Ely, NV 89301

702-289-2622

Schelbourne Service
US Hwy 93, Box 33620
Ely, NV 89301
702-591-0363

Fallon, NV

Valley View RV Park
HC-33, PO Box 33200
Ely, NV 89301
702-289-3303
Fallon, NV

Fallon RV Park
5787 Reno Hwy
Fallon, NV 89406
702-867-2332

Hub Total RV & Mobile Home Park
4800 Reno Hwy
Fallon, NV 89406
702-867-3636

Lahonton State Recreation Area
702-867-3500

Fernley, NV

Fernley RV Park
1405 E. Newlands
Fernley, NV 89408
702-575-6776

Truck Inn
I-80
Fernley, NV 89408
702-575-4800

Gabbs, NV

Berlin-Ichtyosaur State Park
702-964-9440

Gardnerville, NV

Hollbrook Station
1501 US Hwy. 395 S
Gardnerville, NV 89410
702-266-3434

Topaz Lake Park
3700 Topaz Park Road
Gardnerville, NV 89410
702-266-3343

Hawthorne, NV

Desert Lake Campground
US Hwy. 95 Walker Lake, P.O. Box 647
Hawthorne, NV 89415

702-945-3373

Frontier RV Park
Fifth & L St.
Hawthorne, NV 89415
702-945-2733

Jackpot, NV

Spanish Gardens RV Park
Corner of Gurley & US Hwy. 93
Jackpot, NV 89825
702-755-2333

Kiko, NV

R Place
US Hwy 93, HCR 61
Kiko, NV 89017
702-725-3545

Las Vegas, NV

13 Mile Campground
HCR 33, Box 5500
Las Vegas, NV 89124
702-363-1921

Holiday Travel Park
3890 S. Nellis Blvd
Las Vegas, NV 89121-3199
Phone: (702) 451-8005
Fax: (702) 451-5806
beverly@campgroundservices.com

King's Row Trailer Park
3660 Boulder Hwy.
Las Vegas, NV 89121
702-457-3606

Las Vegas KOA
4315 Boulder Hwy.
Las Vegas, NV 89121
702-451-5527

Lee Canyon Recreation Area
702-645-2754

Oasis Las Vegas RV Resort
2711 W. Windmill Lane
Las Vegas, NV 89123
702-260-2000

Red Rock Canyon National Conservation Area
702-363-1921

Riviera RV Resort
2200 Palm St.
Las Vegas, NV 89104

Voice: (702) 457-8700
Fax: (702) 457-1488
rivierarvpark@rasnyder.com

Silverton Hotel Casino RV Park
3333 Blue Diamond Road
Las Vegas, NV 89139
702-263-7777

Spring Mountain National Recreation Area
702-873-8800

Spring Mountain Ranch State Park
702-875-4141

Valley of Fire State Park
702-397-2088

Lovelock, NV

Lazy K Campground & RV Park
1550 Cornell Ave., P.O. Box 1661
Lovelock, NV 89419
702-273-1116

Rye Patch State Recreation Area
702-538-7321

Mina, NV

Sunrise Valley RV Park
U.S. Hwy. 95, P.O. Box 345
Mina, NV 89422
702-573-2214

Waterhole RV Park
U.S.Hwy. 95, P.O. Box 131
Mina, NV 89422
702-573-2445

Moapa, NV

Palm Creek RV Park
3215 Warm Springs, P.O. Box 400
Moapa, NV 89025
702-865-2777

Pahrump, NV

Big 5 Trailer Park
850 S. Big 5 Road
Pahrump, NV 89048
702-727-6490

Preferred RV Resort
1801 E Crawford Way
Pahrump, NV 89048
Voice: (775) 727-6429
Fax: (775) 727-4603
prvresort@pahrump.net

Seven Palms RV Park
101 S. Linda St.
Pahrump, NV 89048
702-727-6091

Terrible's Lakeside Casino & RV Resort
5870 S Homestead Road
Pahrump, NV 89048
Voice: (775) 751-7770 / (888) 558-5253
Fax: (775) 751-7746
lakesiderv@terribleherbst.com

Panaca, NV

Cathedral Gorge State Park
702-728-4467

Pioche, NV

Echo Canyon State Park
702-962-5103

Spring Valley State Park
702-962-5102

Reno, NV

Bonanza Terrace RV Park
4800 Staltz Road
Reno, NV 89506
702-329-9624

Chism Trailer Park
1300 W. 2nd St.
Reno, NV 89503
702-322-2281

Four Seasons RV Park
13109 S. Virginia St.
Reno, NV 89511
702-853-1423

KOA at the Reno Hilton
2500 E 2nd St.
Reno, NV 89595
Voice: (775) 789-2147 / (888) 562-5698
Fax: (775) 322-6061
reno@koa.net

Pyramid Lake State Park
State Rt. 445
775-476-1156

Silver Springs, NV

Fort Churchill State Historical Park
US Hwy 95 Alt.
702-577-2345

Tonopah, NV

Lambertucci Roma
US Hwy. 95 N, P.O. Box 3347
Tonopah, NV 89049
702-482-5312

Twister Inn RV Park
Ketten Road & US Hwy. 6
Tonopah, NV 89049
702-482-9444

The Station House
1137 South Main
Tonopah, NV 89049
775-482-9777

Virginia City, NV

Virginia City RV Park
355 N. "F" St.
Tonopah, NV 89440
702-847-0999

Wadsworth, NV

I-80 Campground
I-80 Exit 43, State Rt. 447
Wadsworth, NV 89442
702-575-2181

Wellington, NV

Wellington Station Resort
2855 State Rt. 208
Wellington, NV 89444
702-465-2304

Wells, NV

Mountain Shadows RV Park
807 Humboldt, P.O. Box 362
Wells, NV 89835
702-752-3525

Ruby Mountains Recreation area
702-752-3357

Welcome Station
I-80 Exit 343, P.O. Box 340
Wells, NV 89835
702-752-3808

Wendover, NV

The Wendover KOA Campground
1250 N. Camper Dr. Exit 410
Wendover, NV 89883
702-664-2221

West Wendover, NV

Wendover KOA
Box 3710
West Wendover, NV 89883

800-562-8552

Winnemucca, NV

Hi Desert RV Park
5575 E. Winnemucca Blvd.
Winnemucca, NV 89445
702-623-4513

Winnemucca RV Park
5255 E. Winnemucca Blvd.
Winnemucca, NV 89445
702-623-3501

Yerlington, NV

Greenfield Mobile Home & RV Park
500 W. Goldfield Ave.
Yerlington, NV 89447
702-463-4912

Zephyr, NV

Zephyr Cove Resort
P.O. Box 830, 760 Hwy. 50
Zephyr, NV 89448
702-588-6644

New Hampshire

Albany, NH

Davies Campground
RFD 1, Box 131B, Route
Albany, NH 03818
603-447-1092

Jigger Johnson Campground
Kancamagus Hwy
Albany, NH 03818
603-447-5448

Allenstown, NH

Bear Brook State Park
157 Deerfield Road
Allenstown, NH 03275
603-485-9869

Ashland, NH

Ames Brook Campground
RFD #1, Box 102NA
Ashland, NH 03217
603-968-7998

Squam Lake Camp Resort
RFD #1, Box 42
Ashland, NH 03217
603-968-7227

Yogi Bear's Jellystone Park
RR1, Box 396
Ashland, NH 03217
603-968-9000

Barnstead, NH

Sun River Campground
Rte 28
Barnstead, NH 03225
603-269-3333

Barrington, NH

Ayers Lake Farm Campground
557 Route 202
Barrington, NH 03825
603-335-1110

Barrington Shores Campground
70 Hall Road
Barrington, NH 03825
603-664-9333

Bartlett, NH

Silver Springs Campground

Box 38
Bartlett, NH 03812
603-374-2221

Bath, NH

Twin River Campground & Cottages
P.O. Box 212
Bath, NH 03740
603-747-3640

Bethlehem, NH

Apple Hill Campground
P.O. Box 388
Bethlehem, NH 03574
603-869-2238

Snowy Mountain Campground & Motel
1225 Main Street
Bethlehem, NH 03574
603-869-2600

Bradford, NH

Lake Massasecum Campground
Massasecum Road, RR1, Bo
Bradford, NH 03221
603-938-2571

Brentwood, NH

Three Ponds Campground
146 North Road
Brentwood, NH 03803
603-679-5350

Bristol, NH

Davidson's Countryside Campgr
RFD #2, Box 485, River
Bristol, NH 03222
603-744-2403

Brookline, NH

Field & Stream Park
5 Dupaw Gould Road
Brookline, NH 03033
603-673-4677

Cambridge, NH

Umbagog Lake Campground
181 North
Cambridge, NH 03579
603-482-7795

Campton, NH

Branch Brook Four Season Camping
P.O. Box 390
Campton, NH 03223
603-726-7001

Goose Hollow Campground
RR2, Box 1600
Campton, NH 03223
800-204-2267

Pemi River Campground
RFD 1, Box 926
Campton, NH 03223
603-726-7015

Canaan, NH

Crescent Campsites
P.O. Box 238
Canaan, NH 03741
603-523-9910

Center Barns, NH

Sun River Campground
P.O. Box 7
Center Barns, NH 03225
603-269-3333

Center Harbor, NH

Camp Iroquois Campground
P.O. Box 150
Center Harbor, NH 03226
603-253-4287

Long Island Bridge Campground
HCR 62, Box 455
Center Harbor, NH 03226
603-253-6053 Center

Terrace Pines Campground
P.O. Box 98Z
Ossipee, NH 03814
603-539-6210

Chester, NH

Silver Sands Campground
603 Raymond Road
Chester, NH 03036
603-887-3638

Chichester, NH

Hillcrest Campground
78 Dover Road
Chichester, NH 03234
603-798-5124

Chocorua, NH

Chocorua Camping Village
893 White Mountain Highway
Tamworth, NH 03886
Toll Free: (888)237-8642
Phone: (603)323-8536

Fax: (603)323-8271
info@chocoruacamping.com

Colebrook, NH

Maplewoods Scenic Camping Area
Route 1, Box 247
Colebrook, NH 03576
603-237-4237

Contocook, NH

Sandy Beach Family Campground
677 Clement Hill Road
Contocook, NH 03229
603-746-3591

Conway, NH

Passaconaway Campground
Rte 12
Conway, NH 03812
603-447-5448

Saco River Camping Area
P.O. Box 546N, Route 16
Conway, NH 03860
603-356-3360

The Beach Camping Area
Box 1007N
Conway, NH 03818
603-447-2723

Derry, NH

Hidden Valley Rec. & Camping
81 Damren Road
Derry, NH 03038
603-887-3767

Dover, NH

Old Stage Campground
46 Old Stage Road
Dover, NH 03820
603-742-4050

Durham, NH

Forest Glen Campground
P.O. Box 676
Durham, NH 03824
603-659-3416

E. Haverhill, NH

Oliverian Valley Campgrounds
P.O. Box 91
E. Haverhill, NH 03765
603-989-3351

E. Wakefield, NH

Beachwood Shores Campground

HC Box 228
E. Wakefield, NH 03830
603-539-4272

Lake Forest Resort
271 North Shore Road
E. Wakefield, NH 03830
603-522-3306

Lake Ivanhoe Campground
631 Action Ridge Road
E. Wakefield, NH 03830
603-522-8824

East Lempster, NH

Tamarack Trails Camping Park
P.O. Box 24
East Lempster, NH 03605
603-863-6443

Enfield, NH

Mascoma Lake Camping Area
RR2, Box 331
Enfield, NH 03748
603-448-5076 Epsom, NH

Blake's Brook Campground
76 Mt. Road
Enfield, NH 03234
603-736-4793

Circle 9 Ranch Campground
P.O. Box 282
Enfield, NH 03234
603-736-9656

Epsom Valley Campground
990 Suncook Valley Hwy.
Enfield, NH 03234
603-736-9758

Lazy River Campground
427 Goboro Road
Enfield, NH 03234
603-798-5900

Epsom, NH

Epsom Valley Campground
990 Suncook Valley Hwy
Epsom, NH 03234
603-736-9758

Errol, NH

Log Haven Campground
P.O. Box 239
Errol, NH 03579

603-482-3294

Mollidgewock State Park
RFD #2, P.O. Box 29
Errol, NH 03579
603-482-3373

Umbagog Lake Campground
Box 181N
Errol, NH 03579
603-482-7795

Exeter, NH

The Exeter Elms Campground
188 Court St.
Exeter, NH 03833
603-778-7631

The Green Gate Camping Area
P.O. Box 185
Exeter, NH 03833
603-772-2100

Fitzwilliam, NH

Hunter's State Line Campground
Rt. 12, Box 132
Fitzwilliam, NH 03447
603-585-7726

Franconia, NH

Fransted Campground
P.O. Box 155
Franconia, NH 03580
603-823-5675

Franklin, NH

Pine Grove Campground
14 Timberland Dr.
Franklin, NH 03235
603-934-4582

Thousand Acres Campground
Route 3, 1079 S. Main S
Franklin, NH 03235
603-934-4440

Fremont, NH

Exeter River Camping Area
13 South Road
Fremont, NH 03044
603-895-3448

Glen, NH

Glen-Ellis Family Campground
P.O. Box 397
Glen, NH 03838

603-383-4567

Green Meadow Camping Area
P.O. Box 246
Glen, NH 03838
603-383-6801

Gorham, NH

Moose Brook State Park
30 Jimtown Road
Gorham, NH 03581
603-466-3860

Timberland Camping Area
Box 303
Gorham, NH 03581
603-466-3872

Greenfield, NH

Greenfield State Park
Box 203
Greenfield, NH 03047
603-547-3496

Hampstead, NH

Emerson's Camping Area
233 Emerson Avenue
Hampstead, NH 03841
603-329-6938

Sanborn Shore Acres Campground
P.O. Box 626 Main St.
Hampstead, NH 03841
603-329-5247

Sunset Park Campground
P.O. Box 16N, 104 Emers
Hampstead, NH 03841
603-329-6941

Hampton, NH

Tidewater Campground
160 Lafayette Road
Hampton, NH 03842
Voice: (603) 926-5474

Hampton Fall, NH

Wakeda Campground
294 Exeter Road
Hampton Fall, NH 03844
603--772-527

Hancock, NH

Seven Maples Camping Area
24 Longview Road
Hancock, NH 03449
603-525-3321

Hanover, NH

Storrs Pond Campground
P.O. Box 106
Hanover, NH 03755
603-643-2134

Henniker, NH

Keyser Pond Campground
47 Old Concord Road
Henniker, NH 03242
603-428-7741

Mile Away Campground
41 Old West Hopkinton R
Henniker, NH 03242
603-428-7616

Mile-Away Best Holiday
41 Old W. Hopkinton Road
Henniker, NH 03242
603-428-7616

Hillsboro, NH

Oxbow Campground
RFD 1, Box 11
Hillsboro, NH 03244
603-464-5952

Holderness, NH

Bethel Woods Campground
Route 3, Box 201
Holderness, NH 03245
603-279-6266

Jaffrey, NH

Emerald Acres Campground
39 Ridgecrest Road
Jaffrey, NH 03452
603-532-8838

Jefferson, NH

Israel River Campgrounds
Box 179A
Jefferson, NH 03583
603-586-7977

Jefferson Campground
Box 112A
Jefferson, NH 03583
603-586-4510

Lantern Motor Inn & Campground
P.O. Box 97
Jefferson, NH 03583
603-586-7151

Keene, NH

Hilltop Campground & Adventure
HCR 33, Box 186
Keene, NH 03431
603-847-3351

Laconia, NH

Gunstock Campground
P.O. Box 1307
Laconia, NH 03247
603-293-4341

Hack-Ma-Tack Campground
RFD 3, Box 90, Weir's B
Laconia, NH 03246
603-366-5977

Paugus Bay Campground
96 Hilliard Road
Laconia, NH 03246
603-366-4757

Lancaster, NH

Beaver Trails Campground
RR #2, Box 315
Lancaster, NH 03584
603-788-3815

Mountain Lake Campground
P.O. Box 475
Lancaster, NH 03584
603-788-4509

Roger's Campground & Motel
10 Roger's Campground R
Lancaster, NH 03584
603-788-4885

Lee, NH

Ferndale Acres Campgrounds
132 Wednesday Hill Road
Lee, NH 03824
603-659-5082

Wadleigh Falls Campground
16 Campground Road
Lee, NH 03824
Voice: (603) 659-1751
info@wadleighfalls.com

Lincoln, NH

Country Bumbkins Campground
RR1, Box 83, Route 3
Lincoln, NH 03251
603-745-8837

Lisbon, NH

Littleton KOA Kampground
2154 Route 302
Lisbon, NH 03585
603-838-5525

Littleton/Lisbon KOA
2154 Route 302
Lisbon, NH 03585
800-562-5386

Mink Brook Family Campground
Route 302, RFD 2
Lisbon, NH 03585
603-838-6658

Littleton, NH

Crazy Horse Campground
788 Hilltop Road
Littleton, NH 03561
603-444-2204

Lochmere, NH

Winnisquam Beach Resort
P.O. Box 67, 2 Grey Roc
Lochmere, NH 03252
603-524-0021

Loudon, NH

Cascade Park Camping Area
Route 106 S.
Loudon, NH 03301
603-224-3212

Meredith, NH

Clearwater Campground
26 Campground Road
Meredith, NH 03253
603-279-7761

Harbor Hill Camping Area
189 NH Route 25
Meredith, NH 03253
603-279-6910

Meredith Woods 4-Season Camping
26 Campground Road
Meredith, NH 03253
603-279-5449

Milton, NH

Mi-Ti-Jo Campground
P.O. Box 830
Milton, NH 03851
603-652-9022

Moultonborough, NH

Pine Woods Campground
P.O. Box 776
Moultonborough, NH 03254
603-253-6251

N. Woodstock, NH

Lost River Valley Campground
RD 1, Box 44
N. Woodstock, NH 03262
603-745-8321

Maple Haven Camping & Cottage
RFD 1, Box 54
N. Woodstock, NH 03626
602-745-3350

New Boston, NH

Friendly Beaver Campground
Old Coach Road
New Boston, NH 03070
603-487-5570

Wildwood Campgrounds
540 Old Coach Road
New Boston, NH 03070
603-487-3300

New Hampton, NH

Twin Tamarack Family Camping
Route 104, Box 121
New Hampton, NH 03265
603-279-4387

New London, NH

Otter Lake Campground
55 Otterville Road
New London, NH 03257
603-763-5600

Newfields, NH

Great Bay Camping Village
P.O. Box 331, #56Rt/108
Newfields, NH 03856
603-778-0226

Newmarket, NH

Wellington Camping Park
P.O. Box D
Newmarket, NH 03857
603-659-5065

Newport, NH

Crow's Nest Campground
529 S. Main St.
Newport, NH 03773

603-863-6170

Loon Lake Campground
P.O. Box 345
Newport, NH 03773
603-863-8176

Northstar Campground
43 Coonbrook Road
Newport, NH 03773
603-863-4001

North Hampton, NH

Shel-Al Camping Area
P.O. Box 700 Rt. 1
North Hampton, NH 03862
603-964-5730

Ogdensburg, NH

Ogdensburg/1000 Islands KOA
4707 St. Hwy.
Ogdensburg, NH 13669
800-562-3962

Ossipee, NH

Deer Cap Campground
P.O. Box 332
Ossipee, NH 03814
603-539-6030

Ossipee Lake Camping Area
Route 25
Ossipee, NH 03814
603-539-6631
Oxford, NH

Jacobs Brook Campground
P.O. Box 167, High Bridge
Oxford, NH 03777
603-353-9210

The Pastures Campground
RR 1, Box 57A, Route 10
Oxford, NH 03777
603-353-4579

Pittsburg, NH

Hidden Acres Campground
P.O. Box 94
Pittsburg, NH 03592
603-538-6919

Lake Francis State Park
285 River Road
Pittsburg, NH 03592
603-538-6965

Mountain View Cabins & Campground
Mountain View RR1, Box
Pittsburg, NH 03592
603-538-6305

Plaistow, NH

Country Shore Camping Area
P.O. Box 559
Plaistow, NH 03865
603-642-5072

Plymouth, NH

Plymouth Sands Campground
RR1, Box 3172
Plymouth, NH 03264
603-536-2605

Raymond, NH

Pine Acres Recreation Area
74 Freetown Road
Raymond, NH 03077
603-895-2519

Richmond, NH

Shir-Roy Camping Area
100 Athol Road
Richmond, NH 03470
603-239-4768

Rochester, NH

Crown Point Campground
44 First Crown Point Road
Rochester, NH 03867
603-332-0405

Grand View Camping Area
51 Four Rod Road
Rochester, NH 03867
603-332-1263

Rumney, NH

Baker River Campground
56 Campground Road
Rumney, NH 03266
603-786-9707

S. Hampton, NH

Tuxbury Pond Camping Area
88 Whitehall Road
S. Hampton, NH 03827
603-394-7660

S. Weare, NH

Autumn Hills Campground
285 South Stark Hwy.

S. Weare, NH 03281
603-529-2425

Shelburne, NH

White Birches Camping Park
218 State Rt 2
Shelburne, NH 03581
603-466-2022

Stewartstown, NH

Coleman State Park
Diamond Pond Road
Stewartstown, NH 03576
603-237-4520

Suncook, NH

Twin Oaks Campground
80 Pinewood Road
Suncook, NH 03275
603-485-2700

Tamworth, NH

Foothills Campground
506 Maple Road
Tamworth, NH 03886
603-323-8322

Tamworth Camping Area
P.O. Box 99
Tamworth, NH 03866
603-323-8031

Twin Mountain, NH

Ammonoosuc Campground
P.O. Box 178N
Twin Mountain, NH 03595
603-846-5527

Beech Hill Campground & Cabin
P.O. Box 129
Twin Mountain, NH 03595
603-846-5521

Dry River Campground Crawford
Box 177
Twin Mountain, NH 03595
603-374-2272

Tarry-Ho Campground & Cottage
P.O. Box 369
Twin Mountain, NH 03595
603-846-5577

Twin Mountain KOA Campground
P.O. Box 148
Twin Mountain, NH 03595

603-846-5559

Warren, NH

Moose Hillcock Campground
RFD 1, Box 96N, Route 1
Warren, NH 03279
603-764-5294

Scenic View Campground
193AA S. Main Street
Warren, NH 03279
603-764-9380

Washington, NH

Recreational Camping at Highland Park
928 Valley Road
Washington, NH 03280
603-495-0150

Weare, NH

Cold Springs Campground
22 Wildlife Dr.
Weare, NH 03281
603-529-2528

Webster, NH

Cold Brook Campground
513 Battle St.
K03303
603-746-3390

Weirs Beach, NH

Pine Hollow Camping World
Route 3, P.O. Box 5024
Weirs Beach, NH 03247
603-366-2222

Weirs Beach Tent & Trailor Pa
198 Endicott St.
Weirs Beach, NH 03246
603-366-4747

Wentworth, NH

Pine Haven Campground
P.O. Box 43N
Wentworth, NH 03282
603-786-9942

Swain Brook Campground
P.O. Box 157, Beech Hil
Wentworth, NH 03282
603-764-5537

West Ossipee, NH

Chocoru Camping Village
Box 118N
West Ossipee, NH 03890

603-323-8536

Whit's End Campground
140 Newman Drew Road
West Ossipee, NH 03890
603-539-5050

Bearcamp River Campground
P.O. Box 104
West Ossipee, NH 03890
603-539-3898

Westward Shores Campground
P.O. Box 308
West Ossipee, NH 03890
603-539-6445

West Sawnzey, NH

Swanzey Lake Camping Area
P.O. Box 115
West Sawnzey, NH 03469
603-352-9880

Whitefield, NH

Burns Lake Campground
R-2, Box 620A
Whitefield, NH 03598
603-837-9037

Winchester, NH

Forest Lake Campground, Inc.
331 Keene Road, Route 10
Winchester, NH 03470
603-239-4267

Wolfeboro, NH

Willey Brook Campground
883 Center St.
Wolfeboro, NH 03894
603-569-9493

Robie's RV Park
139 Governor Wentworth
Wolfeboro, NH 03894
603-569-4354

Wolfeboro Campground
61 Haines Hill Road
Wolfeboro, NH 03894
603-569-9881

Woodstock, NH

Broken Branch KOA Campground
Box 6
Woodstock, NH 03293
603-745-8008

New Jersey

Absecon High, NJ

Shady Pines Campground
443 S. 6th Avenue, Dept
Absecon High, NJ 08201
609-652-1516

Andover, NJ

Columbia Valley Campground
3 Ghost Pony Road
Andover, NJ 07821
973-691-0596

Panther Lake Camping Resort
6 Panther Lake Road
Andover, NJ 07821
973-347-4440

Asbury, NJ

Jugtown Mountain Campsites
1074 State Route 173
Asbury, NJ 08802
908-735-5995

Barnegat, NJ

Brookville Campground
Box 169, 244 Jones Road
Barnegat, NJ 08005
609-698-3134

Bayville, NJ

Cedar Creek Campground
1052 Route 9
Bayville, NJ 08721
732-269-1413

Beach Haven, NJ

Long Beach Island Trailer Park
19 Harding Ave.
Beach Haven, NJ 08008
Voice: (609) 492-9151
Fax: (609) 492-4663
lbitp@worldnet.att.net

Branchville, NJ

Harmony Ridge Farm and Campgr
23 Risdon Drive
Branchville, NJ 07826
973-948-4941

Kymers' Camping Resort
69 Kymer Road
Branchville, NJ 07826

973-875-3167

Buena, NJ

Buena Vista Camping Park
Route 40, Box 144
Buena, NJ 08310
609-697-2004

Cape May, NJ

Beachcomber Camping Resort
462-G Seashore Road
Cape May, NJ 08204
800-233-0150

Cape Island Campground
709 Route 9
Cape May, NJ 08204
609-884-5777

Holly Shores Best Holiday
491 Route 9
Cape May, NJ 08204
609-886-1234

Holly Shores Holiday Trav-L-P
491 Route 9
Cape May, NJ 08204
609-886-1234

Lake Laurie Campground
669 Route 9
Cape May, NJ 08204
609-884-3567

Seashore Campsites
720 Seashore Road, Dept.
08204
609-884-4010

Cape May Court House, NJ

Big Timber Lake Camping Resort
P.O. Box 366
Cape May Court House, NJ 08210
800-542-CAMP

Hidden Acres Campground
1142 Route 83, Box 354-
Cape May Court House, NJ 08210
609-624-9015

King Nummy Trail Campground
205 Route 47 South, Dep
Cape May Court House, NJ 08210
609-465-4242

North Wildwood Camping Resort

240 W. Shellbay Ave.
Cape May Court House, NJ 08210
609-465-4440

Ponderosa Campground
18 West Beaver Dam Road
Cape May Court House, NJ 08210
609-465-7794

Shellbay Family Camping Resor
Shellbay Avenue
Cape May Court House, NJ 08210
609-465-4770

Chatsworth, NJ

Wading Pines Campground
85 Godfrey Bridge Road
Chatsworth, NJ 08019
609-726-1313

Clarksboro, NJ

Timberlane Campground
117 Timber Lane
Clarksboro, NJ 08020
609-423-6677

Clemont, NJ

Avalon Campground
1917 Route 9 North
Clemont, NJ 08210
800-814-2267

Driftwood Camping Resort
1955 Route 9
Clemont, NJ 08210
609-624-1899

Columbia, NJ

Camp Taylor Campground
85 Mt. Pleasant Road
Columbia, NJ 07832
908-496-4333

Delaware, NJ

Delaware River Family Campgro
142 Route 46
Delaware, NJ 07833
908-475-4517

Dennisville, NJ

Holly Lake Condo Camping Reso
P.O. Box 324
Dennisville, NJ 08214
609-861-7144

Dorothy, NJ

Country Mouse Campground

13 South Jersey Avenue
Dorothy, NJ 08317
609-476-2143

Egg Harbor, NJ

Best Holiday Trav-L-Park Holl
218 S. Frankfurt Ave.
Egg Harbor, NJ 08215
609-965-2287

Colonial Meadows Campground
1410 Somers Point Road
Egg Harbor, NJ 08234
609-653-8449

Union Hill Campground
163 Leektown Road
Egg Harbor, NJ 08215
609-296-8599

Elmer, NJ

Yogi Bear's Jellystone Park a
49 Beal Road
Elmer, NJ 08318
609-451-7479

Flanders, NJ

Fla-Net Park
Flanders-Netcong Road
Flanders, NJ 07836
973-347-4467

Flemington, NJ

Camp Carr Campground
144 W. Woodschurch Road
Flemington, NJ 08822
908-782-1030

Freehold, NJ

Pine Cone Campground
P.O. Box 7074, Dept. N
Freehold, NJ 07728
732-462-2230

Goshen, NJ

Green Holly Campground
P.O. Box 193
Goshen, NJ 08218
609-465-9602

Green Creek, NJ

Acorn Campground
P.O. Box 151, Dept. N
Green Creek, NJ 08219
609-886-7119

Greenbank, NJ

Belhaven Lake Resort Campgrou
1213 Route 542
Greenbank, NJ 08215
609-965-2827

Hammonton, NJ
Indian Branch Park Campground
2021 Skip Morgan Drive,
Hammonton, NJ 08037
609-561-4719

Paradise Lake Campground
500 Paradise Drive, Dep
Hammonton, NJ 08037
609-561-7095

Jackson, NJ
Butterfly Camping Resort
360 Butterfly Road, Dept
Jackson, NJ 08527
732-928-2107

Maple Leaf Campground
P.O. Box 1209
Jackson, NJ 08527
732-367-0177

Tip Tam Camping Resort
301 Brewers Bridge Road
Jackson, NJ 08527
732-363-4036

Toby's Hide-Away Campground
380 Clearstream Road
Jackson, NJ 08527
732-363-3662

Yogi Bear's Jellystone Park
P.O. Box 48, Reed Road
Jackson, NJ 08527
609-758-2235Jersey City, NJ

Liberty Harbor RV Park
11 Marin Blvd.
Jackson, NJ 07302
201-451-1000

Little York, NJ
Mountain View Campground
Box 130
Little York, NJ 08834
908-996-2953

Marmora, NJ
Bayberry Cove Condominium Cam
435 South Route 9

Marmora, NJ 08233
609-390-3535

Oak Ridge Condo Campground
516 South Shore Road, P.
Marmora, NJ 08233
609-390-0916

Whipporwill Campground
810 S. Shore Road, Dept.
Marmora, NJ 08223
609-390-3458

Mays Landing, NJ
River Beach Camp II
4678 Mays Landing-Somer
Mays Landing, NJ 08330
609-625-8611

Winding River Campground
6752 Weymouth Road, Dept
Mays Landing, NJ 08330
609-625-3191

Yogi Bear's Jellystone Park
1079 12th Avenue
Mays Landing, NJ 08330
609-476-2811

Monroeville, NJ
Old Cedar Campground
274 Richwood Road, Dept.
Monroeville, NJ 08343
609-358-4881

Oldman's Creek Campground
174 Laux Road
Monroeville, NJ 08343
609-478-4502

Montague, NJ
Cedar Ridge Family Campground
205 River Road
Montague, NJ 07827
973-293-3512

Shippekonk Family Campground
59 River Road
Montague, NJ 07827
973-293-3383

New Gretna, NJ
Chips Folly Family Campground
P.O Box 56
New Gretna, NJ 08224
609-296-4434

Pilgrim Lake Campground
P.O. Box 17A
New Gretna, NJ 08224
609-296-4725

Timberline Lake Camping Resor
P.O. Box 278A
New Gretna, NJ 08224
609-296-7900

Turtle Run Campgroung
Box 129
New Gretna, NJ 08224
609-965-5343

Newton, NJ

Green Valley Beach Campground
68 Phillips Road
Newton, NJ 07860
973-383-4026

Rabbit Patch Campground
974 Route 619
Newton, NJ 07860
973-383-7661

North Bergen, NJ

New Yorker RV Park and Campgr
4901 Tonnelle Avenue
North Bergen, NJ 07047
800-688-5080

Ocean View, NJ

Echo Farm Campground
P.O. Box 610
Ocean View, NJ 08230
609-624-3589

Ocean View Campground
P.O. Box 607, Dept. S.
Ocean View, NJ 08230
609-624-1675

Outdoor World Lake & Shore Re
Corson Tavern Road
Ocean View, NJ 08230
609-624-1494

Pine Haven Campground
P.O. Box 606
Ocean View, NJ 08230
609-624-3437

Plantation Campground
3065 Shore Road, P.O. Bo
Ocean View, NJ 08230

609-624-3528

Resort Campground Country Clu
Box 602
Ocean View, NJ 08230
609-624-3666

Sea Grove Camping Resort
2665 Route 9, Box 603
Ocean View, NJ 08230
609-624-3529

Shady Oaks Campground
64 Route 50
Ocean View, NJ 08230
609-390-0431

Tamerlane Campground
P.O. Box 510, 2241 Rout
Ocean View, NJ 08230
609-624-0767

Parkertown, NJ

Baker's Acres Campground, Inc
230 Willets Ave.
Parkertown, NJ 08087
609-296-2664

Pilesgrove, NJ

Four Seasons Campground
158 Woodstown-Daretown
Pilesgrove, NJ 08098
609-769-3635

Pleasantville, NJ

Pleasantville Campgrounds
408 NOrth Mill Road
Pleasantville, NJ 08232
609-641-3176

Pomona, NJ

Evergreen Woods Lakefront Res
Box 197
Pomona, NJ 08240
609-652-1577

Pomona Campground
Oak Drive, P.O. Box 675
Pomona, NJ 08240
609-965-2123

Port Republic, NJ

Atlantic City Blueberry Hill
Route 624, Dept., SB98,
Port Republic, NJ 08241
609-652-1644

224

Chestnut Lake Resort
631 Old New York Road
Port Republic, NJ 08241
609-652-1005

Thousand Trails-Chestnut Lake
631 Chestnut Neck Road
Port Republic, NJ 08241
609-652-1005

South Seaville, NJ

Jersey Shore Haven
728 Dennisville Road, P.
South Seaville, NJ 08246
609-861-2293

Sussex, NJ

Beaver Hill Campground
P.O. Box 353
Sussex, NJ 07461
973-827-0670

Pleasant Acres Farm Campground
61 DeWitt Road
Sussex, NJ 07461
800-722-4166

Tall Timbers Campground
100 Tall Timbers Road
Sussex, NJ 07461
973-875-1991

Swainton, NJ

Outdoor World Sea Pines Resor
1535 US Highway 9
Swainton, NJ 08210
609-465-4518

Toms River, NJ

Albocondo Campground
1480 Whitesville Road
Toms River, NJ 08755
732-349-4079

Surf and Stream Campground
1801 Ridgeway Road
Toms River, NJ 08757
732-349-8919

Tuckahoe, NJ

Scenic Riverview Campground
465 Route 49, Box 184
Tuckahoe, NJ 08250
609-628-4566

Tuckerton, NJ

Atlantic City North KOA
P.O. Box 242, Stage Road
Tuckerton, NJ 08087
800-562-3315

West Cape May, NJ

Depot Travel Park
800 Broadway
West Cape May, NJ 08204
609-884-2533
West Creek, NJ

Sea Pirate Campground
P.O. Box 271
West Cape May, NJ 08092
609-296-7400

Williamstown, NJ

Hospitality Creek Campground
117 Coles Mill Road
Williamstown, NJ 08094
609-629-5140 Woodbine, NJ

Holiday Haven Family Campgrou
230 Route 50
Williamstown, NJ 08270
609-476-2963

New Mexico

Abiquiu, NM
Riana Campground
Abiquiu Lake Project Office
Abiquiu, NM 87510
505-685-4371

Albuquerque, NM
Albuquerque Central KOA
12400 Skyline Road
Albuquerque, NM 87123
505-296-2729

Almogordo, NM
Alamogordo/White Sands KOA
412 24th St.
Almogordo, NM 88310
800-562-3992

Alamogordo Roadrunner Campground
412 24th St.
Alamogordo, NM 88310
Phone: 505-437-3003
info@roadrunnercampground.com

Angel Fire, NM
Sierra Bonita Cabins and RV Park
PO Box 963
Angel Fire, NM 87710
800-942-1556

Artesia, NM
Artesia RV Park
201 West Hermosa Dr
Artesia, NM 88210
505-746-6184

Bernalillo, NM
Albuquerque N./Bernalillo KOA
P.O. Box 758
Bernalillo, NM 87004
800-562-3616

Bernardo, NM
Kiva RV Park and Horse Motel
21 Old Hwy 60 West
Bernardo, NM 87006
877-374-Kiva

Bloomfield, NM
Bloomfield KOA
1900 E. Blanco Blvd.
Bloomfield, NM 87413

800-562-8513

Caballo, NM
Truth or Consequences KOA
HC 31, Box 105
Caballo, NM 87931
800-562-2813

Carlsbad, NM
Carlsbad RV Park & Campground
4301 National Parks Hwy.
Carslbad, NM 88220
505-885-6333

Carrizozo, NM
Sands RV Park and Motel
South Hwy 54
Carrizozo, NM 88301
800-81Sands

Chama, NM
Rio Chama RV Park
182 North State Hwy17
Chama, NM 87520
505-756-2303

Clayton, NM
Meadowlark KOA
Box 366
Clayton, NM 88415
800-562-9507

Columbus, NM
Pancho Villa State Park
400 Highway 9W
Columbus, NM 88029
505-531-2711

Deming, NM
A Deming Roadrunner RV Park
2849 E Motel Dr.
Deming, NM 88030
Voice: (505) 546-6960 / (800) 226-9937
Fax: (505) 546-6960
roadrunnerrv@zianet.com

Dwyer, NM
Faywood Hot Springs
165 Hwy 61, HC 71
Dwyer, NM 88034
505-536-9663

East Otis, NM
Tolland State Forest
PO Box 342, Tolland Road
East Otis, NM 01029

413-269-6002

Elephant Butte, NM

107 Country Club Blvd
PO Drawer 981
Elephant Butte, NM 87935
800-808-5848

Gallup, NM

Gallup KOA
2925 W. Hwy. 66
Gallup, NM 87301
800-562-3915

Jemez Springs, NM

Trail's End RV Park
37695 Hwy 126
Jemez Springs, NM 87025
505-829-4072

Las Vegas, NM

Las Vegas KOA
HCR 31, Box 16
Las Vegas, NM 87701
800-562-3423

Logan, NM

Ute Lake State Park
PO Box 52
Logan, NM 88426
877-664-7787

Lordsburg, NM

Lordsburg KOA
1501 Lead St.
Lordsburg, NM 88045
800-562-5772

Prewitt, NM

Bluewater Lake State Park
Lake Rte Box 3419
Prewitt, NM 87045
505-876-2391

Raton, NM

Raton KOA
1330 South 2nd St.
Raton, NM 87740
800-562-9033

Santa Fe, NM

Los Campos De Santa Fe RV Resort
3574 Cerrillos Road
Santa Fe, NM 87507
Voice: (505) 473-1949 / (800) 852-8160
Fax: (505) 471-9220
loscampossf@aol.com

Santa Fe KOA
934 Old Las Vegas Hwy.
Santa Fe, NM 87505
800-562-1514

The Trailer Ranch
3471 Cerrillos Road, #27
Santa Fe, NM 87505
Voice: (505) 471-9970
Fax: (505) 424-4460
trailerranch@aol.com

Santa Rosa, NM

Santa Rosa KOA
Box 423
Santa Rosa, NM 88435
800-562-0836

Silver City, NM

Silver City KOA
11824 Hwy. 180 E.
Silver City, NM 88061
800-562-7623 Taos, NM

Manzano's RV Park
103 Flurry Lane
Silver City, NM 88061
505-538-0918

Taos Valley RV Park & Campground
120 Este Es Road
7204 NDCBU
Taos, NM 87571
Toll Free: (800)999-7571
Phone: 505-758-4469
camptaos@newmex.com

Taos, NM

Monte Bello RV Park
24819 Hwy 64 West
Taos, NM 87529
505-751-0774

Tucumcari, NM

Tucumcari KOA
6299 Quay Road AL
K88401
800-562-1871

Whites City, NM

Whites City RV Park
17 Calsbad Caverns Hwy
Whites City, NM 88268
800-Caverns

New York

Ausable Chasm, NY

Ausable Chasm KOA
P.O. Box 390
Ausable Chasm, NY 12911
800-562-9105

Averill Park, NY

Alps Family Campground
1928 NY 43
Averill Park, NY 12018
Voice - (518) 674-5565

Bath, NY

Hickory Hill Family Camping Resort
7531 Mitchellsville Road
Bath, NY 14810
Voice - (607) 776-4345
Toll Free - (800) 760-0947
Fax - (607) 776-9218
camp@hickoryhillcampresort.com
http://www.hickoryhillcampresort.com

Batvia, NY

Lei-Ti Campground
9979 Francis Road
Batavia, NY 14020
Voice - (585) 343-8600
Toll Free - (800) 445-3484
Fax - (585) 345-0713
leiti@leiti.com
http://www.leiti.com

Bridgewater, NY

Lake Chalet Campground and Motel
593 Rt. 8 (PO Box 22)
Bridgewater, NY 13313
Voice - (315) 822-6074
Fax - (315) 822-3267
lakechalet@mailstation.com

Byron, NY

Southwoods RV Resort
6749 Townline Road
Byron, NY 14422
Voice - (716) 548-9002

Caledonia, NY

Genesee Country Campground
40 Flint Hill Road (PO Box 100)
Caledonia, NY 14423
Voice - (585) 538-4200
Fax - (585) 538-9253

jaka401@frontiernet.net

Cambridge, NY

Lake Lauderdale Campground
744 County Rt. 61
Cambridge, NY 12816
Voice - (518) 677-8855
Fax - (518) 677-3133
joanllc@yahoo.com
http://www.lakelauderdalecampground.com

Campbell, NY

Camp Bell Campground
8700 State Rt. 415 (PO Box 463)
Campbell, NY 14821
Voice - (607) 527-3301
Toll Free - (800) 587-3301
Fax - (607) 527-3720
campbellcampground@yahoo.com
http://www.campbellcampground.com

Canandaigua, NY

Bristol Woodlands Campground
4835 S Hill Road
Canandaigua, NY 14424
Voice - (585) 229-2290
Fax - (585) 396-1417
brwoodland@aol.com
http://www.bristolwoodlands.com

Clayton, NY

Birch Haven Campground - Clayton
38191 Rt. 12E
Clayton, NY 13624
Voice - (315) 686-5253
Toll Free - (800) 235-8331

Cooperstown, NY

Cooperstown Beaver Valley Cabins & Campsites
PO Box 704
Cooperstown, NY 13326
Voice - (607) 293-7324
Toll Free - (800) 726-7314
info@beavervalleycampground.com

Cooperstown Famous Family Campground
230 Petkewec Road
Cooperstown, NY 13326
607-293-7766

Cooperstown KOA
P.O. Box 786
Cooperstown, NY 13326
800-562-3402

Corinth, NY

River Road Campgrounds
5254 Rt. 9N
Corinth, NY 12822
Voice - (518) 654-6630
Fax - (518) 654-9995
http://www.theriverroad.com

Corning, NY

Ferenbaugh Campsite
4682 SR 414
Corning, NY 14830
Voice - (607) 962-6193
Fax - (607) 962-6193
ferencamp@aol.com
http://www.ferenbaugh.com

Dansville, NY

Sugar Creek Glen Campground
11288 Poags Hole Road
Dansville, NY 14437
Voice - (585) 335-6294

Delevan, NY

Arrowhead Camping Area
10487 Rte. 16
Delevan, NY 14042
Voice - (716) 492-3715
reservations@arrowheadcamping.com
http://www.arrowheadcamping.com

Dewittville, NY

Chautauqua Heights Camping Resort
5652 Thumb Road
Dewittville, NY 14728
Voice - (716) 386-3804
Fax - (716) 386-3043
contact@chautauquahgts.com
http://www.chautauquahgts.com

Dexter, NY

Black River Bay Campground
(PO Box 541) Foster Park Road
Dexter, NY 13634
Voice - (315) 639-3735

Duane, NY

Deer River Campsite
County Road 14 (Red Tavern Road)
Duane, NY 12953
Voice - (518) 483-0060
Fax - (518) 481-6286
deerriver@westelcom.com
http://www.deerrivercampsite.com

Farmington, NY

Canandaigua/Rochester KOA
5374 Farmington Townline Road

Farmington, NY 14425
800-562-0533

Florida, NY

Black Bear Campground
197 Wheeler Road (PO Box 82)
Florida, NY 10921
Voice - (845) 651-7717
Toll Free - (888) 867-2267
Fax - (845) 651-7918
topcamp@warwick.net
http://www.blackbearcampground.com

Franklin, NY

Unadilla/I-88/Oneonta KOA
Road 1, Box 186
Franklin, NY 13775
800-562-9032

Gainesville, NY

Woodstream Campsite RV Resort
5440 School Road
Gainesville, NY 14066
Voice - (585) 493-5643
Toll Free - (877) 226-7669
camp@woodstreamcampsite.com
http://www.woodstreamcampsite.com

Gilboa, NY

Nickerson Park Campground
378 Stryker Road
Gilboa, NY 12076
Voice - (607) 588-7327

Grand Island, NY

Niagara Falls KOA
2570 Grand Island Blvd.
Grand Island, NY 14072
800-562-0787

Hammond, NY

McLear's Cottage Colony and Campground
2477 County Route 6
Hammond, NY 13646
Voice - (315) 375-6508
Fax - (315) 375-4113
gofishin@mclears.com
http://www.mclears.com

Herkimer, NY

Herkimer KOA
Route 28
Herkimer, NY 13350
800-562-0897

Houghton, NY

Camping at Mariposa Ponds

7632 Centerville Road Box 4
Houghton, NY 14744
Voice - (585) 567-4211
Fax - (585) 567-8211
mariposa@houghton.edu
http://www.mariposaponds.com

Ithaca, NY

Spruce Row Campsite and RV Resort
2271 Kraft Road
Ithaca, NY 14850
Voice - (607) 387-9225
Fax - (607) 387-9225
sprucerow@zoom-dsl.com

Keeseville, NY

Ausable River Campsite
367 Rt. 9 N
Keeseville, NY 12944
Voice - (518) 834-9379

Lake George, NY

Lake George/Saratoga KOA
P.O. Box 533
Lake George, NY 12845
800-562-0368

Adirondack Adventure Resorts of Lake George
291 Fortsville Road
Gansevoort, NY 12832
Toll Free - (800) 340-CAMP
Fax - (518) 893-0120
acinc@net-link.net
http://www.adirondackadventureresorts.com

Adirondack Camping Village
PO Box 406
Lake George, NY 12845
Voice - (518) 668-5226
Fax - (518) 668-4256
info@adirondackcampingvillage.com
http://www.adirondackcampingvillage.com

Lake George Escape Camping Resort
175 E Schroon River Road
Lake George, NY 12845
Voice - (518) 623-3207
Toll Free - (800) 327-3188
Fax - (518) 623-3234
info@lakegeorgeescape.com
http://www.LakeGeorgeEscape.com

Le Roy, NY

Lei-Ti, Too!
8101 Conlon Road
Le Roy, NY 14482

Voice - (585) 768-4883
Toll Free - (800) 445-3484
leiti@leiti.com

Lewiston, NY

Niagara Falls North/Lewiston KOA
1250 Pletcher Road, Box 71
Lewiston, NY 14092
800-562-8715 Livingston Manor, NY

Covered Bridge Casmpsite
68 Conklin Hill Road
Lewiston, NY 12758
845-439-5093 Malone, NY

Deer River Campsite
HCR-01, Box 101A
Lewiston, NY 12953
518-483-0060

Massena, NY

Massena International Kampground
84 County Rte. 42A
Massena, NY 13662
Voice - (315) 769-9483
massenakamp@earthlink,net

Mexico, NY

Mexico KOA
291 Tubbs Road
Mexico, NY 13114
800-562-3967

Yogi Bear's Jellystone Park at Mexico
601 CR 16
Mexico, NY 13114
Voice - (315) 963-7096
Toll Free - (800) 248-7096
Fax - (315) 963-4192
campyogi@dreamscape.com
http://www.jellystonecny.com

Natural Bridge, NY

Adirondack - 1000 Islands Camping
6081 State Rt. 3
Natural Bridge, NY 13665
Voice - (315) 644-4880
Fax - (315) 644-4017
nbwkoa@uasdatanet.net
http://www.aticamping.com

Natural Bridge/Watertown KOA
Box 71 A, Route 3
13665
800-562-4780 Kellystone Park
51 Hawkins Road

Nineveh, NY 13813
Voice - (607) 639-1090
Toll Free - (877) 397-0204
Fax - (607) 639-3810
kellystone_park@yahoo.com
http://www.kellystonepark.com

Niagara Falls, NY

Royal Motel and Campgrounds
3333 Niagara Falls Blvd.
North Tonawanda, NY 14120
Voice - (716) 693-5695
Fax - (716) 693-5695
theroyalmotel@yahoo.com

Old Forge, NY

Old Forge KOA
Box 51
Niagara Falls, NY 13420
800-562-3251

Oneonta, NY

Susquehanna Trail Campground
4292 St. Hwy. 7
Oneonta, NY 13820
Voice - (607) 432-1122
Toll Free - (800) 494-0103
Fax - (607) 431-9858
susqtrls@stny.rr.com
http://www.susquehannatrail.com

Ovid, NY

Sned-Acres Family Campground
6590 S Cayuga Lake Road
Ovid, NY 14521
Voice - (607) 869-9787
sned.acres@fltg.net
http://www.sned-acres.com

Petersburg, NY

Aqua Vista Valley Campground
82 Aemsby Road
Petersburg, NY 12138
518-658-3659

Phelps, NY

Cheerful Valley Campground
1412 Rt. 14
Phelps, NY 14532
Voice - (315) 781-1222
cheerfulvalley@cny.net
Plainville, NY

Syracuse KOA
7620 Plainville Road
Phelps, NY 13137
800-562-9107 Plattekill, NY

Newburgh/New York City KOA
Box 134 D
Phelps, NY 12568
800-562-7220

Poland, NY

West Canada Creek Campsites
12275 State Route 28
Poland, NY 13431
Voice - (315) 826-7390
Toll Free - (888) 461-2267
Fax - (315) 826-5239
camp@westcanadacreekcampsites.com
http://www.westcanadacreekcampsites.com

Portageville, NY

WeFour Winds Campground
7350 Tenefly Road
Portageville, NY 14536
Voice - (585) 493-2794
Toll Free - (877) 777-8655
4winds@wycol.com
Rhinebeck, NY

Interlake Farm Campground
45 Lake Drive
Portageville, NY 12572
914-266-5387 Roscoe, NY

Roscoe Campsites
607-498-5264

Russell Brook C_{ampsite}
101 Russell Brook Road
Roscoe, NY 12776
Voice - (607) 498-5416
russellbrook@hotmail.com
http://www.russellbrook.com

Twin Islands Campsite
607-498-5326

Saugerties, NY

Saugerties/Woodstock KOA
882 Route 212
Saugerties, NY 12477
800-562-4081

Springwater, NY

CaHoliday Hill Campground
7818 Marvin Hill Road
Springwater, NY 14560
Voice - (585) 669-2600
Toll Free - (800) 719-2267
info@holidayhillcampground.com
http://www.holidayhillcampground.com

Stow, NY

Camp Chautauqua Camping Resort
3900 Rt. 394
Stow, NY 14785
Voice - (716) 789-3435
Toll Free - (800) 578-4849
Fax - (716) 789-4415
campchau@cecomet.net
http://www.campchautauqua.com

Swan Lake, NY

Swan Lake Camplands
Box 336, Fulton Road
Swan Lake, NY 12783
914-292-4781

Verona, NY

Peaceful Pines Campground & RV Park
6591 Blackman Corners Road (PO Box 126)
Verona, NY 13478
Voice - (315) 336-7318
Toll Free - (800) 771-7711

Rome/Verona KOA
6591 Blackmans Cor Road
Verona, NY 13478
800-562-7218

Warrensburg, NY

Daggett Lake Campsites
660 Glen Athol Road
Warrensburg, NY 12885
518-623-2198

Lake George / Schroon Valley Resort
1730 Schroon River Road
Warrensburg, NY 12885
Voice - (518) 494-2451
Toll Free - (800) 958-2267
Fax - (518) 494-4715
info@lakegeorgecamping.com
http://www.lakegeorgecamping.com

Watkins Glen, NY

Watkins Glen/Corning KOA
Box 228
Watkins Glen, NY 14891
800-562-7430

Westfield, NY

Westfield/Lake Erie KOA
8001 Route 5
Westfield, NY 14787
800-562-3973

North Carolina

Almond, NC

Tumbling Waters Campground & Trout Farm
52 Panther Creek Road
Almond, NC 28702
828-479-3814

Turkey Creek Campground
135 Turkey Creek Road
Almond, NC 28702
828-488-8966

Apex, NC

Crosswinds Campground
Jordan Lake State Recreation Area
280 State Park Road
Apex, NC 27502
919-362-0586

Poplar Point Campground
Jordan Lake State Recreation Area
280 State Park Road
Apex, NC 27523
919-362-0586

Ashboro, NC

Holly Bluff Family Campground
4846 NC Hwy. 49 South
Ashboro, NC 27203 USA
336-857-2761

Asheville, NC

Asheville Taps RV Park
1327 Tunnel Road
Asheville, NC 28815
704-299-8277

Bear Creek RV Park & Campground
81 S. Bear Creek Road
Asheville, NC 28806
704-253-0798

Campfire Lodgings
7 Appalachian Village Road
Asheville, NC 28804
828-658-80112
800-933-8012

French Broad River Campground
1030 Old Marshall Hwy.
Asheville, NC 288004
704-658-0772Balsam, NC

Moonshine Creek Campground
Dark Ridge Road
Asheville, NC 28707
704-586-6666

Balsam, NC

Moonshine Creek Campground
Dark Ridge Road
Balsam, NC 28707
828-586-6666

Banner Elk, NC

Grandfather Mountain Club
Hw. 105, S. Park Road
Banner Elk, NC 28607
704-963-7275

Boone, NC

Boon KOA Kampground, Inc.
123 Harmony Mtn. Ln.
Boone, NC 28607
704-264-7250

Boonville, NC

Holly Ridge Family Campground
5140 River Road
Boonville, NC 27011
336-367-7756

Brevard, NC

Black Forest Family Camping Resort
Summer Road, Cedar Mtn.
Brevard, NC 28718
704-884-2267

Bryson City, NC

Cooper Creek Campground
122 Cooper Creed Road
Bryson City, NC 28713
704-488-3922

Deep Creek Tube Center & Campground
1090 W. Deep Creek Road
Bryson City, NC 28713
704-488-6055

Lost Mine Campground
1000 Silvermine Road
Bryson City, NC 28713
704-488-6445

Candler, NC

Asheville West KOA Campground
309 Wiggins Road
Candler, NC 28715
704-665-7015

Asheville West KOA
309 Wiggins Road
Candler, NC 28715
800-562-2806Canton, NC

Laurel Bank
350 Campers Lane.
Candler, NC 28716
704-235-8940

Mountain Shadows Campground
3748 Lake Logan Road
Candler, NC 28716
704-648-0132

Riverhouse Acres
4744 Pisgah Dr.
Candler, NC 28716
704-646-0303

Cape Hatteras, NC

Cape Point
Rte 1, Box 675
Cape hatteras, NC 27954
252-473-2111

Ocracoke
Rte 1 Box 675
Cape Hatteras, NC 27954
252-473-2111

Carolina Beach, NC

Carolina Beach State Park
PO Box 475
Carolina Beach, NC 28428
910-458-8206

Cashiers, NC

Singing Waters Camping Resort
1006 Trout Creek Road
Cashiers, NC 28783
704-293-5872

Cedar Mountain, NC

Black Forest Family Camping Resort
P.O. Box 266
Cedar Mountain, NC 28718
828-884-CAMP

Cherokee, NC

Adventure Trail
Camp Creek Road
Cherokee, NC 28719
704-497-3651

Cherokee Campground & Cabins

US 19 N & US 441
Cherokee, NC 28719
704-497-9838

Cherokee/Great Smokies KOA
SR. Box 39
Cherokee, NC 28719
800-562-7784

Cherokee/Great Smokies KOA
Big Cove Road
Cherokee, NC 28719
704-497-9711

Eljawa Campground
Old No. 4 Road
Cherokee, NC 28719
704-497-7204

Happy Holiday RV Park & Campground
Rt. 1, Box 132E, Hwy. 19F
Cherokee, NC 28719
704-497-7250

Indian Creek Campground/Indian Hills Cabins
Bunches Creek Road
Cherokee, NC 28719
704-497-4361

Lost Cove Campground
1591 Hwy. 19
Cherokee, NC 28719
704-497-6168

Mile High Campground
Box 30, Bradley Loop Road
Cherokee, NC 28719
704-497-2230

River Valley Resort
Big Cove Road
Cherokee, NC 28719
704-497-3540

Riverside Campground
Hwy. 441 S. Bypass
Cherokee, NC 28719
701-497-9311

Smokemont Campground
107 Park Headquarters Road
Cherokee, NC 37738
865-436-1200

Twin Forks
Big Cove Road
Cherokee, NC 28719

236

704-497-4330

Wagon Train Campgrounds
US 19, Soco Road
Cherokee, NC 28719
704-497-9502

Welch Campground
P.O. Box 747
Cherokee, NC 28719
704-497-4716

Wolf Campground
102 Adam's Creek
Cherokee, NC 28719
704-497-9868

Yogi in the Smokies
317 Galamore Bridge Road
Cherokee, NC 28719
828-497-9151

Chimney Rock, NC

Hickory Nut Falls Family Campground
P.O. Box 97
Chimney Rock, NC 28720
704-625-4014

Lake Lure RV Park & Campground
176 Boys Camp Road
Chimney Rock, NC 28746
704-625-9160 Chocowinity, NC

Twin Lakes Camping Resort & Yacht Basin
1618 Memory Lane
Chimney Rock, NC 27817
252-946-5700

Cruso, NC

Riverside Campground
6 Happy Camper Dr.
Cruso, NC 28716
704-235-9128

Danbury, NC

Hanging Rock State Park
2005 Visitor Center
Danbury, NC 27016
336-593-8480

Enfield, NC

Enfield/Rocky Mount KOA
101 Bell Acres
Enfield, NC 27823
800-562-5894

Fletcher, NC

Rutledge Lake Travel Park
170 Rutledge Lake Road
Fletcher, NC 28732
828-654-7873
800-368-3209

Franklin, NC

Country Woods RV Park
2887 Georgia Road
Franklin, NC 28734
828-524-4339

Standing Indian
90 Sloan Road
Franklin, NC 28734
828-524-6441

Frisco, NC

Frisco Woods Campground, Inc
Box 159
Frisco, NC 27936
704-955-5208

Four Oaks, NC

Smithfield Best Holiday Trav-L-Park
497 Highway 701 South
Four Oaks, NC 27524
919-934-3181

Franklin, NC

Cartoogechay Creek Campground
91 No Name Road
Franklin, NC 28734
704-524-8553

Country Woods RV Park
2887 Georgia Road
Franklin, NC 28734
704-524-4339

Cullasaja River Campground
6269 Highlands Road
Franklin, NC 28734
704-524-2559

Downtown RV Park
160 Heritage Hollow Dr.
Franklin, NC 28734
704-369-2125

Great Smokey Mountain Fish Camp & Safaris
Hwy. 28N at The Little Tennessee River
Franklin, NC 28734
704-369-5295

Morrison Campground & Rental
29 Bates Branch Road
Franklin, NC 28734
704-524-4783

Mountain Springs Campground
189 Lake Ledford Road
Franklin, NC 28734
704-524-0469

Mt. Mountain Campground
151 Mt. Mtn. Road
Franklin, NC 28734
704-524-6155

Rainbow Springs Campground
7984 W. Old Murphy Road
Franklin, NC 28734
704-524-6376

Rose Creek Mine & Campground
115 Terrace Ridge Dr.
Franklin, NC 28734
704-524-3225

Glenville, NC

Ralph J. Andrews Park
Rt. 66, Box 132E Cullowhee
Franklin, NC 28723
704-743-3923

Greensboro, NC

Greenboro Campgrounds, Inc.
2300 Montreal Avenue
Greensboro, NC 27406
336-274-4143

Hayesville, NC

Rivers Edge RV Park, Inc.
Hwy. 64E
Hayesville, NC 28904
704-389-6781

Sundowner RV Resort
42 Sundowner Circle
Hayesville, NC 28904
704-389-3241

Tusquittee Campground & Cabins
9594 Tusquittee Road
Hayesville, NC 28904
704-389-8520

Hendersonville, NC

Big Willow Mountain Resort, Inc.
Rt. 13, Box 296, Willow Mt. Road
Hendersonville, NC 28739

704-693-0187

Blue Ridge Travel Trailer Park
3576 Chimney Rock Road
Hendersonville, NC 28792
704-685-9207

Lazy Boy Travel Park
110 Old Sunset Hill Road
Hendersonville, NC 28792
704-697-7165

Red Gates RV Park
Sugarloaf Road
Hendersonville, NC 28792
704-685-8787Hiddenite, NC

Hiddenite Family Campground
601 Princess La.
Hendersonville, NC 28636
828-632-3815

Highlands, NC

Sassafras Gap Campground
5920 Walhalla Road
Highlands, NC 28741
704-526-9909

Skyline Lodge & Restaurant
Flat Mtn. Road
Highlands, NC 28741
704-526-2121

Hot Springs, NC

Hot Springs Campground & Spa
300 Bridge St.
Highlands, NC 28743
704-622-7676

Meadow Fork Campground
5995 Meadow Fork Road
Highlands, NC 28743
704-622-9505

Jefferson, NC

Greenfield
Mt. Jefferson Road
Jefferson, NC 28640
704-336-9106

Lake Toxaway, NC

Pounding Branch Campground
Slick Fisher Road
Lake Toxaway, NC 28747
704-966-4359

Riverbend RV Park

Hwy. 281 N.
Lake Toxaway, NC 28747
704-966-4214

Laurel Springs, NC

Miller's Camping
973 Miller Road. Blue Ridge Pkwy. MP 247
Laurel Springs, NC 28644
704-336-8156

Linville Falls, NC

Linville Falls Trailer Lodge & Camp
Gurney Franklin Road
Linville Falls, NC 28647
704-765-2681

Long Beach, NC

Long Beach Campground
5011 East Oak Island Drive
Long Beach, NC 28465
910-278-9905

Maggie Valley, NC

Connie's Campground
68 Leisure Lane
Maggie Valley, NC 28751
704-926-3619

Creekwood Farm RV Park
4096 Jonathan Creek Road
Maggie Valley, NC 28786
704-926-7977

Happy Valley RV Park
40 Happy Valley Circle
Maggie Valley, NC 28751
704-926-0327

Hillbilly Campground & RV Park
4115 Soco Road
Maggie Valley, NC 28751
704-926-3353

Presley Campground & RV Park
1786 Soco Road
Maggie Valley, NC 28751
704-926-1904

Rippling Waters Creekside RV Park
3962 Soco Road
Maggie Valley, NC 28751
704-926-7787

Marion, NC

Hidden Valley Campground
Rt. 1, Box 377, Deacon Dr.
Marion, NC 28752

704-652-7208

Lake James Landing
Rt. 6, Box 862
Marion, NC 28752
704-652-2907

Mountain Laurel Resort
Rt. 3, Poncheon Fork Road
Marion, NC 28754
704-689-5058

Mountain Paradise Campground
Rt. 3, Box 316
Marion, NC 28752
704-756-4085

Mountain Stream RV Park
1820 Buck Creek Road
Marion, NC 28752
828-724-9013

Mocksville, NC

Lake Myers RV Resort
US HWY 64 East
150 Fred Lanier Road
Mocksville, NC 27028
336-492-7736

Morehead City, NC

Whispering Pines Campground
P.O. Box 726
Morehead City, NC 28557
919-726-4902

Morgantown, NC

Daniel Boone Campground
Hwy. 181
Morgantown, NC 28638
704-396-5124

Lake James Family Campground
5786 Benefied Landing Road
Morgantown, NC 28761
704-584-0190

Rose Creek Campground
3471 Rose Creed Road
Morgantown, NC 28655
704-438-4338

Murphy, NC

Circle "J" Family Campground
Rt. 6, Box 289
Murphy, NC 28906
704-494-7042

Hanging Dog
123 Woodland, Dr
Murphy, NC 28906
828-837-5152

Mr. Piper's Campground
Rt. 6, Box 101B
Murphy, NC 28906
704-644-9130

Riverbend Campground
Hwy. 74, 19-129 N. Bypass
Murphy, NC 28906
704-837-6223

Stateline Village RV Park
Hwy. 64 W. Ducktown
Murphy, NC 28906
704-423-5006

Nags Head, NC

Cape Hatteras KOA
Box 100
Nags Head, NC 27968
252-987-2307

Nebo, NC

Paddy Creek Campground
1465 Old NC 105
Nebo, NC 28761
704-584-1346

Newland, NC

Buck Hill Campground
6401 South US 19E Hwy
Newland, NC 28657 USA
828-765-7387

Old Fort, NC

Catawba Falls Family Campground
Rt 3, Box 230
Old Fort, NC 28762
704-668-4831

Pinehurst, NC

Village of Pinehurst RV Park
Hwy 15-501 No.
Pinehurst, NC. 28374
910-295-5452

Pineola, NC

Down by the River Campground
P.O. Box 428
Pineola, NC 28662
704-733-5057

Piney Creek, NC

Rivercamp USA, Inc.
1 River Camp Road At NCSR 1308
Piney Creek, NC 28663
336-359-2267

Robbinsville, NC

Hidden Waters RV Park & Campground
Rt 3, Box 81, Tullulah Hwy. 129 S
Robbinsville, NC 28771
704-479-3509

Shook's RV Park & Trout Ponds
Rt 3., Box 120
Robbinsville, NC 28771
704-479-6930

Rutherfordton, NC

Four Paws Kingdom Campground
335 Lazy Creek Dr.
Rutherfordton, NC 28139
828-287-7324

Saluda, NC

Orchard Lake Campground
231 Orchard Lake Road
Saluda, NC 28773
704-749-3901

Selma, NC

Selma/Smithfield KOA
428 Campground Road
Selma, NC 27576
800-562-5897

Sparta, NC

Hidden Valley Campground
Hidden Valley Road
Sparta, NC 28675
704-336-8911

Spruce Pine, NC

Bear Den Family Campground
Rt.3, Box 284
Spruce Pine, NC 28777
704-765-2888

Buck Hill Campground
6401 US 19E Newland
Spruce Pine, NC 28657
704-765-7387

Statesville, NC

Midway Campground and RV Resort
114 Midway Dr.
Statesville, NC 28677

704-546-7615
1-888-754-4809

Statesville KOA
162 KOA Lane
Statesville, NC 28677
800-562-5705

Swannanoa, NC

Asheville East KOA
Box 485
Swannanoa, NC 28778
800-562-5907

Sylva, NC

Fort Tatham
175 Tatham Creek Road
Sylva, NC 28779
704-586-6662

Topton, NC

Nelson's Nantahala Hideaway
Hwy. 19/74
Topton, NC 28781
704-321-4407

Union Grove, NC

Vanhoy Farms Family Campground
P.O. Box 38
Union Grove, NC 28689
704-539-5493

Wade, NC

Fayetteville/Wade KOA
P.O. Box 67
Wade, NC 28395
800-562-5350

Waynesville, NC

Winngray Family Campground
26 Winngray Lane
28786
704-926-3170

Whittier, NC

Smokey Trails Campground
1385 Shoal Creek Road
Whittier, NC 28789
704-497-6693

Timberlake
3270 Conleys Creed Road
Whittier, NC 28789
704-497-7320

Whispering Pines, NC

The Heritage
253 Sadler Road
Whispering Pines, NC 28387
910-949-3433

Wilkesboro, NC

Bandits Roost
P.O. Box 182
Wilkesboro, NC 28697
704-336-3390

Doughton Park Campground
45356 Blue Ridge Parkway
Wilkesboror, NC 28644
336-372-4499

Warrior Creek
P.O. Box 182
Wilkesboro, NC 28697
704-336-3390

North Dakota

Bismarck, ND

Bismarck KOA
3720 Centennial Road
Bismarck, ND 58501
800-562-2636

Bottineau, ND

Lake Metigoshe State Park
No 2 Lake Metigoshe State Park Road
Bottineau, ND 58318
701-263-4651

Cavalier, ND

Graham's Island State Park
152 South Duncan Drive
Cavalier, ND 58301
701-766-4015

Icelandic State Park
13571 Hwy. 5
Cavalier, ND 58220
701-265-4561

Dickinson, ND

Camp on the Heart
387 S. State Avenue
Dickinson, ND 58602
701-225-9600

Epping, ND

Lewis and Clark State Park
119th Rd NW
Epping, NC 58843
701-859-3071

Garrison, ND

Sportsmen's Centennial Park
PO Box 98
Garrison, ND 58540
701-337-5377

Jamestown, ND

Frontier Fort Campground
PO Box 143
Jamestown, ND 58402
701-252-7492

Jamestown Campground
3605 80th Avenue SE
Jamestown, ND 58401
Voice: (701) 252-6262 / (800) 313-6262
Fax: (701) 252-6249

ahc@mailstation.com

Jamestown KOA
3605 80th Ave., SE
Jamestown, ND 58401
800-562-6350 Minot, ND

Minot KOA
5261 Highway 52 S
Jamestown, ND 58701
800-562-7421

Roughrider Campground
500 54th Street NW
Minot, ND 58703-8614
Voice: (701) 852-8442
Fax: (701) 852-9482
roughrid@minot.com

Larimore, ND

Larimore Dam Recreation Area
PO Box 268
Larimore, ND 58251
701-343-2078

Mandan, ND

Fort Lincoln State Park
4480 Fort Lincoln Road
Mandan, ND 58554
701-667-6340

Ohio

Baltimore, OH

Rippling Stream Campground
3640 Reynoldsburg-Baltimore Road
Baltimore, OH 43105
740-862-6065

Bellville, OH

Yogi Bear's Jellystone Park- Mansfield
6500 Black Road
Bellville, OH 44813
Local Phone: 419-886-2267

Bluffton, OH

Twin Lakes Park
3506 TR 34
Bellville, OH 45817
419-477-5255

Bowling Green, OH

Fire Lake Camper Park
13630 W. Kramer Road
Bowling Green, OH 43402
888-879-2267

Brookville, OH

Dayton KOA
7796 Wellbaum Road
Brookville, OH 45309
Local Phone: 937-833-3888
Toll Free: 800-KOA-331
Fax: 937-833-2477
Email: daytonKOA@aol.com

Dayton Tall Timbers KOA
7796 Welbaum Road
Brookville, OH 45309
937-833-3888

Brunswick, OH

Willow Lake Park
PO Box 102
Brunswick, OH 44212
330-225-6580

Buckeye Lake, OH

Buckeye Lake KOA/Cols. East
4460 Walnut Road
P. O. Box 972
Buckeye Lake, OH 43008
Local Phone: 740-928-0706
Fax: 740-928-0462
Email: mikeandshirleyg@earthlink.net

Butler, OH

Butler/Mohican KOA
6918 Bunker Hill Road S.
Butler, OH 44822
800-562-8719

Cambridge, OH

Hillview Acres Campground
66271 Wolf's Den Road
Cambridge, OH 43725
Local Phone: 740-439-3348

Canton, OH

Bear Creek Resort Ranch KOA
3232 Downing St. S.W.
Canton, OH 44626
Local Phone: 330-484-3901
Toll Free: 800-562-3903
Fax: 330-484-4809
Email: bearcreek@iwon.com

Carroll, OH

Camp Coonpath
4625 Coonpath Road, NW
Carroll, OH 43112
740-756-9218

Chillicothe, OH

Sun Valley Campground
10105 C.R. 550, Box 27
Chillicothe, OH 45601
Local Phone: 740-775-3490

Clyde, OH

Seneca Campground
6955 South S.R. 101
Clyde, OH 43410
419-639-2887

Collville, OH

Carthage Gap Campground
22575 Brimstone Road
Coolville, OH 45723
Local Phone: 740-667-3072
Email: carthagegaprvpark@1st.net

Conneaut, OH

Evergreen Lake Park
703 Center Road
Conneaut, OH 44030
Local Phone: 440-599-8802
Email: camper@suite224.net

Windy Hill Golf Course & Campground
6263 Weaver Road
Conneaut, OH 44030

Local Phone: 440-594-5251
Email: windy@suite224.net

Delaware, OH

Cross Creek Camping Resort
3190 South Old State Road
Delaware, OH 43015
Local Phone: 740-549-2267
Fax: 740-369-4068
Email: crosscreek@alumcreek.com

E. Rochester, OH

Bob Boord Park
25067 Buffalo Road
East Rochester, OH 44625
Local Phone: (330)894-236
Toll Free: (330)894-220

East Sparta, OH

Bear Creek Resort Ranch KOA
3232 Downing St., S.W.
East Sparta, OH 44626
330-484-3901

Canton/East Sparta KOA
3232 Downing SW
East Sparta, OH 44626
800-562-3903

Frankfort, OH

Lake Hill Campground
2466 Musselman Station Road
Frankfort, OH 45628
Local Phone: 740-998-5648
Fax: 740-998-5648
Email: pjwelcome@juno.com

Ft. Loramie, OH

Hickory Hill Lakes
7103 Rt. 66
Ft. Loramie, OH 45845
937-295-3820

Galena, OH

Berkshire Campgrounds
1848 Alexander Road
Galena, OH 43021
740-965-2321

Geneva, OH

Audobon Lakes Campground
3935 N. Broadway
Geneva, OH 44041
440-466-1293

Glenmont, OH

Mohican Wilderness

22462 Wally Road
Glenmont, OH 44628
Local Phone: 740-599-6741
Email: wilderness@ecr.net

Guernsey, OH

Paradise Valley Campground
74131 Plum Road
6690 Lawnwood Ave, Parma Heigh
Guernsey, OH 43749-
Local Phone: 440-888-1260

Hillsboro, OH

Shady Trails Family Campground
11145 North Shore Dr.
1580 Springdale, Cincinnati OH
Hillsboro, OH 45133
Local Phone: 937-393-5618
Toll Free: 740-773-4985
Fax: 937-393-1692
Email: shadytrails@aol.com

Homerville, OH

Wild Wood Lakes, Inc.
11450 Crawford Road, Box 26
Homerville, OH 44235
Local Phone: 330-625-2817
Fax: 330-625-5502
Email: wwlakes@bright.net

Hubbard, OH

Chestnut Ridge Park & Campground
6486 Chestnut Ridge Road
Hubbard, OH 44425
Local Phone: 330-534-2352

Homestead Family Campground
1436 St Rt 7 SE
Hubbard, OH 44425
Local Phone: 330-448-2938
Fax: 330-448-4869
Email: info@homesteadrv.net

Jefferson, OH

Buccaneer Campsites
PO Box 352
Jefferson, OH 44047
440-576-2881

Kings Island, OH

Jellystone Park at Paramount's Kings Island
Yogi Bear's Campground
Kings Island, OH 45034
513-398-2901

Long Lake Park
Rt. 3, 8974 Long Lake Drive

Kings Island, OH 44638
419-827-2278

Logan, OH

Logan/Hocking Hills KOA
29150 Pattor Road
Logan, OH 43138
800-562-4208

Lore City, OH

Campbell Cove Camping
30775 Wintergreen Road
Lore City, OH 43755
740-489-5837

Loudonville, OH

Camp Toodik Family Campground, Cabins and Canoeing
7700 Twp. Road 462
Loudonville, OH 44842
Local Phone: 877-885-7866
Toll Free: 877-886-7866
Fax: 419-994-4093
Email: mrtoodik@bright.net

Mohican Reservation Campgrounds
23270 Wally Road South
Loudonville, OH 44842
800-766-6631

River Run Family Campground
3175 Wally Road
Loudonville, OH 44842
419-994-5257

Smith's Pleasant Valley Family Campground
Box 356
Loudonville, OH 44842
419-994-4024

Mantua, OH

Yogi Bear's Jellystone Park Camp Resort
3392 S.R. 82
Mantua, OH 44255
330-562-9100

Marion, OH

Hickory Grove Lake Campground
805 Hoch Road
Marion, OH 43302
740-382-8584

Medina, OH

Pier-Lon Park
5960 Vandemark Road
Medina, OH 44256

Local Phone: 330-667-2311
Fax: 330-667-2319
Email: info@pier-lonpark.com

Milan, OH

Milan Travel Park Best Holiday
11404 Highway 250 N.
Medina, OH 44846
419-433-4277

Millersburg, OH

Scenic Hills RV Park
4483 TR 367
Millersburg, OH 44654
Local Phone: 330-893-3607
Toll Free: 330-893-3258
Email: shrvp@wifi7.com

Mogadore, OH

Countryside Campground
2687 SR 43
Mogadore, OH 44260
Local Phone: 330-628-1212
Fax: 330-628-3149
Email: gtbrain@aol.com

Montville, OH

Country Lakes Family Campground
17147 G.A.R Highway
Montville, OH 44064
Local Phone: 440-968-3400
Fax: 440-639-8770

Tri-Country Kamp Inn
17147 Gar. Hwy
Montville, OH 44064
440-968-3400

Mt. Gilead, OH

Dogwood Valley Camp
4185 T.R. 99
Mt. Gilead, OH 43338
419-946-5230

Mt. Gilead/Columbus North KOA
5961 State Route 95
Mt. Gilead, OH 43338
800-562-3428

Mt. Vernon, OH

8664 Keys Road
Mount Vernon, OH 43050
Local Phone: 740-397-9318
Email: RusticKnolls@ecr.net

N. Ridgeville, OH

Crystal Springs
31478 Bagley Road
N. Ridgeville, OH 44039
440-748-3200

Nelsonville, OH

Happy Hills Family Campground
22245 S.R. 278
Nelsonville, OH 45764
740-385-6720

New London, OH

Indian Trail Campground
1400 Rt. 250
mailing - 189 Benedict Ave, No
New London, OH 44851
Local Phone: 419-929-1135
Fax: 419-499-9047
Email: camp@northcoastmarketplace.com

New Paris, OH

Natural Springs Resort
500 South Washington Street
New Paris, OH 45347
Local Phone: 937-437-5771
Toll Free: 888-330-5771
Fax: 937-437-5771
Email: webmaster@naturalspringsresort.com

New Waterford, OH

Terrace Lakes Camping
6157 SL Rt. 7
New Waterford, OH 44445
Local Phone: 330-227-9606
Fax: 330-227-9606
Email: ginger@raex.com

Newton Falls, OH

Ridge Ranch Campground
5219 SL Rt. 303, N.W.
Newton Falls, OH 44444
Local Phone: 330-898-8080
Email: starmor@msn.com

North Benton, OH

McDermott's Lakefront Campground
8999 German Church Road
8350 Boston Road North Royalto
North Benton, OH 44449
Local Phone: 216-396-1500
Fax: 440-230-2440
Email: lrmcdermott@sbcglobal.net

Nova, OH

Country Stage Campground
40-C Township Road 1031
Nova, OH 44859-9721

Local Phone: 419-652-2267
Fax: 419-652-2567
Email: lamamama@bright.net

Oregonia, OH

Olive Branch Campground
6985 Wilmington Road
Oregonia, OH 45054
Local Phone: 513-932-CAMP
Email: olivebranch@campohio.com

Orwell, OH

Pine Lakes Campground
3001 Hague Road
Orwell, OH 44076
Local Phone: 440-437-6218
Email: kathleen@orwell.net

Parkman, OH

Kool Lakes Family Camping
12990 S.R. 282, Box 673
Parkman, OH 44080
440-548-8436

Parma Heights, OH

Paradise Valley Campground
6690 Lawnwood Ave.
Parma Heights, OH 44130
440-888-1260

Peninsula, OH

Tamsin Park Camping Resort
5000 Akron=Cleveland Road
Peninsula, OH 44264
330-656-2859

Perrysburgh, OH

Toledo East/Stony Ridge KOA
24787 Luckey Road
Perrysburgh, OH 43551
800-562-6831

Port Clinton, OH

Chet's Place
7154 W. Harbor Road
Port Clinton, OH 43452
Local Phone: 419-898-1104
Toll Free: 419-734-5580
Email: chetsplace@cros.net

Put-in-Bay, OH

Fox's Den Campground
PO Box 345
Put-in-Bay, OH 43456
419-285-5001

S. Bloomingville, OH

Top O' The Caves
26780 Chapel Ridge Road
S. Bloomingville, OH 43152
800-967-2434

Salem, OH

Chaparral Family Campground
10136 Middletown Road
Salem, OH 44460
Local Phone: 330-337-9381

Stoneridge Terrace Campground
33807 Winona Road
Salem, OH 44460
Local Phone: 330-222-1201
Fax: 330-222-1201
Email: barb@infinitytvl.webmail.com

Shelby, OH

Wagon Wheel Campground
6787 Baker 47
Shelby, OH 44875
419-347-1392

Shreve, OH

Whispering Hill Recreation
PO Box 607
Shreve, OH 44676
330-567-2137

Spencer, OH

Honey-Do Campground
6794 Avon Lake Road
Spencer, OH 44275
Local Phone: 330-667-2295
Fax: 330-667-2295

Sunset Lake Campground
5566 Root Road
Spencer, OH 44275
Local Phone: 330-667-2686
Fax: 330-667-9201

Springfield, OH

Enon Beach
2401 Enon Road
Springfield, OH 45502
Local Phone: 937-882-6431

Sullivan, OH

Rustic Lakes Campgrounds Inc.
44901 New London Eastern Road
Sullivan, OH 44880
Local Phone: 440-647-3804

Sunbury, OH

Autumn Lakes Campground
8644 Porter Central Road
Sunbury, OH 43074
Local Phone: 740-625-6600
Email: hanawalt5@msn.com

Swanton, OH

Toledo/Maumee KOA
4035 St. Route 295
Swanton, OH 43558
800-562-8748

Thompson, OH

Heritage Hills Campground
6445 Ledge Road
Thompson, OH 44086
440-298-1311

Toronto, OH

Austin Lake Park and Campground
1002 Twp Hwy 285A
Toronto, OH 43964
740-544-LAKE

Upper Sandusky, OH

Smokey's Mini Lake
9527 St Hwy 199
Upper Sandusky, OH 43351
Local Phone: 419-294-1759
Email: barbara1@bright.net

Van Buren, OH

Pleasant View Recreation
12611 Twp Rd 218, P.O. Box 255
PO Box 255
Van Buren, OH 45889
Local Phone: 419-299-3897
Fax: 419-299-3842
Email: pvrcamp@bright.net

Wapakoneta, OH

Wapakoneta/Lima KOA
14719 Cemetery Road
Wapakoneta, OH 45895
800-562-9872

Wellington, OH

Clare-Mar Lakes Campground
PO Box 226
Wellington, OH 44090
440-647-3318

Panther Trails
48081 Peck Wadsworth Road
Wellington, OH 44090
Local Phone: 440-647-5453

Wooster, OH

Beck's Family Campground
8375 Friendsville Road
Wooster, OH 44691
330-264-9930

Meadow Lake Park
8970 Canaan Center Road
Wooster, OH 44691
330-435-6652

Oklahoma

Ardmore, OK

Lake Murray Resort Park
3310 South Lake Murray Drive #12-A
Ardmore, OK 73401
580-223-4044

Atoka, OK

Boggy Depot State Park
PO Box 1020
Atoka, OK 74525
405-889-5625

McGee Creek State Park
HC 82, Box 572
Atoka, OK 74525
405-889-5822

Bartlesville, OK

Riverside RV Resort
1211 SE Adams Blvd.
Bartlesville, OK 74003
Voice: (918) 336-6431 / (888) 572-1241
Fax: (918) 336-3892
riversidervrst@yahoo.com

Beaver, OK

Beaver State Park
PO Box 1190
Beaver, 73932
405-625-3373

Broken Bow, OK

Beavers Bend Resort Park
PO Box 10
Broken Bow, OK 74728
580-494-6300

Reiger RV Park
Hwy 259
Broken Bow, OK 74728
800-550-6521

Canadian, OK

Arrowhead State Park
HC 67, Box 57
Canadian, OK 74425
918-339-2204

Canute, OK

Elk City/Clinton KOA
P.O. Box 137
Canute, OK 73626

800-562-4149

Catoosa, OK

Tusa NE KOA
19605 E. Skelly Dr.
Catoosa, OK 74015
800-562-7657

Checotah, OK

Checotah/Henryetta KOA
HC 68, Box 750
Checotah, OK 74426
800-562-7510

Fountainhead State Park
HC 60, Box 1340
Checotah, OK 74426
918-689-5311

Choctaw, OK

Oklahoma City East KOA
6200 S. Choctaw Road
Choctaw, OK 73020
800-562-5076

Clayton, OK

Clayton Lake State Park
Route 1, Box 33-10
Clayton, OK 74536
918-569-7981

Clinton, OK

Wink's RV Park
1410 Neptune Road
Clinton, OK 73601
580-323-1664

Colbert, OK

Colbertv
Route 2, Box 500
Colbert, OK 74733
800-562-2485

Sherrard RV and KOA
411 Sherrard St
Colbert, OK 74733
580-296-2485

Copan, OK

Wah-Sha-She
Route 1, Box 301
Copan, OK 74022
918-532-4627

Disney, OK

Cherokee State Park

PO Box 220
Disney, OK 74340
918-435-8066

Riverside Campground
Cherokee State Park
Disney, OK 74340
918-435-8066

Elk City, OK

Elk Creek RV Park
I-40 Exit 38 - S Main & 20th
Elk City, OK 73644
Voice: (580) 225-7865 / (888) 478-6552
Fax: (580) 225-1008
hubb@itlnet.net

Elk Run RV Park
Hwy 34 and I-40
Elk City, OK 73644
580-225-4888

El Reno, OK

El Reno West KOA
Box 6
El Reno, OK 73036
800-562-5736

Enid, OK

High Point RV Park
2700 North Van Buren, No. 933
Enid, OK 73703
580-234-1726

Fairland, OK

Spring River Canoe Trails
Route 1, Box 170
Fairland, OK 74343
918-540-2545

Twin Bridges State Park
14801 South Highway 137
Fairland, OK 74343
918-540-2545

Fort Cobb, OK

Fort Cobb Lake State Park
PO Box 297
Fort Cobb, OK 73038
405-643-2249

Fort Towson, OK

Raymond Gary State Park
HC 63, Box 1450
Fort Towson, OK 74735
405-873-2307

Foss, OK

Foss State Park
HC 66, Box 111
Foss, OK 73647
405-592-4433

Freedom, OK

Alabaster Caverns State Park
Route 1, Box 32
Freedom, OK 73842
405-621-3381

Gore, OK

Marval Family Resort
Route 1
Box 314 M
Gore, OK 74435
Phone: (918)489-2295
Fax: (918)489-2671
info@marvalresort.com

Grove, OK

Bernice State Park
Route 5, Box 209
Grove, OK 74344
918-786-9447

Cedar Oaks RV Resort
1550 83rd Street
Grove, OK 743344
918-786-4303

Honey Creek State Park
Route 5, Box 209
Grove, OK 74344
918-786-9447

Guthrie, OK

Pioneer RV Park
1601 Seward Road
Guthrie, OK 73044
405-282-3557

Henryetta, OK

Henryetta RV Park
800 W Corporation
Henryetta, OK 74437
Voice: (918) 652-9111
Fax: (918) 652-9111
henryettarvpark@prodigy.net

Hinton, OK

Red Rock Canyon State Park
PO Box 502
Hinton, OK 73047
405-542-6344

Hodgen, OK

Big Cedar RV Park
.3 mi West of 259 on SH 63
Hodgen, OK 74939
918-651-3271

Jet, OK

Great Salt Plains State Park
Route 1, Box 28
Jet, OK 73749
405-626-4731

Kenton, OK

Black Mesa State Park
HCR 1, Box 8
Kenton, OK 73946
405-426-2222

Kingfisher, OK

Sleepe Hollo RV Park
918 North Main
Kingfisher, OK 73750
405-375-5010

Kingston, OK

Lake Texoma Resort Park
Box 248
Kingston, OK 73439
405-564-2566

Lone Wolf, OK

Quartz Mountain Resort Park
Route 1
Lone Wolf, OK 73655
405-563-2238

Mannford, OK

Lake Keystone State Park
PO Box 147
Mannford, OK 74044
918-865-4477

Marietta, OK

Ardmore/Marietta KOA
Route 1, Box 640
Marietta, OK 73448
800-562-5893

Mountain Park, OK

Great Plains State Park
Route 1, Box 52
Mountain Park, OK 73559
405-569-2032

New Prue, OK

Walnut Creet State Park
PO Box 26
New Prue, OK 74060
918-242-2362

Norman, OK

Little River State Park
Route 4, Box 277
Norman, OK 73071
405-360-3572

Oklahoma City, OK

Abe's RV Park
12115 N I-35 Service Road
Oklahoma City, OK 73131
Voice: (405) 478-0278
Fax: (405) 478-3327

Roadrunner RV Park
4800 S Hattie Ave.
Oklahoma City, OK 73129
Voice: (405) 677-2373

Rockwell RV Park
720 S Rockwell
Oklahoma City, OK 73128
Voice: (405) 787-5992 / (888) 684-3251
Fax: (405) 787-5992
dmlrokrv@aol.com

Sands Motel
721 South Rockwell Ave
Oklahoma City, OK 73128
405-787-7353

Okmulgee, OK

Okmulgee-Dripping Springs State Park
210 Dripping Spring Lake Road
Okmulgee, OK 74447
918-756-5971

Park Hill, OK

Cheokee Landing State Park
HC 73, Box 510
Park Hill, OK 74451
918-457-5716

Pawhuska, OK

Osage Hill State Park
HC 73, Box 84
Pawhuska, OK 74056
918-336-5635

Salina, OK

Snowdale State Park
PO Box 6

Salina, OK 74365
918-434-2651

Sallisaw, OK

Sallisaw KOA
P.O. Box 88
Sallisaw, OK 74955
800-562-2797

Sallisaw State Park at Brushy Lake
PO Box 527
Sallisaw, OK 74955
918-775-6507

Sawyer, OK

Sawyer RV Park
HC 66 Box 1430
Sawyer, OK 74756
580-326-0830

Spiro, OK

Rockin' Horse RV Park
Rte 1 Box 267
Spiro, OK 74959
918-962-2524

Stilwell, OK

Adair State Park
Route 2, Box 8
Stilwell, OK 74960
918-696-6613

Tulsa, OK

Mingo RV Park
801 North Mingo Road
Tulsa, OK 74116
Toll Free: (800)932-8824
Phone: (918)832-8824
Fax: (918)836-7371
Mingorv@sbcglobal.net

Vian, OK

Lake Tenkiller State Park
HCR 68, Box 1095
Vian, OK 74962
918-489-5643

Wagoner, OK

Sequoyah Bay State Park
Route 2, Box 252
Wagoner, OK 74467
918-683-0878

Sequoyah State Park
Box 509
Wagoner, OK 74477
918-772-2046

Watonga, OK

Roman Nose Resort Park
Route 1
Watonga, OK 73772
405-623-4215

Waurika, OK

Moneka Park
1545 South 101st Ave
Waurika, OK 73573
580-963-2111

Waynoka, OK

Little Sahara State Park
Route 2, Box 132
Waynoka, OK 73860
405-824-1471

Wilburton, OK

Robbers Cave State Park
PO Box 9
Wilburton, OK 74578
918-465-2565

Wister, OK

Lake Wister State Park
Route 2, Box 6B
Wister, OK 74966
918-655-7756

Woodward, OK

Boiling Springs State Park
Box 965
Woodward, OK 73802
405-256-7664

Oregon

Albany, OR

Albany / Corvallis KOA
33775 Oakville Road, S
Albany, OR 97321
Voice: (541) 967-8521
Fax: (541) 535-8302
pvgreig@proaxis.com

Baker City, OR

Mountain View Holiday Trav-L-Park
2845 Hughes Lane
Baker City, OR 97814
541-523-4824

Bend, OR

Bend Kampground
63615 Highway 97 N.
Bend, OR 97701
541-382-7738

Sisters/Bend KOA
67667 Hwy. 20 W.
Bend, OR 97701
800-562-0363

Brookings, OR

Driftwood RV Park
16011 Lower Harbor Road
Brookings, OR 97415
Voice: (541) 469-9089
Fax: (541) 412-0156
rsvp@driftwoodrvpark.com

Canby, OR

Riverside RV Park
24310 Hwy. 99E
Canby, OR 97013

Cascade, OR

Cascade Locks/Portland East KOA
841 NW Forest Lane
Cascade, OR 97014
800-562-8698

Culver, OR

Madras/Culver KOA
2435 SW Jericho Lane
Culver, OR 97734
800-562-1992

Eugene, OR

Premier RV Resort - Eugene

33022 Van Duyn Road
Eugene, OR 97408
Voice: (541) 686-3152 / (888) 710-8451
Fax: (541) 344-7067
premiereugene@msn.com

Foster, OR

Sweet Home/Foster Lake KOA
6191 Hwy. 20 East
Foster, OR 97345
800-562-0367

Gold Hill, OR

Medford-Gold Hill KOA
Box 320
Gold Hill, OR 97525
800-562-7608

Hammond, OR

Astoria/Seaside KOA
1100 Ridge Road
Hammond, OR 97121
800-562-8506

Idleyld Park, OR

Elk Haven RV Resort
22020 N. Umpqua Hwy
Idleyld Park, OR 97447
541-496-3090

Klamath Falls, OR

Klamath Falls KOA
3435 Shasta Way
Klamath Falls, OR 97603
800-562-9036

Langlois, OR

Bandon/Port Orford KOA
46612 Hwy 101
Langlois, OR 97450
800-562-3298

Medford, OR

Fish Lake Resort
PO Box 990
Eagle Point, OR 97524
Phone: (541) 949-8500
fishlakeresort@aol.com

North Bend, OR

Oregon Dunes KOA
4135 Coast Hwy.
North Bend, OR 97459
800-562-4236

Otis, OR

Lincoln City KOA
5298 NE Park Lane
Otis, OR 97368
800-562-2791

Voice: (503) 682-7829 / (800) 532-7829
Fax: (503) 682-9043
terri@pheasantridge.com

Reedsport, OR

Loon Lake Lodge & RV Park
9011 Loon Lake Road
Reedsport, OR 97467
Phone: (541)599-2244
Fax: (541)599-2274
loonlake@mpam.com

Salem, OR

Salem Campground & RVs
3700 Hagers Grove SE
Salem, OR 97301
Voice: (503) 581-6736 / (800) 825-9605
Fax: (888) 827-9605

Sunny Valley, OR

Grants Pass/Sunny Valley KOA
140 Old Stage Road
Sunny Valley, OR 97497
800-562-7557

Tualatin, OR

RV Park of Portland
6645 SW Nyberg Road
Tualatin, OR 97062
Voice: (503) 692-0225 / (800) 856-2066
Fax: (503) 691-8452
rvpp@rvparkofportland.com

Roamer's Rest RV Park LLC
17585 SW Pacific Hwy.
Tualatin, OR 97062
Voice: (503) 692-6350 / (877) 478-7275
Fax: (503) 691-6996
info@roamersrestrvpark.com

Waldport, OR

Waldport/Newport KOA
P.O. Box 397
Waldport, OR 97394
800-562-3443

Wilderville, OR

Grants Pass/Redwood Hwy. KOA
13370 Redwood Hwy.
Wilderville, OR 97543
800-562-7566

Wilsonville, OR

Pheasant Ridge RV Park
8275 SW Elligsen Road
Wilsonville, OR 97070

Pennsylvania

Adamstown, PA

Sill's Family Campground
PO Box 566
Adamstown, PA 19501
Voice: (717) 484-4806 / (800) 325-3002
Fax: (717) 484-6132

Airville, PA

Otter Creek Campground
1101 Furnace Road
Airville, PA 17302
Voice: (717) 862-3628 / (877) 336-8837
ottercreek@ottercreekcamp.com

Bellefonte, PA

Bellefonte/State College KOA
2481 Jacksonville Road
Bellefonte, PA 16823
800-562-8127

Blakeslee, PA

WT Family Camping, Inc.
Box 1486 Rt. 115
Blakeslee, PA 18610
Voice: (570) 646-9255
Fax: (570) 646-6317
wtcamp@epix.net

Bradford, PA

Indian Head Campground
340 Reading St.
Bloomsburg, PA 17815
Voice: (570) 784-6150
Fax: (570) 356-3157
tal@sunlink.net

Bowmansville, PA

Oak Creek Campground, Inc.
PO Box 128
Bowmansville, PA 17507
Voice: (717) 445-6161 / (800) 446-8365
oakcreek@ptd.net

Sun Valley Campground
451 E Maple Grove Road
Bowmansville, PA 17507
Voice: (717) 445-6262 / (800) 700-3370
Fax: (717) 445-5854
sunvalleycampground@sunvalleycampground.net

Bradford, PA

Kinzua East KOA

Kinzua Heights
Bradford, PA 16701
800-562-3682

Carlisle, PA

Carlisle Campground
1075 Harrisburg Pike
Carlisle, PA 17013
717-249-4563

Western Village RV Park
200 Greenview Drive
Carlisle, PA 17013
Phone: (717)243-1179
5412none@parkname.com

Cedar Run, PA

Pettecote Junction Campground
Box 14 Beach Road
Cedar Run, PA 17727
Voice: (570) 353-7183

Coatesville, PA

Birchview Farm Campground
100 Birchview Dr.
Coatesville, PA 19320
Voice: (610) 384-0500

Hidden Acres Campground
103 Hidden Acres Road
Coatesville, PA 19320
Voice: (610) 857-3990

Denver, PA

Lancaster/Reading KOA
3 Denber Road
Denver, PA 17517
800-562-1621

Hickory Run Campground
285 Greenville Road
Denver, PA 17517
Voice: (717) 336-5564 / (800) 458-0612
Fax: (717) 336-7759
stanst@ptd.net

Drums, PA

81-80RV Park & Campground
RR 1, Box 1405
Drums, PA 18222
570-788-3382

E. Stroudsburg, PA

Delaware Water Gap KOA
KOA RD 6, Box 6196
E. Stroudsburg, PA 18301

800-562-0375

Gettysburg, PA

Drummer Boy Camping Resort
1300 Hanover Road
Gettysburg, PA 17325
800-336-3269

Gettysburg/Battlefield KOA
20 Konx Road
Gettysburg, PA 17325
800-562-1869

Granite Hill Campground
3340 Fairfield Road
Gettysburg, PA 17325
Voice: (717) 642-8749 / (800) 642-8368
Fax: (717) 642-8025
gburggrass@aol.com

Round Top Campground
180 Knight Road
Gettysburg, PA 17325
Voice: (717) 334-9565
Fax: (717) 334-9946
info@roundtopcamp.com

Hershey, PA

Hershey KOA
P.O. Box 449
Hershey, PA 17033
800-562-4774

Honesdale, PA

Ponderosa Pines Campground
RR 3
Honesdale, PA 18431
Voice: (570) 253-2080

Jonestown, PA

Jonestown/I-81 KOA
145 Old Route 22
Jonestown, PA 17038
800-562-1501

Lancaster, PA

Old Mill Stream Camping Manor
2249 Rte. 30 E
Lancaster, PA 17602
Voice: (717) 299-2314
Fax: (717) 291-1595
infooc@oldmillstreamcamping.com

Lenhartsville, PA

Blue Rocks Family Campground
341 Sousley Road
Lenhartsville, PA 19534

Voice: (610) 756-6366
Fax: (610) 756-3006
camp@bluerockscampground.com

Robin Hill Camping Resort
149 Robin Hill Road
Lenhartsville, PA 19534
Voice: (610) 756-6117 / (800) 732-5267
Fax: (610) 756-3434
robinhill@intergate.com

Lewisburg, PA

River Edge RV Camp & Marina
443 River Edge Lane
Winfield, PA 17889
Voice: (570) 524-0453
Fax: (570) 524-0453
riveredgervcamp@aol.com

Liverpool, PA

Ferryboat Campsites
32 Ferry Lane
Liverpool, PA 17045
Voice: (717) 444-3200 / (800) 759-8707
ferryboat@tricountyi.net

McKean, PA

Erie KOA
6645 West Road
McKean, PA 16426
800-562-7610

Mercer, PA

Junction 19-80 Campground
1266 Old Mercer Road
Mercer, PA 16137
Voice: (724) 748-4174
Fax: (724) 748-5998
Outside Link: www.junction19-
80campground.com

Mercer/Grove City KOA
1337 Butler Pike
Mercer, PA 16137
800-562-2802

Rocky Springs Campground
84 Rocky Springs Road
Mercer, PA 16137
Voice: (724) 662-4415
Fax: (724) 662-4390
rockysprings@nowonline.net
Outside Link:
users.nowonline.net/rockysprings/rocky.htm

RV Village Camping Resort
235 N Skyline Dr.

Mercer, PA 16137
Voice: (724) 662-4560 / (866) 978-2267

Milford, PA

River Beach Campsites
PO Box 382
Milford, PA 18337
Voice: (570) 296-7421 / (800) 356-2852
Fax: (570) 828-2165
floatkc@warwick.net

Morris, PA

Twin Streams Campground
2143 Rt. 287
Morris, PA 16938
Voice: (570) 353-7251
Fax: (570) 353-7819

New Columbia, PA

Nittany Mountain Campground
2751 Millers Bottom Road
New Columbia, PA 17856
Voice: (570) 568-5541
Fax: (570) 568-1232
nittanycg@aol.com

New Tripoli, PA

Allentown KOA
6750 KOA Dr.
New Tripoli, PA 18066
800-562-2138

Portersville, PA

Bear Run Campground
184 Badger Hill Road
Portersville, PA 16051
412-368-3564

Yogi Bear's Jellystone Park Lancaster
South/Quarryville
340 Blackburn Road
Quarryville, PA 17566
Voice: (717) 786-3458
Fax: (717) 786-2310
yogilanc@aol.com

Ruffsdale, PA

Madison/Pittsburgh SE KOA
RR 2, Box 560
Ruffsdale, PA 15679
800-562-4034

Saylorsburg, PA

Silver Valley Best Holiday
RR 4, Box 4214
Saylorsburg, PA 18353

717-992-4824

Selinsgrove, PA

Penn Avon Campground
RR 1, Box 366-D
Selinsgrove, PA 17870
Voice: (570) 374-9468
Fax: (570) 374-2281
pennavon@ptdprolog.net

Stroudsburg, PA

Pocono Vacation Park
Shafer School House Road
RD 5, Box 5214
Stroudsburg, PA 18360
Phone: (570)424-2587
carlet_2001@yahoo.com

Tamaqua, PA

Rosemount Camping Resort
285 Valley Road
Tamaqua, PA 18252
Voice: (570) 668-2580

Tunkhannock, PA

Tunkhannock KOA
Box 768
Tunkhannock, PA 18657
800-562-5856

Unionville, PA

Philadelphia/West Chester KOA
P.O. Box 920D
Unionville, PA 19375
800-562-1726

Upper Black Eddy, PA

Colonial Woods Campground
545 Lonely Cottage Drive
Upper Black Eddy, PA 18972
610-847-5808

Washington, PA

Washington KOA
7 KOA Road
Washington, PA 15301
800-562-0254

Waymart, PA

Keen Lake Camping and Cottage Resort
RR 3 (PO Box 1976) Keen Lake Road
Waymart, PA 18472
Voice: (570) 488-5522 / (800) 443-0412
Fax: (570) 488-7077
keenlake@socantel.net

Wellsboro, PA

Canyon Country Campground
130 Wilson Road
Wellsboro, PA 16901
Voice: (570) 724-3818
Outside Link: www.campinpa.com

Rhode Island

Exeter, RI

Peeper Pond Campground
159 Liberty Church Road
Exeter, RI 02822
401-294-5540

Foster, RI

Ginny-B Campground
46 Johnson Road
Foster, RI 02825
Voice: (401) 397-9477 / (401) 397-7982
gnnyb@aol.com

Hope Valley, RI

Whispering Pines Campground
41 Saw Mill Road
Hope Valley, RI 02832
Voice: (401) 539-7011
wpinesri@aol.com

Jamestown, RI

Fort Getty Recreation Area
PO Box 377
Jamestown, RI 02835
401-423-7211

Pascoag, RI

Buck Hill Family Campground
464 Wakefield Pond Road
Pascog, RI 02859
401-568-0456

Portsmouth, RI

Melville Ponds Campground
181 Bradford Ave
Portsmouth, RI 02871
401-682-2424

West Kingston, RI

Wamaloam Campground
510 Gardnier Road
West Kingston, RI 02892
401-294-3039

South Carolina

Anderson, SC

Anderson/Lake Hartwell KOA
200 Wham Road
Anderson, SC 29625
800-562-5804

Sadlers Creek State Park
940 Sadlers Creek Park Road
Anderson, SC 29626
864-226-8950

Springfield Campground
Hartwell Lake
Providence Church Road
Anderson, SC 29625
877-444-6777

Bishopville, SC

Lee State Park
Route 2, Box 1212
Bishopville, SC 29010
803-428-3833

Blacksburg, SC

Kings Mountain State Park
1277 Park Road
Blacksburg, SC 29702
803-222-3209

Blackville, SC

Barnwell State Park
223 State Park Road
Blackville, SC 29817
803-284-2212

Calhoun Falls, SC

Calhoun Falls State Park
46 Maintenance Shop Road
Calhoun Falls, SC 29628
864-447-8267

Canadys, SC

Colleton State Park
803-538-8206

Chapin, SC

Dreher Island State Park
3677 State Park Road
Chapin, SC 29127
803-364-4152

Charleston, SC

Lake Aire RV Park
4375 Hwy 162
Hollywood, SC 29449
Phone: 843-571-1271
uzmom@mindspring.com
Cheraw, SC

Cheraw State Park
100 State Park Road
Charleston, SC 29520
800-868-9630

Chester, SC

Chester State Park
759 State Park Drive
Chester, SC 29706
803-385-2680

Cleveland, SC

Caesars Head State Park
8155 Geer Hwy
Cleveland, SC 29635
864-836-6115

Columbia, SC

Sesquicentennial State Park
9564 Two Notch Road
Columbia, SC 29223
803-788-2706

Conway, SC

Big Cypress Lake RV Park & Fishing Retreat
6531 Brownsway Shortcut Road
Conway, SC 29527
Voice: (843) 397-1800
rvpark@sccoast.net

Dillon, SC

Little Pee Dee State Park
1298 State Park Road
Dillon, SC 29536
803-774-8872

Edisto Island, SC

Edisto Beach State Park
8377 State Cabin Road
Edisto Island, SC 29438
803-869-2156

Ehrhardt, SC

Rivers Bridge State Park
Route 1
Ehrhardt, SC 29081
803-267-3675

Eutawville, SC

Rocks Pond Campground and Marina
235 Rocks Pond Road
Eutawville, SC 29048
803-492-7711

Fair Play, SC

Lake Hartwell State Park
19138-A South Hwy 11
Fair Play, SC 29643
864-972-3352

Florence, SC

Florence KOA
1115 E. Campground Road
Florence, SC 29506
800-562-7807

Greenville, SC

Paris Mountain State Park
2401 State Park Road
Greenville, SC 29609
864-244-5565

Hilton Head, SC

Outdoor Resorts Motorcoach Resort
133 Arrow Road
Hilton Head Island, SC 29928
Voice: (843) 785-7699
Fax: (843) 785-7643
outdooresort@hargray.com

Hunting Island, SC

Hunting Island State Park
2555 Sea Island Pkwy
Hunting Island, SC 29920
803-838-2011

Ladson, SC

Charleston KOA
9494 Hwy. 78
Ladson, SC 29456
800-562-5812

Lancaster, SC

Andrew Jackson State Park
196 Andrew Jackson Park Road
Lancaster, SC 29720
803-285-3344

Marietta, SC

Jones Gap State Park
303 Jones Gap Road
Marietta, SC 29661
864-836-3647

McCormick, SC

Baker Creek State Park

Route 3, Box 50
McCormick, SC 29835
864-443-2457

Hickory Knob State Park
Route 1, Box 199-B
McCormick, SC 29835
800-491-1764

Modoc, SC

Modoc Campground
J. Strom Thurmond Lake
Rte 1, Box 2-D
Modoc, SC 29821
864-333-2272

Mountain Rest, SC

Oconee State Park
624 State Park Road
Mountain Rest, SC 29664
864-638-5353

Mt. Pleasant, SC

Mt. Pleasant/Charleston KOA
P.O. Box 248
Mt. Pleasant, SC 29466
800-562-5796

Myrtle Beach, SC

Apache Family Campground
9700 Kings Road
Myrtle Beach, SC 29572
Toll Free: (800)553-1749
Phone: (843) 449-7323
Fax: (843)497-3018
apache843@aol.com

Barefoot RV Resort, Inc.
4825 Hwy. 17 S
North Myrtle Beach, SC 29598
Voice: (843) 272-1790 / (800) 272-1790
Fax: (843) 272-4208
requests@barefootrvresort.com

Lakewood Camping Resort
5901 S Kings Hwy.
Myrtle Beach, SC 29575
Voice: (843) 238-5161 / (877) 525-3966
Fax: (843) 447-7350
info@lakewoodcampground.com

Myrtle Beach KOA
5th Avenue S.
Myrtle Beach, SC 29577
800-562-7790

Myrtle Beach State Park

4401 S. Kings Hwy
Myrtle Beach, SC 29575
803-238-5325

Myrtle Beach Travel Park
10108 Kings Road
Myrtle Beach, SC 29572
Voice: (843) 449-3714 / (800) 255-3568
Fax: (843) 497-8521
mbtpark@myrtlebeachtravelpark.com

Ocean Lakes Family Campground
6001 S Kings Hwy.
Myrtle Beach, SC 29575
Voice: (843) 238-5636 / (800) 722-1451
Fax: (843) 238-1890
camping@oceanlakes.com

Ninety Six, SC

Lake Greenwood State Park
302 State Park Road
Ninety Six, SC 29666
864-543-3535

Pickens, SC

Table Rock State Park
246 Table Rock State Park Road
Pickens, SC 29671
864-878-9813

Plum Branch, SC

Hamilton Branch State Park
Rout 1, Box 97
Plum Branch, SC 29845
864-333-2223

Prosperity, SC

Dreher Island State Park
3677 State Park Road
Prosperity, SC 29127
803-364-4152

Ridgeville, SC

Givhans Ferry State Park
746 Givhans Ferry Road
Ridgeville, SC 29472
803-873-0692

Salem, SC

Devils Fork State Park
161 Holcombe Circle
Salem, SC 29676
864-944-2639

Spartanburg, SC

Croft State Park

450 Croft State Park Road
Spartanburg, SC 29302
864-585-1283

Summerton, SC

Santee Lake Campground
1268 Gordon Road
Summerton, SC 29148
803-478-2262

Sunset, SC

Keowee-Toxaway State Park
108 Residence Drive
Sunset, SC 29685
864-868-2605

Swansea, SC

River Botton Farms RV Park & Campground
357 Cedar Creek Road
Swansea, SC 29160
Voice: (803) 568-4182

Taylors, SC

The Flowermill RV Park
23 Stallings Road
Taylors, SC 29687
864-877-5079

Wedgefield, SC

Poinsett State Park
6660 Poinsett Park Road
Wedgefield, SC 29168
803-827-1473

Windsor, SC

Aiken State Park
1145 State Park Road
Windsor, SC 29856
803-649-2857

Winnsboro, SC

Lake Wateree State Park
Route 4, Box 282 E-5
Winnsboro, SC 29180
803-482-6401

Yemassee, SC

Point South KOA Kampground
PO Box 1760
Yemassee, SC 29945
843-726-5733

South Dakota

Black Hawk, SD
Fort Welikit Family Campground
PO Box 381
Black Hawk, SD 57718
605-787-7898

Brookings, SD
Oakwood Lakes State Park
46109 202nd Street
Brookings, SD 57220
605-627-5441

Custer, SD
Beaver Lake Campground
12005 W Hwy 16
Custer, SD 57730
Voice: (605) 673-2464 / (800) 346-4383
Fax: (605) 673-2308
beaverlake@gwtc.net

Big Pine Campground
Route 1 Box 52 mi W of Custer on US 16
Custer, SD 57730
Voice: (605) 673-4054

Custer - Crazy Horse Campground
Route 2 Box 3030
Custer, SD 57730
Voice: (605) 673-2565 / (866) 526-7377
cchkampground@hotmail.com

Custer Mountain Cabins and Campground
PO Box 472
Custer, SD 57730
605-673-5440

Custer State Park
HC 83 Box 70
Custer, SD 57730
605-255-4515

Deadwood, SD
Deadwood KOA
Box 451
Deadwood, SD 57732
800-562-0846

Garretson, SD
Palisades State Park
25495 485th Ave
Garretson, SD 57030
605-594-3824

Gettysburg, SD
West Whitlock Recreation Area
16157A West Whitlock Road
Gettysburg, SD 57442
605-765-9410

Hill City, SD
Crooked Creek Campground
PO Box 603
Hill City, SD 57745
Voice: (605) 574-2418 / (800) 252-8486

Horse Thief Campground and Resort
(Box 307) 24391 Hwy. 87
Hill City, SD 57745
Voice: (605) 574-2668 / (800) 657-5802
camp@horsethief.com

Mt. Rushmore/Hill City KOA
Box 295K
Hill City, SD 57745
800-562-8503

Rafter J Bar Ranch
US Hwy 16 & 385 (PO Box 128)
Hill City, SD 57745
Voice: (605) 574-2527 / (888) 723-8375
Fax: (605) 574-4882
info@rafterj.com

Hot Springs, SD
Hot Springs KOA
HCR 52, Box 112C
Hot Springs, SD 57747
800-562-0803

Interior, SD
Badlands / Interior Campground
HC 54, Box 115
Interior, SD 57750
Voice: (605) 433-5335

Kennebec, SD
Kennebec KOA
P.O. Box 248
Kennebec, SD 57544
800-562-6361

Midland, SD
Belvidere East KOA
HCR 62, Box 108
Midland, SD 57552
800-562-2134

Mitchell, SD
Mitchell KOA

41244 SD Hwy. 38
Mitchell, SD 57301
800-562-1236

RonDees Campground
I-90 Exit 32
Mitchell, SD 57301
Voice: (605) 996-0769 / (866) 747-2267
Fax: (605) 996-5220

N. Sioux City, SD

Sioux City North KOA
Box 846
N. Sioux City, SD 57049
800-562-5439

Rapid City, SD

Happy Holiday
8990 S. Highway 16
Rapid City, SD 57701
605-342-7635

Hart Ranch Camping Resort Club
23756 Arena Dr.
Rapid City, SD 57702
Voice: (605) 399-2582
Fax: (605) 348-4570
hartclub@rapidnet.com

Lake Park Campground and Cottages
2850 Chapel Ln.
Rapid City, SD 57702
Voice: (605) 341-5320 / (800) 644-2267
Fax: (605) 394-8871
campnelson@rapidnet.com

Rapid City KOA
3010 East Highway 44
Rapid City, SD 57709
Toll Free: (800)562-8504
Phone: (605)348-2111
rckoa@aol.com

Sioux Falls, SD

Sioux Falls KOA
Box 963
Sioux Falls, SD 57101
800-562-9865

Spearfish, SD

Spearfish KOA
Box 429
Spearfish, SD 57783
800-562-0805

Watertown, SD

Dakota Sioux Casino

Sioux Conifer Road
Watertown, SD 57201
605-882-2051

Lake Pelican Recreation
Hwy 212
Watertown, SD 57201
605-882-5200

Memorial County Park
North Lake Drive & Hwy 139
Watertown, SD 57201
605-882-6290

Sandy Shores State Park
Highway 212
Watertown, SD 57201
605-882-5200

Stokes-Thomas Lake City Park
South Lake Drive & Hwy 20
Watertown, SD 57201
605-882-6264

Yankton, SD

Lewis and Clark Recreation Area
43349 SD 52
Yankton, SD 57078
605-668-2985

Tennessee

Ashland City, TN

Cheatham Lake Lock A Campground
1798 Cheatham Dam Road
Ashland City, TN 37015
615-792-3715

Benton, TN

Chilhowee Campground
Cherokee National Forest
Rte 1, Box 348-D
Benton, TN 37307
423-338-5201

Hiwassee State Scenic River & Ocoee River
Camping
423-338-4133

Blountville, TN

Rocky Top Best Holiday Trav-L-Park
496 Pearl Lane
Blountville, TN 37617
423-323-2535

Buchanan, TN

Paris Landing KOA
6290 E. Antioch Road
Buchanan, TN 38222
800-562-2815

Paris Landing State Park
Hwy. 79
Buchanan, TN
901-642-4311

Burns, TN

Montgomery Bell State Park
Hwy. 70
Burns, TN
615-797-9052

Camden, TN

Nathan Bedford Forrest State
Hwy. 191
Camden, TN
901-584-6356

Caryville, TN

Cove Lake State Park
Hwy. 25W
Caryville, TN
423-566-9701

Chapel Hill, TN

Henry Horton State Park
Hwy. 31A
Chapel Hill, TN
931-364-2222

Chattanooga, TN

Harrison Bay State Park
Hwy. 58
Chattanooga, TN

Holiday Trav-L-Park
1709 Mack Smith Road
Chattanooga, TN 37412
706-891-9766

Clarksville, TN

Clarksville RV Park and Campground
1270 Tylertown Road
Clarksville, TN 37040
Voice: (931) 648-8638
Fax: (931) 648-8639
info@clarksvillervpark.com

Cleveland, TN

Chattanooga North/Cleveland KOA
Box 3232
Cleveland, TN 37320
800-562-9039

Clinton, TN

Fox Inn Campground
2423 Andersonville Hwy.
Clinton, TN 37716
Voice: (865) 494-9386 / (888) 803-9883
Fax: (865) 494-6794
foxinncamp@comcast.net
Outside Link: www.foxinncampground.com

Cosby, TN

Cosby Campground
Great Smoky Mountains National Park
Hwy 32
Cosby, TN 37738
865-436-1200

Counce, TN

TVA Pickwick Dam Campground
Park Road
Counce, TN 38326
256-386-2228

Crossville, TN

Ballyhoo Family Campground
256 Werthwyle Drive
Crossville, TN 38555
Voice: (931) 484-0860 / (888) 336-3703

Fax: (931) 484-8070
ballyhoo@multipro.com

Bean Pot Holiday Trav-L-Park
23 Bean Pot Campground Loop
Crossville, TN 38558
931-484-7671

Crossville KOA
256 Werthwyle Dr.
Crossville, TN 38555
800-562-8153

Cumberland Mountain State Park
Hwy. 127
Crossville, TN
931-484-6138

Roam & Roost RV Campground
255 Fairview Dr.
Crossville, TN 38558
Voice: (931) 707-1414
Fax: (877) 707-1414

Eva, TN

Nathan Bedford Forrest State Park
1825 Pilot Knob Road
Eva, TN 38333
731-584-1841

Gallatin, TN

Bledsoe Creek State Park
Hwy. 25
Gallatin, TN
615-452-3706

Gatlinburg, TN

Crazy Horse Campground & RV Resort
4609 East Parkway
Gatlinburg, TN 37738
423-436-4434

Elkmont Campground
Great Smoky Mountain National Park
Gatlinmburg, TN 37738
865-436-1200

Smoky Bear Campground
Hwy. 321 East
Gatlinburg, TN 37738
Voice: (865) 436-8372 / (800) 850-8372
Fax: (865) 436-3008

Twin Creek RV Resort
1202 East Pkwy
Gatlinburg, TN 37738
865-436-7081

Harrison, TN

Harrison Bay State Park
8411 Harrison Bay
Harrison, TN 37341
423-344-2272

Henning, TN

Fort Pillow State Historic Park
Hwy. 51
Henning, TN
901-738-5581

Hilham, TN

Standing Stone State Park
1674 Standing Stone Park Hwy
Hilham, TN 38568
931-823-6347

Hurricane Mills, TN

Buffalo/I-40/Exit 143 KOA
473 Barren Hollow Road
Hurricane Mills, TN 37078
800-562-0832

Loretta Lynn Dude Ranch
1-40 West Exit 143
Hurricane Mills, TN 37078
931-296-7700

Jamestown, TN

Pickett State Park
Hwy. 154
Jamestown, TN 37243
931-879-5821

Jellico, TN

Indian Mountain State Park
I-75
Jellico, TN
423-784-7958

Kingsport, TN

Bristol/Kingsport KOA
Box 5024
Kingsport, TN 37663
800-562-7640

Warrior's Path State Park
Hemlock Road, Box 5026
Kingsport, TN 37663
423-239-8531

Kingston Springs, TN

Harpeth Scenic River and Narrows
Hwy. 70
Kingston Springs, TN

615-797-9052

Kodak, TN
Knoxville East KOA
241 KOA Dr.
Kodak, TN 37764
800-562-8693

Lake City, TN
Mountain Lake Marina and Campground
136 Campground Road
Lake City, TN 37769
Toll Free: (877)686-2267
Phone: (865)426-6510
mtnlaketn@aol.com
Lakeland, TN

Memphis East KOA
3291 Shoehorn Dr.
Lake City, TN 38002
800-562-8753

Lawrenceburg, TN
David Crockett State Park
Hwy. 64
Lawrenceburg, TN
931-762-9408

Lebanon, TN
Cedars of Lebanon State Park
Hwy. 231
Lebanon, TN
615-443-2769

Limestone, TN
Davy Crockett Birthplace Statr Park
Hwy. 11E
Limestone, TN
423-257-2167

Linden, TN
Mousetail Landing State Park
Hwy. 50
Linden, TN
901-847-0841

Livingston, TN
Standing Stone State Park
Hwy. 136
Livingston, TN
931-823-6347

Manchester, TN
Manchester KOA
586 Kampground Road
Manchester, TN 37355

800-562-7785

Old Stone Fort Archaeological Park
Hwy. 41
Manchester, TN
931-723-5073

Maynardville, TN
Big Ridge State Park
Hwy. 61
Maynardville, TN
423-992-5523

Memphis, TN
Memphis/Graceland KOA
3691 Elvis Presley Blvd.
Memphis, TN 38116
800-562-9386

T.O. Fuller State Park
Hwy. 61
Memphis, TN
901-543-7581

Millington, TN
Meeman-Shelby Forest State Park
Hwy. 388
Millington, TN
901-876-5215

Morristown, TN
Panther Creek State Park
Hwy. 11E
Morristown, TN
423-587-7046

Nashville, TN
Holiday Nashville Travel Park
2572 Music Valley Drive
Nashville, TN 37214
615-889-4225

Nashville Country RV Park
1200 Louisville Hwy.
Millersville, TN 37072
Voice: (615) 859-0348
Fax: (615) 859-0366
nashvillecountry@bellsouth.net

Nashville/Opryland KOA
2626 Music Valley Drive
Nashville, TN 37214
800-562-7789

Radnor State Natural Area
1160 Otter Creek Road

Nashville, TN 37243
615-373-3467

Two Rivers Campground
2616 Music Valley Dr.
Nashville, TN 37214
Voice: (615) 883-8559
Fax: (615) 889-0045
trcg@bellsouth.net
Outside Link: www.tworiverscampground.com

New Johnson, TN

Johnsonville State Historic Park
Hwy. 70
New Johnson, TN
931-535-2789

Newport, TN

Newport/I-40/Smoky Mountains KOA
240 KOA Lane
Newport, TN 37821
800-562-9016

Oneida, TN

Bandy Creek Campground
Big South Fork National River
4563 Leatherwood Road
Oneida, TN 37841
931-879-4869

Pickwick, TN

Pickwick Landing State Park
Hwy. 57
Pickwick, TN
901-689-3135

Pigeon Forge, TN

Eagles Nest Campground
1111 Wears Valley Road
Pigeon Forge, TN 37863
Voice: (865) 428-5841 / (800) 892-2714
Fax: (865) 428-8699
encamp@webtv.net

Pigeon Forge/Gatlinburg KOA
Box 310
Pigeon Forge, TN 37868
800-562-7703

Pikeville, TN

Fall Creek Falls State Park
Hwys. 111 and 30
Pikeville, TN
423-881-5241

Pocohontas, TN

Big Hill Pond State Park

Hwy. 57
Pocohontas, TN
931-645-7967

Pulaski, TN

Pulaski/I-65 Exit 14 KOA
5701 Fayettville Hwy.
Pulaski, TN 38478
800-562-4063

Tennessee Valley RV Park
2289 Hwy 64
Pulaski, TN 38478
931-363-4600

Roan Mountain, TN

Roan Mountain State Park
Hwy. 143
Roan Mountain, TN
423-772-3303

Rock Island, TN

Rock Island State Park
Hwy. 70S
Rock Island, TN
931-686-2471

Silver Point, TN

Edgar Evins State Park
Hwy. 96
Silver Point, TN
931-858-2446

Sweetwater, TN

Sweetwater/I-75/Exit 62 KOA
269 Murray's Chapel Road
Sweetwater, TN 37874
800-562-9224

Tellico Plains, TN

Indian Boundary Campground
Cherokee National Forest
250 Ranger Station Road
Tellico Plains, TN 37385
423-253-2520

Tiptonville, TN

Reelfoot Lake State Park
Hwy. 21
Tiptonville, TN
901-253-7756

Townsend, TN

Big Meadow Family Campground
8215 Cedar Creek Road
Townsend, TN 37882
Voice: (865) 448-0625 / (888) 497-0625

Fax: (865) 448-3346
bigmeadow@msn.com

Cades Cove Campground
Great Smoky Mountains National Park
Laurel Creek Road
Townsend, TN 37738
85-65-436-1200

Lazy Daze Campground
8429 State Hwy. 73 (PO Box 214)
Townsend, TN 37882
Voice: (865) 448-6061
Fax: (865) 448-9060
lazydazetn@aol.com

Little River Village
8533 State Highway 73
Townsend, TN 37882
Toll Free: (800)261-6370
Phone: (865)448-2241
Fax: (865)448-6052
littlerivervillage@comcast.net

Tremont Hills Campground & Log Cabins
PO Box 5
Townsend, TN 37882
423-448-6363

Tracy City, TN

South Cumberland Recreation Area
Hwy. 41A
Tracy City, TN
931-924-2980

Warthburg, TN

Frozen Head State Natural Area
Hwy. 62
Warthburg, TN
423-346-3318

Waverly, TN

Tennessee River Mountain Getaways
270 Riverwind Dr.
Waverly, TN 37185
888-332-4919

Wildersville, TN

Natchez Trace State Park
I-40
Wildersville, TN
901-968-3742

Pin Oak Campground
Natchez Trace State Resort Park
Natchez Trace Road

Wildersville, TN 38388
731-968-3742

Winchester, TN

Tims Ford State Park
570 Tims Ford Drive
Winchester, TN 37398

Texas

Abilene, TX

Abilene KOA
4851 W. Stamford St.
Abilene, TX 79603
800-562-3651

Amarillo, TX

Overnite RV Park
900 S. Lakeside Drive
Amarillo, TX 79118
806-373-1431

Amarillo KOA
1100 Folsom Road
Amarillo, TX 79108
800-562-3431

Austin, TX

Austin Lone Star RV Resort
7009 S. Ih 35
Austin, TX 78744

Lake Travis Inn and RV Park
4511 Doss Road
Austin, TX 78734

Oak Forest RV Park
8207 Canoga Ave.
Austin, TX 78724

Balmorhea, TX
Saddleback Mt RV Park
EXIT 212 I-10
Balmorhea, TX 79718

Bastrop, TX

Bastrop River RV Park
98 Hwy 71 West
Bastrop, TX 78602

Baytown, TX

Houston East/Baytown KOA
11810 I-10 East
Baytown, TX 77520
800-562-3418

Belton, TX

Belton/Temple/Killeen KOA
P.O. Box 118
Belton, TX 76513
800-562-1902

Big Spring, TX

Texas RV Park of Big Spring
4100 South US 87
Big Spring, TX 79720
915-267-7900

Whip In RV Park
7000 I-20
Big Spring, TX 79720
915-393-5242

Boerne, TX

Alamo Fiesta RV Resort
33000 IH-10 West
Boerne, TX 78006

Brookshire, TX

Houston West/Brookshire KOA
35303 Cooper Road
Brookshire, TX 77423
800-562-5417

Buchanan Dam, TX

Beachcomber RV Park
8138 Ranch Road 261
Buchanan Dam, TX 78609

Burkburnett, TX

Wichita Falls/Burkburnett KOA
1202 E 3rd St.
Burkburnett, TX 76354
800-562-2649

Burleson, TX

Mockingbird Hill MH and RV Park
1990 S. IH-35W
Burleson, TX 76028

Cleburne, TX

RV Ranch Of Cleburne
2230 Hwy 67 E
Cleburne, TX 76031

Columbus, TX

Columbus RV Park & Campground
2800 Hwy 71 South
Columbus, TX 78934
979-732-6455

Corpus Christi, TX

Laguna Shore Village RV Park
3828 Laguna Shores Road
Corpus Christi, TX 78418
361-937-6035

Crockett, TX

Crockett Family Resort

Rt 3, Box 460
Crockett, TX 75835

Crystal Beach, TX

Crystal Canal RV Resort
1300 Monkhouse Drive
Crystal Beach, TX 77650

Crystal City, TX
Triple R Resort RV Park
3766 Hwy 65
Crystal City, TX 78839

Denton, TX

Dallas KOA
7100 S. Stemmons
Denton, TX 76205
800-562-1893

Destiny Dallas
7100 S. I-35 E
Denton, TX 76210

Dickinson, TX

Bay Colony RV Resort
217 FM 517 W
Dickinson, TX 77539

Fentress, TX

Leisure Camp and RV Park
P.O. Box 277
Fentress, TX 78622

Fort Stockton, TX

Fort Stockton KOA
Box 627
Fort Stockton, TX 79735
800-562-8607

Fort Worth, TX

Fort Worth Midtown RV Park
2906 W. 6Th St
Fort Worth, TX 76107

RV Ranch of South Ft Worth
2301 S. IH 35W
Fort Worth, TX 76028
817-426-5037

Frankston, TX

SKYTRAQs Resort
23202 Gatlin Road
Frankston, TX 75763
903-876-4607

Glenn Heights, TX

Dallas Hi Ho RV Park

200 W. Bear Creek
Glenn Heights, TX 75154

Grand Prairie, TX

Traders Village RV Park Dallas
2602 Mayfield Road
Grand Prairie, TX 75052
972-647-8205

Hico, TX

Ez Duz It RV Park
East State Highway 6
Hico, TX 76457

Houston, TX

Houston Central KOA
1620 Peachleaf
Houston, TX 77039
800-562-2132

Traders Village RV Park Houston
7979 N. Eldridge
Houston, TX 77041
281-890-8846

Jacksonville, TX

Shady Pines RV Park
Rt. 2 Box 999
Jacksonville, TX 75766

Johnson City, TX

Miller Creek RV Park
5618 US Hwy 281 S
Johnson City, TX 78636
830-868-2655

Junction, TX

Junction KOA
2145 N. Main Street
Junction, TX 76849
800-562-7506

Kerrville, TX

Kerrville KOA
2950 Goat Creek Road
Kerrville, TX 78028
800-562-1665

Kilgore, TX

DandD RV Park
23500 Fm 2767
Kilgore, TX 75662

Lubbock, TX

Lubbock KOA
5502 County Road 6300
Lubbock, TX 79416

800-562-8643

Lubbock RV Park
4811 N. I-27
Lubbock, TX 79403

Madisonville, TX
Home on the Range RV Park
3239 Interstate 45 South
Madisonville, TX 77864
936-348-9470

Mathis, TX
Lake Corpus Christi/Mathis KOA
Route 1, Box 158B
Mathis, TX 78368
800-562-8601

Montgomery, TX
Havens Landing
19785 Hwy 105 W
Montgomery, TX 77356

Mt. Pleasant, TX
Mt. Pleasant KOA
P.O. Box 387
Mt. Pleasant, TX 75456
800-562-5409

Newton, TX
Whispering Creek RV Park/Motel
3713 Hwy 190 East
Newton, TX 75966
409-379-8400

Odessa, TX
Midland/Odessa KOA
4220 S. County Road 1290
Odessa, TX 79765
800-562-9168

Princeton, TX
Hidden Acres RV Park
10364 County Road 740 W
Princeton, TX 75407

San Angelo, TX
San Angelo KOA
6699 Knickerbocker Road
San Angelo, TX 76904
800-562-7519

Spring Creek Marina and RV Park
45 Fishermans Road
San Angelo, TX 76904

San Antonio, TX
Admiralty RV Resort
1485 N. Ellison Dr.
San Antonio, TX 78251

Blazing Star Luxury RV Resort
1120 West Loop 1604 N.
San Antonio, TX 78251
210-680-7827

San Antonio KOA
602 Gemberl Road
San Antonio, TX 78219
800-562-7783

Sargent, TX
Caney Creek RV
P.O. Box 4312
Sargent, TX 77404

Schulenburg, TX
Schulenburg RV Park
65 N. Kessler Ave.
Schulenburg, TX 78956
979-743-4388

Tarpley, TX
Caribbean Cowboy RV Resort
10965 FM 470
Tarpley, TX 78883
830-562-3233

Tyler, TX
Whispering Pines RV Resort
5583 FM 16 East
Tyler, TX 75706

Victoria, TX
Dads RV Park
203 Hopkins
Victoria, TX 77901

Uvalde, TX
Chalk Bluff Park
1108 Chalk Bluff Road
Uvalde, TX 78801
830-278-5515

Van Horn, TX
Van Horn KOA
P.O. Box 265
Van Horn, TX 79855
800-562-0798

West, TX

Waco North KOA
P.O. Box 157
West, TX 76691
800-562-4199

Willis, TX

Park On The Lake
12351 Fm 830
Willis, TX 77378

Utah

Arches National Park, UT

Devil's Garden Campground
Hwy 191
Arches National Park 84532
435-719-2299

Beaver, UT

Beaver KOA
P.O. Box 1437
Beaver, UT 84713
800-562-2912

Minersville State Park
PO Box 1521
Beaver, UT 84713
435-438-5472

United Beaver Campground
1603 South Campground Road
Beaver, UT 84713
435-438-2808

Bluff, UT

Cadillac Ranch RV Park
Hwy 191
Bluff, UT 84512
435-672-2262

Brigham City, UT

Brigham City/Perry South KOA
Box 579
Brigham City, UT 84302
800-562-0903

Bryce Canyon, UT

Ruby's Inn RV Park & Campground
1280 South State Hwy 63
Bryce Canyon, UT 84764
435-834-5301

Sunset Campground
Bryce Canyon National Park
Bryce Canyon, UT 84717
435-834-5322

Canyonlands National Park, UT

Squaw Flat Campground
Needles District, Hwy 211
Canyonlands National Park, UT 84532
319-259-7164

Willow Flat Campground

Island in the Sky District, Hwy 313
Canyonlands National Park, UT 84532
435-259-4712

Cedar City, UT

Cedar Canyon Campground
1789 North Wedgewood Lane
Cedar City, UT 84721
435-865-3200

Cedar City KOA
1121 N Main St.
Cedar City, UT 84720
Voice: (435) 586-9872
Fax: (435) 865-9009
koa@skyviewmail.com

Duck Creek Campground
PO Box 627
Cedar City, UT 84721
435-865-3200

Point Supreme Campground
Cedar Breaks National Monument
2390 West Hwy 56
Cedar City, UT 84720
435-586-9451

Escalante, UT

Broken Arrow RV Camp
495 Main St
Escalante, UT 84726
888-241-8785

Calf Creek Campground
PO Box 225
Escalante, UT 84726
435-826-5400

Fillmore, UT

Fillmore KOA
900 South 410 West
Fillmore, UT 84631
800-562-1516

Garden City, UT

Bear Lake/Garden City KOA
US 89
Garden City, UT 84028
800-562-3442

Glendale, UT

Glendale KOA
Box 189
Glendale, UT 84729
800-562-8635

Green River, UT

Green River KOA
P.O. Box 14
Green River, UT 84525
800-562-3649

Green River State Park
PO Box 637
Green River, UT 84525
435-564-3633

Shady Acres RV Park and Campground
350 Main St
Green River, UT 84525
800-537-8674

United Campground
910 East Main St
Green River, UT 84545

Kanab, UT

Coral Pink Sand Dunes State Park
12500 Sand Dunes Road
Kanab, UT 84741
435-648-2800

Kaysville, UT

Cherry Hill Campground
1325 South Main
Kaysville, UT 84037
801-451-5379

Leeds, UT

Leeds RV Park and Motel
97 S Valley Road (PO Box 461149)
Leeds, UT 84746
Voice: (435) 879-2450
leedsrv@infowest.com

Manila, UT

Flaming Gorge/Manila KOA
Box 157
Manila, UT 84046
800-562-3254

Mexican Hat, UT

Goosenecks State Park
UT 316, off UT 261
Mexican Hat, UT 84511
435-678-2238

Moab, UT

Dead Horse Point State Park
SR 313 PO Box 609
Moab, UT 84532
435-259-2614

Moab Rim Campark and Cabins
1900 South Hwy 19
Moab, UT 84532
435-259-5002

Pack Creek Campgound
1520 Murphy Lane #6
Moab, UT 84532
435-259-2982

Portal RV Park
1261 North Hwy 191
Moab, UT 84532
435-259-6108

Monument Valley, UT

Monument Valley Simpson's Trailhandler Tours
PO box 360377
Monument Valley, UT 84536
435-727-3362

Panguitch, UT

Panguitch KOA
P.O. Box 384
Panguitch, UT 84759
800-562-1625

Red Canyon RV Park
3279 Hwy 12
Panguitch, UT 84759
435-676-2690

Provo, UT

Provo KOA
320 N. 2050 W
Provo, UT 84601
800-562-1894

Richfield, UT

Richfield KOA
600 W 600 S
Richfield, UT 84701
800-562-9382

Vernal, UT

Vernal KOA
1800 West Sheraton Ave.
Vernal, UT 84078
800-562-7574

Virgin, UT

Zion River Resort-RV Park & Campground
730 East Highway 9 - PO Box 790219
Virgin, UT 84779
Voice: (435) 635-8594 / (800) 838-8594
Fax: (435) 635-3934

info@zrr.com

Washington, UT
Redlands RV Park
650 W. Telegraph St.
Washington, UT 84780
435-673-9700

Zion, UT
Zion National Park
435-648-2154

Zion National Park, UT
Mukuntuweep RV Park & Campground
Zion East Gate
Zion National Park, UT
435-648-2154

Vermont

Addison, VT

Griffin's Ten Acre Campground
RD 1, Box 3560
Addison, VT 05491
802-759-2662

Alburg, VT

Alburg RV Resort
PO Box 50
Alburg, VT 05440
802-796-3733

Andover, VT

Horeshoe Acres
RD 1, Box 206
Andover, VT 05143
802-875-2960

Arlington, VT

Camping on the Battenkill
RD 2, Box 3310
Arlington, VT 05250
802-375-6663

Ascutney, VT

Getaway Mountain Campground
PO Box 372
Ascutney, VT 05030
802-674-2812

Running Bear Camping Area
PO Box 378
Ascutney, VT 05030
802-674-6417

Wilgus State Park
PO Box 196
Ascutney, VT 05030
802-674-5422

Barnard, VT

Silver Lake Family Campground
Box 11
Barnard, VT 05031
802-234-9974

Barton, VT

Belview Campground
Rt. 16 East
Barton, VT 05822
802-525-3242

Bennington, VT

Greenwood Lodge & Campsites
Route 9 (Mail Only: PO Box 246, Bennington, VT 05201)
Woodford, VT 05201
Voice: (802) 442-2547
Fax: (802) 442-2547
campgreenwood@aol.com

Woodford State Park
HCR 65, Box 928
Bennington, VT 05201
802-447-7169

Brandon, VT

Brandbury State Park
RR 2, Box 242
Brandon, VT 05743
802-247-5925

Smokerise Family Campground
2145 Grove Street
Brandon, VT 05733
802-247-6984

Brattleboro, VT

Fort Drummer State Park
434 Old Guilford Road
Brattleboro, VT 05301
802-254-2610

Moss Hollow Campground
RD 4, Box 723
Brattleboro, VT 05301
802-368-2418

Bristol, VT

Elephant Mountain Campground
RD 3, Box 850
Bristol, VT 05443
802-453-3123

Burlington, VT

Burlington's North Beach Campground
60 Institute Road
Burlington, VT 05401
802-862-0942

Cavendish, VT

Caton Place Campground
RR 1, Box 107
Cavendish, VT 05142
802-226-7767

Charlotte, VT

Mt. Philo State Park
5425 Mt. Philo Road

Charlotte, VT 05445
802-425-2390

Concord, VT

Breezy Meadows Campground
23 Wendel Road
Concord, VT 05824
Phone: (802)695-9949
breezy@together.net

Rustic Haven Campground
Rte 2
Concord, VT 05824
802-695-9933

Derby, VT

Char-bo Campground
PO Box 438
Derby, VT 05829
802-766-8807

Fireside Campground
Box 340
Derby, VT 05829
802-766-5109

Dorset, VT

Dorset RV Park
RR 1, Box 180
Dorset, VT 05251
802-867-5754

East Dorset, VT

Emerald Lake State Park
RD Box 485
East Dorset, VT 05253
802-362-1655

East Montpelier, VT

Green Valley Campground
PO Box 21
East Montpelier, VT 05651
802-223-6217

East Thetford, VT

Rest N' Nest
PO Box 258
East Thetford, VT 05043
802-785-2997

Enosburg Falls, VT

Brookside Campground
RD 2, Box 3300
Enosburg Falls, VT 05450
802-933-4376

Lake Carmi State Park

460 Marsh Road
Enosburg Falls, VT 05450
802-933-8383

Fair Haven, VT

Half Moon Pond
RR 1, Box 2730
Fair Haven, VT 05743
802-273-2848

Franklin, VT

Mill Pond Campground
RR 1, Box 2335
Franklin, VT 05452
802-285-2240

Grand Isle, VT

Champlain Adult Campground
3 Silent Cedars
Grand Isle, VT 05458
802-372-5938

Grand Isle State Park
36 East Shore Road, South
Grand Isle, VT 05458
802-372-4300

Graniteville, VT

Lazy Lions Campground
PO Box 56
Graniteville, VT 05654
802-479-2823

Groton, VT

Ricker Pond State Park
Groton, VT 05046
802-584-3821

Stillwater State Park
RD 2, Box 332
Groton, VT 05046
802-584-3822

Guildhall, VT

Maidstone State Park
RD Box 455
Guildhall, VT 05905
802-676-3930

Hardwick, VT

Idle Hours Campground
PO Box 1053
Hardwick, VT 05843
802-472-6732

Island Pond, VT

Brighton State Park

Island Pond, VT 05846
802-479-4280

Lakeside Camping
RR 1, Box194
Island Pond, VT 05846
802-723-6649

Jamaica, VT

Jamaica State Park
Box 45
Jamaica, VT 05343
802-874-4600

Killington, VT

Gifford Woods State Park
Killington, VT 05751
802-775-5354

Killington Campground
Alphenhof Lodge, Box 2880
Killington, VT 05751
802-422-9787

Lake Elmore, VT

Elmore State Park
Box 93
Lake Elmore, VT 05657
802-888-2982

Ludlow, VT

Hideaway "Squirrel Hill" Campground
PO Box 176
Ludlow, VT 05149
802-228-8800

Marshfield, VT

Groton Forest Road Campground
RR 1, Box 402
Marshfield, VT 05658
802-426-4122

Kettle Pond State Park
RD Box 600
Marshfield, VT 05658
802-584-3820

New Discovery State Park
4239 VT 232
Marshfield, VT 05658
802-426-3042

Middlebury, VT

Fall of Lana
RR 4 Box 1260
Middlebury, VT 05753

802-388-4362

Lake Dunmore Kampersville
Box 214
Middlebury, VT 05753
802-352-4501

Mount Moosalamo
RR 4 Box 1260
Middlebury, VT 05753
802-388-4362

Morrisville, VT

Mountain View CG & Cabins
Rt. 15
Morrisville, VT 05661
802-888-2178

New Haven, VT

Rivers Bend Campground
PO Box 9, Dog Team Rd & Rt. 7
New Haven, VT 05472
802-388-9092

Newfane, VT

Kenolie Village Campground
RR 1, Box 810
Newfane, VT 05345
802-365-7671

North Hero, VT

Carry Bay
PO Box 207
North Hero, VT 05474
802-372-8233

Kings Bay Campground
Lakeview Drive, PO Box 169
North Hero, VT 05474
802-372-3735

North Hero State Park
RD Box 259, Lakeview Road
North Hero, VT 05474
802-373-8389

Orleans, VT

White Caps Campground
RD 2, Box 626
Orleans, VT 05860
802-467-3345

Will-O-Wood Campground
RD 2, Box 316
Orleans, VT 05860
802-525-3575

Plainfield, VT
Onion River Campground
RR 1, Box 1205
Plainfield, VT 05667
802-426-3232

Plymouth, VT
Coolidge State Park
HCR 70, Box 105
Plymouth, VT 05056
802-672-3612

Poultney, VT
Lake St. Catherine State Park
RD 2, Box 1775
Poultney, VT 05764
802-287-9158

Randolph Center, VT
Lake Champagne Campground
PO Box C, Furnace Road
Randolph Center, VT 05061
802-728-5293

Randolph, VT
Allis State Park
RD 2, Box 192
Randolph, VT 05060
802-276-3175

Rochester, VT
Mt. Trails Campground
RFD 1, Box 7, Quarry Road
Rochester, VT 05767
802-767-3352

Salisbury, VT
Branbury State Park
3570 Lake Dunmore, Rte 53
Salisbury, VT 05733
802-247-5925

Lake Dunmore Kampersville Campground
PO Box 56, Rte 53
Salisbury, VT 05769
802-352-4501

Waterhouse Campground and Marina
937 West Shore Road
Salisbury, VT 05769
802-352-4433

Shelburne, VT
Shelburne Camping Area
2056 Shelburne Road
Shelburne, VT 05482

802-985-2540

Springfield, VT
Tree Farm Campground
53 Skitchewaug Trail
Springfield, VT 05156
802-885-2889

St. Johnsbury, VT
Moose River Campground
RR 3, Box 197
St. Johnsbury, VT 05819
802-748-4334

Stowe, VT
Smugglers' Notch
7248 Mountain Road
Stowe, VT 05672
802-253-4014

Swanton, VT
Champlain Valley Campground
RD 1, Box 4255
Swanton, VT 05448
802-524-5146

Lakewood Campground
RFD 2, Box 482
Swanton, VT 05488
802-868-7270

Thetford, VT
Thetford Hill State Park
Box 132
Thetford, VT 05074
802-785-2266

Townshend, VT
Camperama Campground
PO Box 282, Depot Road
Townshend, VT 05353
802-365-4315

Townshend State Park
RR 1, Box 2650
Townshend, VT 05353
802-365-7500

Underhill, VT
South Hill Riverside Campground
RR 2, Box 287
Underhill, VT 05489
802-899-2232

Underhill Center, VT
Underhill State Park
PO Box 249

Underhill Center, VT 05490
802-899-3022

Vergennes, VT

Button Bay State Park
RD 3, Box 4075
Vergennes, VT 05491
802-475-2377

DAR State Park
RD 2, Box 3493
Vergennes, VT 05491
802-759-2359

Waterbury, VT

Little River State Park
RD 1, Box 1150
Waterbury, VT 05676
802-244-7013

West Danville, VT

Indian Joe Court
US Rt. 2, PO Box 126
West Danville, VT 05873
802-684-3430

Westfield, VT

Barrewwod Campground
HCR 13, Box 4
Westfield, VT 05874
802-744-6340

Mill Brook Campground
PO Box 133
Westfield, VT 05874
802-744-6673

White River Junction, VT

Maple Leaf Motel & Campground
406 N. Harland Road
White River Junction, VT 05001
802-295-2817

Pine Valley RV Resort
400 Woodstock Road
White River Junction, VT 05001
802-296-6711

Quechee Gorge State Park
190 Dewey Mill Road
White River Junction, VT 05001
802-295-2990

Williamstown, VT

Limehurst Lake Campground
RR 1, Box 462

Williamstown, VT 05679
802-433-6662

Wilmington, VT

Molly Stark State Park
705 Rt. 9 East
Wilmington, VT 05363
802-464-5460

Windsor, VT

Ascutney State Park
Box 186, HCR 71
Windsor, VT 05089
802-886-2060

Woodford, VT

Woodford State Parkl
142 State Park Road
Woodford, VT 05201
802-447-7169

Virginia

Appomattox, VA
Holiday Lake State Park
Rte 2, Box 622
Appomattox, VA 24522
434-248-6308

Ashland, VA
Americamps, Richmond North
11322 Air Park Road
Ashland, VA 23005
804-798-5298

Bedford, VA
Peaks of Otter Campground
Blue Ridge Pkwy.-Rte 2
Bedford, VA 24523
540-586-4357

Bowling Green, VA
Bowling Green/Richmond KOA
Box 1250
Bowling Green, VA 22427
800-562-2482

Breaks, VA
Breaks Interstate Park
Rte 80
Breaks, VA 24607
276-865-4413

Broadway, VA
Harrisonburg/New Market KOA
12480 Mountain Valley Road
Broadway, VA 22815
800-562-5406

Charlottesville, VA
Charlottesville KOA
3825 Red Hill Road
Charlottesville, VA 22903
800-562-1743

Chesapeake, VA
Chesapeake Campground
693 S George Washington Hwy.
Chesapeake, VA 23323
Voice: (757) 485-0149 / (888) 584-2267

Dublin, VA
Claytor Lake State Park
4400 State Park Road
Dublin, VA 24084

804-225-3867

Dumfries, VA
Prince William Travel Trailer Village
16058 Dumfries Road
Dumfries, VA 22026
Voice: (703) 221-2474 / (888) 737-5730
Fax: (703) 670-4706
traveltrailervillage@yahoo.com

Edinburg, VA
Creekside Campground
108 Palmyra Road
PO Box 277
Edinburg, VA 22824
540-984-4299

Emporia, VA
Yogi Bear's Jellystone Park & Emporia
2940 Sussex Dr.
Emporia, VA 23847
Voice: (434) 634-3115 / (800) 545-4248
Fax: (434) 634-6560
info@campingbear.com

Fredericksburg, VA
Fredericksburg/Washington DC KOA
7400 Brookside Lane
Fredericksburg, VA 22408
800-562-1889

Front Royal, VA
Front Royal/Washington DC KOA
P.O. Box 274
Front Royal, VA 22630
800-562-9114

Haymarket, VA
Greenville Farm Family Campground
14004 Shelter Ln.
Haymarket, VA 20169
Voice: (703) 754-7944

R-J Ranch RV Resort
8736 Double Cabin Road
Hillsville, VA 24343
Voice: (276) 766-3703
Fax: (276) 766-3759
miller921@aol.com

Huddleston, VA
Smith Mountain Lake State Park
1235 State Park Road
Huddleston, VA 24104
804-225-3867

Luray, VA

Luray RV Resort Country Waye
3402 Kimball Road
Luray, VA 22835
Voice: (540) 743-7222 / (888) 765-7222
Fax: (540) 743-1803
camp@countrywaye.com

Madison, VA

Shenandoah Hills Campground
110 Campground Lane
Madison, VA 22727
Toll Free: (800)321-4186
Phone: (540)948-4186
ateam143@msn.com

Marion, VA

Hungry Mother State Park
2854 Park Blvd.
Marion, VA 24354
804-225-3867

Meadows of Dan, VA

Meadows of Dan Campground
2182 Jeb Stuart Highway
Meadows of Dan, VA 24120-4182
Voice: (276) 952-2292
Fax: (276) 952-2392

Middletown, VA

Battle of Cedar Creek Campground
249 Waterland Road
Middletown, VA 22645
Voice: (540) 869-1888 / (800) 343-1562

Millboro, VA

Douthat State Park
Route 1, Box 212
Millboro, VA 24460
804-225-3867

Monroe, VA

Wildwood Campground
6252 Elon Road
Monroe, VA 24574
434-299-5228

Montross, VA

Westmoreland State Park
1650 State Park Road
Montross, VA 22520
804-225-3867

Natural Bridge, VA

Natural Bridge/Lexington KOA
Box 148

Natural Bridge, VA 24578
800-562-8514

Petersburg, VA

Petersburg KOA
2809 Courtland Road
Petersburg, VA 23805
800-562-8545

Picture Lake Campground
7818 Boydton Plank Road
Petersburg, VA 23803
Voice: (804) 861-0174

Reedville, VA

Chesapeake Bay/Smith Island KOA
382 Campground Road
Reedville, VA 22539
800-562-9795

Scottsburg, VA

Staunton River State Park
1170 Staunton Trail
Scottsburg, VA 24589
804-225-3867

Stafford, VA

Aquia Pines Camp Resort
3071 Jefferson Davis Highway
Stafford, VA 22554
540-659-2447

Staunton, VA

Walnut Hills Campground
391 Walnut Hills Road
Staunton, VA 24401
540-337-3920

Stuart, VA

Fairy Stone State Park
907 Fairy Stone Lake Drive
Stuart, VA 24171
804-225-3867

Triangle, VA

Prince William Forest Park
PO Box 209
Triangle, VA 22172
703-221-7181

Urbana, VA

Bethpage Camp-Resort
Route 602 (PO Box 178)
Urbanna, VA 23175
Voice: (804) 758-4349
Fax: (804) 758-0209
bethpage@oonl.com

Verona, VA

Staunton/Verona/I-81 Exit 227 KOA
P.O. Box 98
Verona, VA 24482
800-562-9949

Virginia Beach, VA

First Landing State Park
2500 Shore Drive
Virginia Beach, VA 23451
804-225-3867

Best Holiday Trav-L-Park
1075 General Booth Blvd.
Virginia Beach, VA 23451
757-425-0249

Virginia Beach KOA
1240 General Booth Blvd.
Virginia Beach, VA 23451
800-562-4150

Williamsburg, VA

American Heritage RV Park
146 Maxton Lane
Williamsburg, VA 23188
757-566-2133

Anvil Campground
5243 Mooretown Road
Williamsburg, VA 23188
800-633-4442

Fair Oaks Family Campground
901 Lightfoot Road
Williamsburg, VA 23188
757-565-2101

Williamsburg/Busch Gardens KOA
5210 Newman Road
Williamsburg, VA 23188
800-562-1733

Williamsburg/Colonial KOA
4000 Newman Road
Williamsburg, VA 23188
800-562-7609

Winchester, VA

Candy Hill Campground
165 Ward Ave.
Winchester, VA 22602
Voice: (540) 662-8010 / (800) 462-0545
Fax: (540) 662-8010
karl-littman@hotmail.com

Wytheville, VA

Wytheville KOA
RR 2, Box 122
Wytheville, VA 24382
800-562-3380

Washington

Anacortes, WA

Pioneer Trails Campground
7337 Miller Road
Anacortes, WA 98221
Voice: (360) 293-5355 / (888) 777-5355
Fax: (360) 299-2240
pioneertrails@pioneertrails.com

Bay Center, WA

Bay Center/Willapa Bay KOA
P.O. Box 315
Bay Center, WA 98527
800-562-7810

Bellevue, WA

Trailer Inns RV Park / Bellevue
15531 SE 37th
Bellevue, WA 98006
Voice: (425) 747-9181 / (800) 659-4684
Outside Link: www.trailerinnsrv.com

Bothell, WA

Lake Pleasant RV Park
24025 Bothel Everett Hwy.
Bothell, WA 98021
Voice: (425) 487-1785 / (800) 742-0386
Fax: (425) 487-1785

Chehalis, WA

Cherhalis/Hwy 12 KOA
118 US Hwy. 12
Chehalis, WA 98532
800-562-9120

Cheney, WA

Klink's Williams Lake Resort
18617 Williams Lake Road
Cheney, WA 99004
Voice: (509) 235-2391 / (800) 274-1540
Fax: (509) 235-2817
jfklink@earthlink.net

Electric City, WA

Coulee Playland Resort
Box 457, Hwy. 155 #1
Electric City, WA 99123
Voice: (509) 633-2671
Fax: (509) 633-2133
cpr139@couleeplayland.com

Ellensburg, WA

Ellensburg KOA

32 Thorp Hwy S.
Ellensburg, WA 98926
800-562-7616

Fall City, WA

Snoqualmie River RV Park & Campground
34807 SE 44th Pl.
Fall City, WA 98024
Voice: (425) 222-5545

Hoquiam, WA

Hoquiam River RV Park
425 Queen Ave.
Hoquiam, WA 98550
Voice: (360) 538-2870
Fax: (360) 538-2871
information@hoquiamriverrvpark.com

Ilwaco, WA

Ilwaco KOA
Box 549
Ilwaco, WA 98624
800-562-3258

Issaquah, WA

Blue Sky RV Park
9002 302nd Ave., SE
Issaquah, WA 98027
Voice: (425) 222-7910
Fax: (425) 222-5177

Kent, WA

Seattle Tacoma KOA
5801 South 212th Street
Kent, WA 98032
Phone: (253)872-8652
seattlekoa@aol.com

Leavenworth, WA

Leavenworth/Wenatchee KOA
11401 Riverbend Dr.
Leavenworth, WA 98826
800-562-5709

Long Beach, WA

Anderson's On the Ocean
1400 138th St.
Long Beach, WA 98631
360-642-2231

Lynden, WA

Lynden KOA
8717 Line Road
Lynden, WA 98264
800-562-4779

Oak Harbor, WA

North Whidbey RV Park
565 Cornet Bay Road
Oak Harbor, WA 98277
Voice: (360) 675-9597 / (888) 462-2674
Fax: (360) 679-1665
managers@northwhidbeyrvpark.com

Ocean Park, WA

Ocean Park Resort
25904 R St.
Ocean Park, WA 98640
Voice: (360) 665-4585 / (800) 835-4634
Fax: (360) 665-4130
info@opresort.com

Olympia, WA

American Heritage Holiday Trav-L-Park
9610 Kimmie St., SW
Olympia, WA 98512
360-943-8778

Olympia Holiday Trav-L-Park
1441 83rd Ave., SW
Olympia, WA 98512
360-352-2551

Otis Orchards, WA

Spokane KOA
N 3025 Barker Road
Otis Orchards, WA 99027
800-562-3309

Pasco, WA

Sandy Heights RV Park
8801 St. Thomas Dr.
Pasco, WA 99301
Voice: (509) 542-1357
Fax: (509) 543-8335
sandyheightsrv@urx.com

Port Angeles, WA

Port Angeles/Sequim, KOA
80 O'Brien Road
Port Angeles, WA 98362
800-562-7558

Richland, WA

Horn Rapids RV Resort / Richland RV Park, LLC
2640 Kingsgate Way
Richland, WA 99352
Voice: (509) 375-9913 / (866) 557-9637
Fax: (509) 375-9953
info@hornrapidsrvresort.com

Seaview, WA

Seaview Motel & RV Park
3728 Pacific Highway
Seaview, WA 98644
360-642-2450

Vantage, WA

Vantage KOA
Box 135
Vantage, WA 98950
800-562-7270

Westport, WA

American Sunset RV Resort
1209 N Montesano Ave.
Westport, WA 98595
Voice: (360) 268-0207 / (800) 569-2267
Fax: (360) 268-0207
info@americansunsetrv.com

Winthrop, WA

Winthrop/N. Cascades Nat'l Park KOA
Box 305
Winthrop, WA 98862
800-562-2158

Yakima, WA

Yakima KOA
1500 Keys Road
Yakima, WA 98901
800-562-5773

West Virginia

Alderson, WV

Greenbrier River Campground
282 Greenbrier Road
Alderson, WV 24343
800-775-2203

Barboursville, WV

Beech Fork State Park
5601 Long Branch Road
Barboursville, WV 25504
304-528-5794

Buckhannon, WV

Audra State Park
Rte 4, Box 564
Buckhannon, WV 26201
304-457-1162

Clarksburg, WV

Wilderness Waterpark and Campground
Wolf Summit
Clarksburg, WV 26301
304-622-7528

Elkins, WV

Alpine Shores Campground
HC 73, Box 3
Elkins, WV 26254
304-636-4311

Fayetteville, WV

Rifrafters Campground
Route 2, Box 140A
Fayetteville, WV 25840
Voice: (304) 574-1065
Fax: (304) 574-1007
rifrafters@hotmail.com

Harpers Ferry, WV

Harpers Ferry Koa
343 campground Road
Harpers Ferry, WV 25425
Phone: (304)535-6895
hfkoa@intrepid.net

Gap Mills, WV

Moncove Lake State Park
Rte 4 Box 73-A
Gap Mills, WV 24941
304-772-3450

Hacker Valley, WV

Holly River State Park
PO Box 70
Hacker Valley, WV 26222
304-493-6353

Lansing, WV

Extreme Expeditions
PO Box 9
Lansing, WV 25862
304-574-2827

Summersville Lake Retreat
PO Box 212
Lansing, WV 25862
304-72-5975

Pipestem, WV

Pipestem KOA
HC 78, Box 37B
Pipestem, WV 25979
800-562-5418

Roncevert, WV

Organ Cave Campground
417 Masters Road
Ronceverte, WV 24970
304-647-5551

Weston, WV

Whisper Mountain Campground and RV Park
Rte 1 Box 65
Weston, WV 26423
304-452-8847

Wisconsin

Algoma, WI

Ahnapee River Trails Campground
E6053 W. Wilson Road
Algoma, WI 54201
920-487-5777

Timber Trail Campground
N8326 Co. M
Algoma, WI 54201
920-487-3707

Alma Center, WI

Hixton/Alma Center KOA
N9657 State Hwy. 95f
Alma Center, WI 54611
800-562-2680

Arbor Vitae, WI

Arbor Vitae Campground
10545 Big Arbor Vitae Dr.
Arbor Vitae, WI 54568
715-356-5146

Fox Fire Campground, Inc.
11180 Fox Fire Road
Arbor Vitae, WI 54568
715-356-6470

Athelstane, WI

Mountain Jed's Camping and Canoeing
W13364 Cty., C
Athelstane, WI 54104
715-757-2406

Augusta, WI

Sandy Hill Campground
E21100 ND Road
Augusta, WI 54722
715-286-2495

Bagley, WI

Wyalusing State Park
13342 County Hwy. C
Bagley, WI 53801
608-996-2261

Yogi Bear's Jellystone Park-Bagley
11354 County Highway X
Bagley, WI 53801
608-996-2201

Bailey's Harbor, WI

Bailey's Bluff Campground
2701 County Road EE
Bailey's Harbor, WI 54202
920-839-2109

Bailey's Grove Travel Park and Campground
2552 CR F and EE
Baileys Harbor, WI 54202
866-839-2559

Bancroft, WI

Vista Royalle Campground
8025 Isherwood Road (MAIL 8151 County Hwy BB)
Bancroft, WI 54921
Voice: (715) 335-6860

Baraboo, WI

Baraboo Hills Campground
E10545 Terrytown Road
Baraboo, WI 53913
608-356-8505

Devil's Lake State Park
S5975 Park Road
Baraboo, WI 53913
608-356-6618

Fox Hill RV Park
E11371 N. Reedsburg Road
Baraboo, WI 53913
608-356-5890

Mirror Lake State Park
E10320 Ferndell Road
Baraboo, WI 53913
608-254-2333

Rocky Arbor State Park
c/o E10320 Ferndell Road
Baraboo, WI 53913
608-254-8001

Bayfield, WI

Big Bay State Park
P.O. Box 589
Bayfield, WI 54814
715-747-6425

Beaver Dam, WI

Willow Mill Campsites
P.O. Box 312
Beaver Dam, WI 53916
920-887-1420

Belmont, WI

Lake Joy Campground
24192 Lake Joy Lane
Belmont, WI 53510
608-762-5150

Black River Falls, WI

Lost Falls Resort & Campground
436 S. Third St.
Black River Falls, WI 54615
715-284-7133

Parkland Village Campground
Route 2, Box 7V
Black River Falls, WI 54615
715-284-9700

Blanchardville, WI

Yellowstone Lake State Park
7896 Lake Road
Blanchardville, WI 53516
608-523-4427

Blue Mound, WI

Blue Mound State Park
P.O. Box 98
Blue Mound, WI 53517
608-437-5711

Boulder Junction, WI

Camp Holiday
Box 67 WA
Boulder Junction, WI 54512
715-385-2264

N. Highland/American Legion St. Forest
4125 Co. Hwy. M
Boulder Junction, WI 54512
715-385-2704

Bristol, WI

Happy Acres Kampground
22230 45th St.
Bristol, WI 53104
414-857-7373

Brodhead, WI

Crazy Horse Campground
W741 City F
Brodhead, WI 53520
608-897-2207

Butternut, WI

Butternut Lake Campground
Route 1, Box 129A
Butternut, WI 54514
715-769-3448

Brussels, WI

Quietwoods South Camping Resort
9245 Lovers Ln.
Brussels, WI 54204
Voice: (920) 825-7065

Caledonia, WI

Yogi Bear's Jellystone Camp-Resort
8425 Hwy. 38
Caledonia, WI 53108
414-835-2565

Cambria, WI

Deer Creek Campground
N8129 Larson Road
Cambria, WI 53923
920-348-6413

Camp Douglas, WI

Mill Bluff State Park
Rt. 1, Box 268
Camp Douglas, WI 54618
608-427-6692

Campbellsport, WI

Benson's Century Camping Resort
N3845 Hwy. 67
Campbellsport, WI 53010
920-533-8597

Kettle Moraine State Forest
N1765 Hwy. G.
Campbellsport, WI 53010
414-626-2115

Cascade, WI

Hoeft's Resort & Campground
W9070 Crooked Lake Drive
Cascade, WI 53011
414-626-2221

Cassville, WI

Nelson Dewey State Park
Box 658
Cassville, WI 53806
608-725-5274

Chetek, WI

Ken's Kampsites
P.O. Box 222
Chetek, WI 54822
715-859-2887

Chippewa Falls, WI

Lake Wissota State Park
18127 County Hwy. O

Chippewa Falls, WI 54729
715-382-4574

Comell, WI

Brunet Island State Park
23125 25th St.
Comell, WI 54732
715-239-6888

Conover, WI

Buckatabon Lodge & Lighthouse Inn
5630 Rush Road
Conover, WI 54519
715-479-4660

Crivitz, WI

High Falls Family Campground
11594 Archer Lane
K54114
715-757-3399

Peshtigo River Campground
Rt. 1, Box 243
Crivitz, WI 54114
715-854-2986

Dalton, WI

Grand Valley Campground
W5855 County Road B
Dalton, WI 53926
920-394-3643

DeForest, WI

Madison KOA
4859 CTH-V
DeForest, WI 53532
800-562-5784

DePere, WI

Happy Hollow Camping Resort
3831 County Road U
DePere, WI 54115
920-532-4386

Delavan, WI

Snug Harbor Inn Campground on Turtle Lake
W7772-2C Wisconsin Parkway
Delavan, WI 53115
608-883-6999

Dodgeville, WI

Tom's Campground
2751 CTH BB
Dodgeville, WI 53533
Voice: (608) 935-5446

E. Black River Falls, WI

Black River State Forest Castle Mound
910 Hwy. 54
E. Black River Falls, WI 54615
715-284-4103

Eagle, WI

Kettle Moraine State Forest
S91 W39091 Hwy. 59
Eagle, WI 53119
414-594-6200

Eagle River, WI

Chain-O-Lakes Resort & Camping
3165 Nine Mile Road
Eagle River, WI 54521
715-479-6708

Pine-Aire Resort & Campground
4443 Chain O'Lakes Road
Eagle River, WI 54521
715-479-9208

Edgerton, WI

Hickory Hills Campground
856 Hillside Road
Edgerton, WI 53534
Voice: (608) 884-6327
camphickoryhills@aol.com

Egg Harbor, WI

Door County Kamping Resort
4906 Court Road
Egg Harbor, WI 54209
920-868-3151

Frontier Wilderness Campground
4375 Hillside Road
Egg Harbor, WI 54209
920-868-3349

Elkhart Lake, WI

Plymouth Rock Camping Resort
P.O. Box 445
Elkhart Lake, WI 53020
920-892-4252

Ellison Bay, WI

Hy-Land Court
11563 Hwy 42
Ellison Bay, WI 54210
920-854-4850

Newport State Park
475 County Hwy. NP
Ellison Bay, WI 54210

920-854-2500

Wagon Trail Campground
1190 Hwy. ZZ
Ellison Bay, WI 54210
Voice: (920) 854-4818
wtc@dcwis.com

Fence, WI

Lake Hilbert Campground
N2490 Town Park Road
Fence, WI 54120
715-336-3013

Florence, WI

Keyes Lake Campground
HCI Box 162
Florence, WI 54121
715-528-4907

Fond Du Lac, WI

Fond Du Lac KOA
W. 5099 Hwy. B
Fond Du Lac, WI 54935
800-562-3912

Westward Ho Camp-Resort
N 5456 Division Road
Glenbeulah, WI 53023
Voice: (920) 526-3407
Fax: (920) 526-3332
westwardho@westwardhocampresort.com

Fort Atkinson, WI

Jellystone Park of Fort Atkinson
N551 Wishing Well Drive
Fort Atkinson, WI 53538
920-568-4100

Pilgrims Campground LLC
W7271 Cty. Hwy. C
Fort Atkinson, WI 53538
800-742-1697

Fountain City, WI

Merrick State Park
Box 127
Fountain City, WI 54629
608-687-3025

Fremont, WI

Blue Top Resort & Campground
1460 Wolf River Drive
Fremont, WI 54940
920-446-3343

Yogi Bear's Jellystone Park Camp Resort

P.O. Box 155
54940
800-258-3315
Fremont, WI

Friendship, WI

Roche-A-Cri State Park
1767 Hwy. 13
Friendship, WI 53934
608-339-6881

Galesville, WI

Pow Wow Campground
W16751 Pow Wow Lane
Galesville, WI 54630
608-582-2995

Glenbeulah, WI

Westward Ho Camp-Resort
N5456 Division Road
Glenbeulah, WI 53023
920-526-3407

Grantsburg, WI

James McNally Campground
416 S. Pine St.
Grantsburg, WI 54840
715-463-2405

Green Lake, WI

Green Lake Campground
W2360 Hwy. 23
Green Lake, 54941
920-294-3543

Hancock, WI

Tomorrow Wood Campground
N3845 S. Fish Lake Road
Hancock, WI 54943
715-249-5954

Hartford, WI

Pike Lake STate Park
3544 Kettle Moraine Road
Hartford, WI 53027
414-670-3400

Haugen, WI

Rice Lake-Haugen KOA
P.O. Box 3
Haugen, WI 54841
715-234-2360

Hayward, WI

Everson's Nelson Lake Lodge Resort &
Campground
R 3, Box 3100

300

Hayward, WI 54843
715-634-3750

Hayward KOA
11544 N US Hwy. 63
Hayward, WI 54843
800-562-7631

Lake Chippewa Campground
Rt. 9, Box 9345
Hayward, WI 54843
715-462-3672

Trails End Camping Resort
Rt. 2, Box 2339 WA
Hayward, WI 54843
715-634-2423

Hazelhurst, WI

Cedar Falls Campground
6051 Cedar Falls Road
K54531
715-356-4953

Hiles, WI

Hiles Pine Lake Campground
Rt. 2, Box 440
Hiles, WI 54511
715-649-3319

Hixton, WI

Hixton / Alma Center KOA
N 9657 State Hwy. 95
Alma Center, WI 54611
Voice: (715) 964-2508 / (800) 562-2680
koajimdj@cuttingedge.net

Triple R Resort
N11818 Hixton-Levis Road, Rt. 2
Hixton, WI 54635
715-964-8777

Horicon, WI

The Playful Goose Campground
2001 S. Main St.
Horicon, WI 53032
920-485-4744

Hudson, WI

Willow River State Park
1034 County Trunk A
Hudson, WI 54016
715-386-5931

Iron River, WI

Wildwood Campgrounds

Rt. 2, Box 18
Iron River, WI 54847
715-372-4072

Kansasville, WI

Bong State Recreation Area
26313 Burlington Road
Kansasville, WI 53139
414-878-5600

Kewaunee, WI

Kewaunee Village Camping Resort
333 Terraqua Drive
Kewaunee, WI 54216
920-388-4851

Mapleview Campsites
N1460 Hwy. B
Kewaunee, WI 54216

LaCrosse, WI

Bluebird Springs Recreational Area, Inc.
N2833 Smith Valley Road
LaCrosse, WI 54601
608-781-2267

Pettibone RV Park & Campground
333 Park Plaza Dr.
LaCrosse, WI 54601
608-782-5858

Lac Du Flambeau, WI

Broken Bow Campground
P.O. Box 716, 14855 Deer Trail Road
Lac Du Flambeau, WI 54538
715-588-3844

Ladysmith, WI

Thornapple River Campground
N6599 Hwy. 27
Ladysmith, WI 54848
715-532-7034

Lake Mills, WI

Glacial Drumlin State Trail
1213 S. Main
Lake Mills, WI 53551
920-648-8774

Lakewood, WI

Heaven's Up North Family Campground
18344 Lake John Road
Lakewood, WI 54138
715-276-6556

Maple Heights Campground

P.O. Box 201
Lakewood, WI 54138
715-276-6441

Lancaster, WI

Klondyke Secluded Acres
10161 Quarry Road
Lancaster, WI 53813
608-723-2844

Laona, WI

Camp Five Museum
RFD 1
Laona, WI 54541
715-674-3414

Ham Lake Campground
RR 1 Box 434
Laona, WI 54566
715-674-2201

Lodi, WI

Smokey Hollow Campground, Inc.
W9935 McGowan Road
Lodi, WI 53555
608-635-4806

Lyndon Station, WI

Bass Lake Campground
N1497 Southern Road
Lyndon Station, WI 53944
608-666-2311

Bass Lake Campground
N1497 Southern Road
Lyndon Station, WI 53944
608-666-2311

River Bay Resort & Campground
W1147 River Bay Road
Lyndon Station, WI 53944
608-254-7193

Yukon Trails Camping
N2330 Cty. Road HH
Lyndon Station, WI 53944
608-666-3261

Madison, WI

Camperland
5498 Co. Road CV
Madison, WI 53704
608-241-1636

Manawa, WI

Bear Lake Campground
N4715 Hwy. 22-110

Manawa, WI 54949
920-596-3308

Menomonie, WI

Menomonie KOA
2501 Broadway St. N
Menomonie, WI 54751
800-562-3417

Twin Springs Resort Campground
3010 Cedar Falls Road
Menomonie, WI 54751
715-235-9321

Milton, WI

Blackhawk Campground, Inc.
3407 E. Blackhawk Dr.
Milton, WI 53563
608-868-2586

Hidden Valley RV Resort
872 E. Hwy. 59
Milton, WI 35563
608-868-4141

Lakeland Camping Resort
2803 East State Road 59
Milton, WI 53563
608-868-4700

Minocqua, WI

Patricia Lake Campground
8505 Camp Pinemere Road
Minocqua, WI 54548
715-356-3198

Monroe, WI

Cadiz Hills Campground
W7542 Hwy. 11
Monroe, WI 53566
608-966-3310

Montello, WI

Buffalo Lake Camping Resort
555 Lake Ave.
Montello, WI 53949
608-297-2915

Kilby Lake Campground
N4492 Fern Ave.
Montello, WI 53949
608-297-2344

Lake Arrowhead Campground
W781 Fox Ct.
Montello, WI 53949
920-295-3000

Puckaway Shores Campground
N3510 E. Tomahawk
Montello, WI 53949
920-295-3389

Wilderness Campgrounds
N1499 State Hwy. 22
Montello, WI 53949
608-297-2002

Mosinee, WI

Lake DuBay Campgrounds
1713 DuBay Drive
Mosinee, WI 54455
715-457-2484

N. Dodgeville, WI

Governor Dodge State Park
4175 State Road 23
N. Dodgeville, WI 53533
608-935-3325

Necedah, WI

Buckhorn State Park
W8450 Buckhorn Park Ave.
Necedah, WI 54646
608-565-2789

Ken's Marina Campground & Pontoon Rental
W4240 Marina Lane
Necedah, WI 54646
608-565-2426

St. Joseph Resort
W5630 Hwy. 21
Necedah, WI 54646
608-565-7258

Nekoosa, WI

Deer Trail Park Campground
13846 Cty. Road Z
Nekoosa, WI 54457
715-886-3871

New Glarus, WI

New Glarus Woods State Park
P.O. Box 805
New Glarus, WI 53574
608-527-2335

New London, WI

Wolf River Trips and Campground
E8041 Cty. X
New London, WI 54961
920-9822458

Oakdale, WI

Kamp Dakota Campground
P.O. Box 150
Oakdale, WI 54649
608-372-5622

Oakdale KOA
P.O. Box 150
Oakdale, WI 54649
800-562-1737

Ontario, WI

Brush Creek Campground
S190 Opal Road
Ontario, WI 54651
608-337-4344

Oshkosh, WI

Circle R. Campground
1185 Old Knapp Road
Oshkosh, WI 54901
920-235-8909

Kalbus' Country Harbor Inc.
5309 Lake Road
Oshkosh, WI 54901
920-426-0062

Osseo, WI

Osseo Camping Resort
50483 Oak Grove Road
Osseo, WI 54758
715-597-2102

Oxford, WI

Coon's Deep Lake Campground
360 Fish Lane
Oxford, WI 53952
608-586-5644

Palmyra, WI

Circle K Campground
W1316 Island Road
Palmyra, WI 53156
414-495-2896

Pardeeville, WI

Duck Creek Campground
W6560 Co. Hwy. G
Pardeeville, WI 53954
608-429-2425

Indian Trails Campground
W6445 Haynes Road
Pardeeville, WI 53954
608-429-3244

Pelican Lake, WI

Weaver's Resort & Campground
1001 Weaver Road
Pelican Lake, WI 54463
715-487-5217

Phillips, WI

Comfort Cove Campground & Resort
N10149 E. Solberg Lake Road
Phillips, WI 54555
715-339-3360

Plover, WI

Ridgewood Campground
4800 River Ridge Road
Plover, WI 54467
715-344-8750

Portage, WI

Pride of America Campground-Lake George
P.O. Box 403
Portage, WI 53901
608-742-6395

Sky High Camping
N5740 Sky High Dr.
Portage, WI 53901
608-742-2572

Readstown, WI

Crooked River Resort
RR1, Box 1026
Readstown, WI 54652

Redgranite, WI

Flanagan's Pearl Lake Campsite
4585 Pearl Lake Road
Redgranite, WI 54970
920566-2758

Reedsburg, WI

Lighthouse Rock Campground
S2330 Co. Hwy. V
Reedsburg, WI 53959
608-524-4203

Lighthouse Rock Campground
S2330 Co. Hwy. V
Reedsburg, WI 53959
608-524-4203

Reedsville, WI

Rainbow's End Campground
18227 US Hwy. 10
Reedsville, WI 54230
920-754-4142

Rice Lake, WI

Rice Lake KOA
1876 29-3/4 Ave.
Rice Lake, WI 54868
Voice: (715) 234-2360 / (888) 562-4501
Fax: (715) 234-7865
ricelakekoa@aol.com

Rio, WI

Silver Springs Campsites
N5048 Ludwig Road
Rio, WI 53960
920-992-3537

Saxon, WI

Frontier Bar & Campground
HC 1, Box 477
Saxon, WI 54559
715-893-2461

Shawano, WI

Brady's Pine Grove Campground
N5999 Campground Road
Shawano, WI 54166
715-787-4555

Sheboygan, WI

Kohler-Andrae State Park
1520 Old Park Road
Sheboygan, WI 53081
920-451-4080

Shell Lake, WI

Red Barn Campground
W6820 Cty Road B
Shell Lake, WI 54871
715-468-2575

Sherwood, WI

High Cliff State Park
N7630 State Park Road
Sherwood, WI 54169
920-989-1106

Sister Bay, WI

Aqualand Camp Resort
Box 538
Sister Bay, WI 54234
920-854-4573

Sparta, WI

Leon Valley Campground
9050 Jancing Ave.
Sparta, WI 54656
608-269-6400

Spring Green, WI

Valley RV Park
E5016 Hwy. 14 & 23
Spring Green, WI 53588
608-588-2717

St. Croix Falls, WI

Interstate State Park
Box 703
St. Croix Falls, WI 54024
715-483-3742

St. Germain, WI

Lynn Ann's Campground
P.O. Box 8
St. Germain, WI 54558
715-542-3456

Stevens Point, WI

Rivers Edge Campground
3368 Campsite Drive
Stevens Point, WI 54481
715-344-8058

Stoughton, WI

Kamp Kegonsa
2671 Circle Dr.
Stoughton, WI 53589
608-873-5800

Lake Kegosa State Park
2405 Door Creek Road
Stoughton, WI 53589
608-873-9695

Viking Village Campground & Resort
1648 County Trunk N.
Stoughton, WI 53589
608-873-6601

Sturgeon Bay, WI

Potawatomi State Park
3740 Park Dr.
Sturgeon Bay, WI 54235
920-746-2891

Quietwoods North Camping Resort
3668 Grondin Road
Sturgeon Bay, WI 54235
920-743-7115

Yogi Bear's Jellystone Park
3677 May Road
Sturgeon Bay, WI 54325
920-743-9001

Sturtevant, WI

Travelers' Inn Motel and Campground
14017 Durand Ave.
Sturtevant, WI 53177
414-878-1415

Sullivan, WI

Concord Center Campground
Q901 Concord Center Drive
Sullivan, WI 53178
414-593-2707

Superior, WI

Amnicon Falls State Park
6294 S. State Road 35
Superior, WI 54880
715-398-3000

Pattison State Park
6294 S. State Road 35
Superior, WI 54880
715-399-3111

Tilleda, WI

Tilleda Falls Campground
P.O. Box 76
Tilleda, WI 54978
715-787-4143

Trego, WI

Bay Park Resort & Campground
N8347 Bay Park Road
Trego, WI 54888
715-635-2840

Log Cabin Resort and Campground
N7470 Log Cabin Drive
Trego, WI 54888
715-635-2959

Trempealeau, WI

Perrot State Park
W26247 Sullivan Road, P.O. Box 407
Trempealeau, WI 54661
608-534-6409

Turtle Lake, WI

Turtle Lake RV Park
PO Box 526
Turtle Lake, WI 54889
715-986-4140

Two Rivers, WI

Point Beach State Forest
9400 County Trunk O
Two Rivers, WI 54241

920-794-7480

Wabeno, WI

Ham Lake Campground
RR1, Box 434
Wabeno, WI 54566
715-674-2201

Warrens, WI

Yogi Bear's Jellystone Park Campground Resort
P.O. Box 67
Warrens, WI 54666
608-378-4977

Wasau, WI

Rib Mountain State Park
4200 Park Road
Wasau, WI 54401
715-842-2522

Washington Island, WI

Island Camping & Recreation
RR1, Box 144
Washington Island, WI 54246
920-847-2622

Rock Island State Park
Rt. 1, Box 1118A
Washington Island, WI 54246
920-847-2235

Waupaca, WI

Hartman Creek State Park
N2480 Hartman Creek Road
Waupaca, WI 54981
715-258-2372

Rustic Woods
E2585 Southwood Drive
Waupaca, WI 54981
715-258-2442

Waupaca Camping Park
E2411 Holmes Road
Waupaca, WI 54981
715-258-8010

Wautoma, WI

Lake of the Woods
N9070 14th Ave.
Wautoma, WI 54982
920-787-3601

West Bend, WI

Lake Lenwood Beach and Campground
7053 Lenwood Drive
West Bend, WI 53090

414-334-1335

Lazy Days Campground
1475 Lake View Road
West Bend, WI 53090
414-675-6511

Timber Trail Camp Resort
7590 Good Luck Lane
West Bend, WI 53095
414-282-6394

West Salem, WI

Neshonoc Lakeside Campgrounds
N 5334 Neshonoc Road
West Salem, WI 54669
608-786-1792

Veterans Memorial Campground
N4668 CR VP
West Salem, WI 54669
608-786-4011

White Lake, WI

River Forest Campground
N2755 Sunny Waters Lane
White Lake, WI 54491
715-882-3351

Wolf River Nicolet Forest Outdoor Center
N3116 Hwy. 55
White Lake, WI 54491
715-882-4002

Whitewater, WI

Scenic Ridge Campground
W7991 Town Line Road
Whitewater, WI 53190
608-883-2920

Wilton, WI

Tunnel Trail Campground
Rte 1 Box 185
Wilton, WI 54670
608-435-6829

Wisconsin Dell, WI

K & L Campground
3503 County Road G
Wisconsin Dell, WI 53965
608-586-4720

Wonewoc, WI

Chapparal Campground
S320 Hwy. 33
Wonewoc, WI 53968
608-464-3944

Woodruff, WI

Hiawatha Trailer Resort
P.O. Box 590
Woodruff, WI 54568
715-356-6111

Indian Shores
P.O. Box 12
Woodruff, WI 54568
715-356-5552

Wyoming

Buffalo, WY

Buffalo KOA
Box 189
Buffalo, WY 82834
800-562-5403

Deer Park Campground
146 Hwy. 16E - PO Box 568
Buffalo, WY 82834
Voice: (307) 684-5722 / (800) 222-9960
information@deerparkrv.com

Lake DeSmet, Lake Stop Resort
PO Box 578
Buffalo, WY 82834
307-684-9051

Casper, WY

Casper KOA
2800 E. Yellowstone
Casper, WY 82609
800-562-3259

Cheyene, WY

A.B. Camping
1503 West College Drive
Cheyenne, WY 82007
307-634-7035

Cheyenne KOA
P.O. Box 20341
Cheyene, WY 82003
800-562-1507

Terry Bison Ranch
51 I-25 Service Road, E
Cheyenne, WY 82007
Voice: (307) 634-4171
Fax: (307) 634-9746

Cody, WY

Cody KOA
5561 Greybull Highway
Cody, WY 82414
Toll Free: (800)562-8507
Phone: (800)562-8507
codykoa@aol.com

Devils Tower, WY

Devils Tower KOA
Box 100
Devils Tower, WY 82714

800-562-5785

Douglas, WY

Douglas KOA
Hwy. 91, Box 1190
Douglas, WY 82633
800-562-2469

Glenrock, WY

Deer Creek Village RV Park
PO Box 1003
Glenrock, WY 82637
307-436-8121

Greybull, WY

Greybull KOA
Box 387
Greybull, WY 82426
800-562-7508

Jackson, WY

Jackson South/Hoback Junction KOA
9705 S. Hwy. 89
Jackson, WY 83001
800-562-1878

Lander, WY

Sleeping Bear RV Park
715 E Main St.
Lander, WY 82520
Voice: (307) 332-5159 / (888) 757-2327
Fax: (307) 332-3937
slpbear@yahoo.com

Lyman, WY

Lyman KOA
Star Route, Box 55
Lyman, WY 82937
800-562-2762

Moose, WY

Grand Tetons
PO Drawer 170
Moose, WY 83012
307-739-3300

Moran, WY

Grand Teton Park RV Resort
PO Box 83013
Moran, WY 83013
800-563-6469

The Flagg Ranch Resort
PO Box 187
Moran, WY 83013
800-443-2311

Rawlins, WY

Western Hills Campground
2500 Wagon Circle Road
Rawlins, WY 82301
307-324-2592

Rawlins KOA
205 E. Hwy. 71
Rawlins, WY 82301
800-562-7559

Riverton, WY

Wind River RV Park
1618 E Park Ave.
Riverton, WY 82501
Voice: (307) 857-3000 / (800) 528-3913
Fax: (307) 856-9559
windriverrvpark@wyoming.com

Rock Springs, WY

Rock Springs KOA

P.O. Box 2910
Rock Springs, WY 82902
800-562-8699

Sheridan, WY

Sheridan/Big Horn Mountains KOA
63 Decker Road, Box 35 A
Sheridan, WY 82801
800-562-7621

Teton Village, WY

Teton Village/Jackson West KOA
Box 38
Teton Village, WY 83025
800-562-9043

Thermopolis, WY

Eagle RV Park
204 Hwy20 South
Thermopolis, WY 82443
307-864-5262

INDEX